TEN CONSECUTIVE YEARS LIVING IN CARS:
Living, Traveling, Camping, Attending College and Performing Surveillance in Cars---and Loving It!

Craig Roberts

NOTICE TO THE READER

Printed and published in the Republic of the United States
BookSurge.com
Charleston, South Carolina

ISBN: 0-9676248-2-7
ISBN-13: 978-0967624822

Visit www.booksurge.com to order additional copies.

DEDICATION

To all those living in cars making it happen—Rock On!

To Aaron Russo's greatest work to date: <u>AMERICA: FREEDOM TO FASCISM.</u>

www.GiveMeLiberty.org   www.FreedomToFascism.com

To Alex Jones & associates—for their never-ending quest to educate U.S. Citizens so our Constitutional Republic can be fully restored.

www.INFOWARS.COM   www.PRISONPLANET.COM
www.PRISONPLANET.TV   www.JONESREPORT.COM

TABLE OF CONTENTS

CHAPTER 1

OUTFITTING A CAR FOR COMFORTABLE LIVING

1.1 CHAPTER INTRODUCTION

Before modifying a car to live in, one has to figure out what kind of living environment will best meet one's needs. Over the years, my needs have best been met by creating a comfortable, private, quiet, spacious, insulated, easily organized living area inside my cars. In creating this type of environment, two main areas need to be addressed. The first deals with minor modifications used to create maximum privacy, making a car's living area hidden from view from anyone outside, while still maintaining a car's normal looking appearance. The second addresses modifying a car's living area to provide the benefits of: (1) preventing condensation from forming during cool and cold weather; (2) allowing for more comfortable car living area temperatures during any temperature weather; (3) adding comfortable physical characteristics to a car's living area, such as softness, spaciousness, quietness, etc.; and (4) reducing any unusual infrared signature emitted from a car that is being lived in.

When outfitting a car for comfortable living, I've desired to use non-permanent, non-damaging modifications that can easily be undone whenever desired, such as when wanting to sell the car. Another reason to use non-damaging, non-permanent modifications is that using permanent damaging modifications, such as drilling holes in car body metal or chipping of car body paint, could eventually result in severe car body corrosion problems, because a car being lived in has an extremely humid interior. The non-permanent, non-damaging car modifications presented in this chapter and the comfort enhancing information in Chapters 2 and 3 can all be used to make any car comfortable to live in without damaging the car.

WHAT AREAS OF A CAR ARE SUITABLE FOR LIVING IN The front seat, rear seat, and trunk area (if applicable) can all be lived in. However, since the front seat area can't be completely insulated to prevent condensation from forming during cold weather, and because a car's living area needs to be completely private from outside view, all areas aft of the front seat are better suited for living in.

To minimize condensation from forming in the front seat area during cold weather, and to gain maximum warmth in the aft car living area(s), I usually have separated the minimally insulated front seat area from the thoroughly insulated aft car living area(s) by installing a "privacy/insulating partition" (more later) directly behind the front seats. Except when living in subcompact cars, which requires removal of the front passenger seat to allow for stretching out comfortably, I mainly use the front seat area as a storage area and the aft car area(s) for living space.

CREATING MAXIMUM CAR LIVING AREA SPACE To create maximum car living area storage and living space, along with making a car's living area easier to insulate, I've generally removed all aft seats and sometimes have removed the front passenger seat. Following the seat removal instructions disclosed in the car manufacturer service/repair manual is recommended.

The only permanent damaging car modification I've used when outfitting a car for comfortable living, and only when absolutely necessary, is to remove a portion of the barrier wall that separates the rear seat and trunk area in applicable cars. Removing a portion of the barrier wall allows the trunk area to be accessed from inside the car, and it allows one to stretch out comfortably without having to use the front seat area. Fortunately, many cars that have trunks aren't constructed with a permanent barrier . . . simply removing the back seat gives complete access to the trunk area.

ARE ALL CARS SUITABLE FOR LIVING IN? Although every car model has its own advantages and disadvantages pertaining to car living situations, I personally have never found a car that couldn't be outfitted for comfortable living. Car size mainly determines how much of one's possessions will have to be stored at an external storage location. To a lesser degree, car size determines how easy a car's living area will be to cool during hot weather and warm during cold weather. Car shape mainly affects how easy it will be to insulate the aft car living area(s). I've lived and worked comfortably in most every size and shape car from subcompacts to full-size cars.

1.2 CAR "PRIVATIZATION"

"PRIVATIZING" A CAR FOR COMFORTABLE LIVING
    To comfortably live inside a car, a car's living area(s), areas aft of the front seat area, need to be made completely private. Also, while parked with car windshield shade installed, it's best if anyone outside can't see into a car's front-seat area. If anyone outside looking at a car's front tinted side window can see the silhouette of anyone inside the front seat area, such as when just after entering the car, unwanted attention will be drawn (one really needs to disappear completely). Car "privatization" needs to be done in such a way as to keep the car's appearance legal and normal looking so that the car can't be easily identified and so that it won't attract undesirable attention.

WHY "PRIVATIZE" A CAR'S LIVING AREA(S)? Since people can cause problems for just about anything that is exposed to them, such as one's political views, religion, race, employment, salary, etc., it is essential that one fully "privatize" one's car so that one's secret living/working situation can be kept secret. For the same reasons conventional residences are made private, a car used as a residence should be made private, too. Some physical reasons to "privatize" a car include preventing excessive sunlight from adversely affecting one's skin, eyesight, sleep, and to prevent UV degradation of things stored inside the car. Because one would be severely limited in one's "secret" parking options, and because it would be impossible to enjoy living in a car if people outside could see inside--car "privatization" is the first thing one will want to address in outfitting a car for comfortable living.
    Keeping one's car living situation secret will be beneficial if one is ever involved in a car accident, as many car insurance policies contain an "exclusion of coverage" clause pertaining to cars being lived in. Another financial reason to "privatize" and keep one's car living situation secret is that many cities have local ordinances making it illegal to sleep/camp/live on

city/government property, no matter if one is inside a car or not. In preventing financial loss, a thoroughly "privatized" car has the benefit of preventing thieves from knowing whether there is anything inside worth stealing.

THREE THINGS TO IMPLEMENT IN "PRIVATIZING" A CAR'S LIVING AREA(S)

In privatizing a car, I've basically used three non-permanent, non-damaging modifications that can easily be undone whenever desired. The first is legally tinting a car's side windows and back window, and then legally blocking out the rear side and back windows so that a car's living area(s) can't be seen by anyone outside. Although less darkly tinted than the rear car window(s) so as to remain legal, after legally tinting the front seat area side windows, I sometimes have chosen to farther darken them by temporarily using static window tint which is held on by static electricity, allowing it to being removed or replaced as often as desired.

The second car privatizing modification, the privacy/insulating partition will be beneficial in preventing anyone outside from seeing into a car's aft living area(s) via the windshield, opened front side window, or through an opened front car door.

The third car privatizing modification is installing a windshield shade in a parked car. With windshield shade installed, it's best if anyone outside can't see into any area of the car interior.

•WINDOW TINTING OPTIONS

STICK-ON WINDOW TINT Conventional stick-on window tint can be purchased from automotive suppliers, car and home window tinting businesses, and possibly directly from the window tint manufacturer. The application of conventional stick-on window tint consists of: (1) cutting the tint to the appropriate size so that it will fit against the interior side of the window being tinted, (2) thoroughly cleaning the window's surface (any particles left will form air bubbles in the tint) (3) lightly spraying the surface of the window with water, (4) peeling away the tint's clear plastic sheet exposing the tint's sticky side, and then spraying the tint's sticky side with water, (5) applying the moist sticky side of the tint to the moistened window surface, and (6) moistening the back side of the tint and then using a small squeegee to iron out air bubbles and water caught between the window and tint.

STICK-ON WINDOW TINT ADVANTAGES Stick-on window tint can be applied to most any flat or slightly round, smooth surface window. It adheres extremely well when properly applied and given enough time to cure, thus it can be used on roll up/down car windows and in windy applications without peeling away. Stick-on window tint is offered in a variety of light transmission (darkness) and heat rejection (reflection) ratings and colors--not all are car legal. Stick-on type window tint can be layered to obtain that extra degree of darkness desired, but doing so may be illegal, and it will probably cause much more heat to be generated during sunny days. Quality stick-on window tint lasts an extremely long time.

STICK-ON WINDOW TINT DISADVANTAGES Stick-on window tint is a bit difficult to apply: the hardest part is making a window's surface completely free of dust and other small particles that will cause air bubbles in the tint. Stick-on tint is easily scratched. It is fairly expensive, and it is somewhat expensive to have it professionally applied.

All car legal window tint I've used has heated up considerably in sunny weather (cold weather advantage). Mirror tint reflects most of the sun's solar energy remaining very cool, but mirror tint is illegal to use on cars because of the blinding effect it would have on other drivers.

Although stick-on window tint has a few disadvantages, I've always used it at least minimally on every car I've owned.

•OBTAINING THE DESIRED DEGREE OF WINDOW NON-TRANSPARENCY
MULTIPLE LAYERS OF STICK-ON WINDOW TINT The goal in privatizing car windows is to make a car's living area(s) hidden from view from anyone outside, especially when the car windshield shade is in place. Applying more than one layer of tint is one way of achieving the degree of darkness desired, but may be illegal on certain car windows. In applying multiple layers of stick-on tint, each layer can be applied to a window one layer at a time, or the layers can be stuck together first and then applied as a single layer. Combining the window tint layers together first helps to eliminate dust particles and other tiny debris that would otherwise form air bubbles between the layers of tint.

Unfortunately, the laws regulating window tint darkness are very restrictive, and the fines for breaking the law can be excessive. Therefore, it is important that car window tint is legal, as some police carry light meters in their patrol cars. Passing a vehicle inspection is another problem I've had with excessively dark window tint on certain vehicle windows.

STATIC WINDOW TINT Static tint adheres to a window by the force of static electricity; it has no sticky side or clear, peel away, plastic layer. Static tint looks very much like stick-on window tint but is a bit thicker and softer. Cutting static tint in the shape of a window and then placing it against a clean moistened window is all that is required to apply it.

When entering a parked privatized car with windshield shade installed, it's desirable that one completely disappears from view after closing the door. If the front-seat area side windows are legally lightly tinted, allowing people outside to see one's silhouette after closing the door, undesirable attention will be drawn to one's silhouette. Using static tint to excessively darken legally tinted windows is OK when the vehicle is parked.

MANUFACTURED TINTED WINDOWS: TINT INTEGRAL WITH GLASS (SELF-EXPLANATORY)

WINDOW SPRAY PAINT "PRIVATIZATION" OPTION Because all windows aft of the front-seat driving area will probably be insulated with "tube/shell" insulating foam (soon to be disclosed), I've sometimes chosen to "privatize" my cars' rear windows by spraying a couple coats of spray paint on their interior surface). Surprisingly, spray-painting the inside of a car window gives a smooth professional appearance that may look just like an extremely dark tinted window, depending on the color used.

HANGING TOWELS OR SHEETING BEHIND WINDOWS WHILE PARKED Hanging sheeting in back of usable side widows can be beneficial in certain parking situations, such as when desiring privacy while side windows are slightly opened. Hanging sheeting behind front side windows while parked prevents anyone outside during the night from using a flashlight to see into the car interior. Wooden clothespin halves or plastic shoehorns may work well in hanging sheeting by trapping it in the upper door crevice.

•WINDSHIELD PRIVATIZATION
USE WINDSHIELD SHADE WHILE PARKED A non-transparent windshield shade of the appropriate size placed behind the

windshield of a parked car will substantially increase interior privacy by (1) preventing anyone outside from seeing in through the windshield, (2) limiting sunlight into the car, and (3) helping to prevent interior light from being seen by anyone outside at night.

Windshield shades are inexpensive and readily available from many automotive suppliers. Although there are many types available, non-transparent windshield shades that can be made to fully cover the interior side of a car's windshield (remove rearview mirror) provide the most interior privacy. Purchasing a truck/van size windshield shade and then trimming/folding the windshield shade to fit fully behind a car's windshield can be done if regular size shades won't fully cover the windshield.

Two types of windshield shades I've used are the cardboard windshield shade and the reflective synthetic windshield shade. The cardboard windshield shade is beneficial to use in surveillance applications for a number of reasons: (1) It can be trimmed to fully and exactly cover the backside of a windshield; (2) because of its perfect custom cut fit, the shade's outer edge can be sealed to the windshield's outer edge or plastic trim using silicon sealant for the purpose of preventing window condensation formation during cold weather car living (include a pouch of drying agent between the windshield and shade to farther reduce the possibility of condensation formation); (3) the shade is cheap and disposable; (4) it helps make a car appear ordinary (less identifiable); (5) bore scope or camera viewing holes can easily be cut into the shade; (6) the picture on the front of the shade tends to camouflage any surveillance modifications; and (7) the shade is very non-transparent.

For non-surveillance applications, the reflective synthetic windshield shade (thin foam covered with shiny reflective covering) has several advantages: (1) It's extremely durable and long-lived; (2) its softness makes it comfortable to store inside a car and come in contact with; (3) its edges can be folded over to give it a nearly perfect fit behind a car's windshield; (4) it's extremely non-transparent; (5) its shiny reflective surface reflects sunlight, helping to keep a car cooler in hot sunny weather; and (6) it is extremely moisture resistant.

CUSTOMER'S METHOD OF PRIVATIZING HIS VAN

A customer sent me an e-mail disclosing how he privatizes his van to make it look like a work van. He places construction materials in front of side and rear windows to make it look like the van is full of building materials. He says that police never stop to investigate his van, because it looks just like a loaded work van.

1.3 INSULATING A CAR FOR COMFORTABLE LIVING

To gain maximum comfort while living in a car, the car living area(s) must be insulated. The main reasons for doing so are: (1) to make a car's living area(s) maintain more comfortable temperatures during extreme temperature weather; (2) to prevent condensation from forming on cold hard plastic, glass, and metal interior surfaces during cold weather; (3) to create a soft, spacious, easily-organized living environment; (4) to reduce the outside noise entering a car's living area(s); (5) to help prevent breech of privacy by preventing interior noise and lighting from being heard or seen by anyone outside; (6) to more thoroughly privatize a car's living area from possible view of anyone outside; and (7) to reduce any unnatural infrared signature emitted from a car that is being lived in (viewed by a infrared imager).

PREVENTING CONDENSATION During cold weather, cold temperatures easily transfer through a car body and into the interior hard plastic, glass, and metal surfaces. Warm moist air created by one's body will cause condensation to form on most non-insulated, cold, non-porous interior surfaces. The only suitable option in preventing condensation from forming on the cold glass, metal, and hard plastic surfaces located in a car's living area is to cover them with suitable insulating material. Since glass, metal, and plastic surfaces in a car's front seat driving area can't be thoroughly insulated, a privacy/insulating partition (more later) will need to be installed to separate the minimally insulated front seat driving area from the heavily insulated rear car living area(s).

BEST INSULATING MATERIAL TO USE IN INSULATING A CAR'S LIVING AREA

In creating a soft, condensation-less, low noise, non-toxic, private, well-insulated car living area, I've tried a variety of insulating materials, a few of which are disclosed in Chapter Two. However, the insulating material that has worked best in insulating my cars' living areas is high-density, pink upholstery foam.

EXTRA: Placing Mylar laminated bubble-pack insulation sheeting or metal roofing bubble-pack insulation sheeting underneath the upholstery foam will substantially increase overall insulation.

High density, pink upholstery foam is most suitable to use in insulating a car's living area(s) for a number of reasons: (1) It is non-toxic and extremely safe to be around; (2) it is extremely soft and comfortable to contact; (3) its good "breathing" characteristic helps prevent condensation and moisture buildup; (4) it is extremely mold/mildew resistant; (5) it holds up to moisture (spills) and humidity extremely well; (6) it is extremely durable, long-lived, and has relatively good anti-wear characteristics; (7) it doesn't shed or come apart easily; (8) it maintains its shape extremely well; (9) it can be stored rolled up without adverse effect (tie off with a belt and place in a trash bag); (10) it attenuates sound fairly well; (11) it's very easy to install and remove; (12) it can be obtained (ordered) in most any size and thickness needed in car living insulating applications; and (13) it has good temperature insulating properties. The only insignificant disadvantage of high density, pink upholstery foam is that it is fairly expensive.

High density, pink upholstery foam can be ordered/purchased from upholstery shops or possibly directly from the manufacturer. Be aware that upholstery shops and department stores sometimes offer an inferior yellowish/whitish colored foam that seems to be less dense, less durable, and more susceptible to dry rotting (see right wall in Ch. 1 picture); therefore, purchasing the higher quality pink upholstery foam is what I recommend. Also, I recommend never gluing two pieces of foam together when an application really requires a single piece of the appropriate dimensions.

Metal Roof Insulation

1/4" (6mm) thick bubble-pack with shiny silver and non-reflective

TUBE/SHELL CAR LIVING AREA INSULATING OPTION

The most effective, non-damaging, non-permanent way I've found to insulate a car's living area(s) is by performing what I call the "tube/shell" insulating option. It consists of wrapping a car's living area(s) (rear seats removed) using one piece of 6-12 inches thick, high density, pink upholstery foam (single piece isn't possible on all cars). The single piece of foam is wrapped around the car's living area starting at the center of the ceiling, extending to either side wall, covering the side wall and floor, then extending up the other side wall and back to the center ceiling starting point, thus creating a foam tube/shell of a car's living area. A slightly oversized piece of 6-10 inches thick foam can be inserted to cover the rear opening of the tube/shell. The front tube/shell opening can be covered with a "privacy/insulating partition." The floor foam can be covered with an appropriately sized piece of carpet.

Like most of the information in this book, the tube/shell insulating option can be altered and enhanced in any number of ways to better meet one's application.

TUBE/SHELL PRE-INSTALLATION PREPARATION Car living area windows should be legally blocked out as previously described. All rear car seats should be removed (following the seat removal procedures disclosed in the car manufacturer's service/repair manual is best).

The only permanent, damaging car modification I've used on applicable cars, and only when absolutely necessary, is to remove a portion of the wall barrier that separates the rear seat and trunk areas for the purpose of incorporating the trunk area into a car's overall useable living space. After removing a portion of the barrier wall, the trunk area can then be insulated separately (Mylar laminated bubble-pack insulating sheeting is excellent to use for insulating the trunk area, but thinner metal roofing bubble-pack insulation sheeting may be more suitable--a fairly thick layer of upholstery foam will have to be placed over bubble-pack floor insulation to prevent the air bubbles from popping). Fortunately, many cars that have trunks are built without a barrier wall; simply removing the rear seats fully exposes the trunk area.

FILLING IN EXCESSIVE FLOOR AND SIDE WALL INDENTATIONS Car living area floor and sidewalls generally have indentations or excessive curves that may need filling in to make the overall surface fairly flat before covering it with tube/shell insulating

foam. Filling in excessive floor and sidewall indentations will minimize condensation formation during cold weather that would otherwise form on cold glass, metal, and plastic surfaces located within an unfilled air pocket area (air pockets may also create unnatural infrared emissions). Filling in floor indentation will also help make the car floor flat and more comfortable to lie on.

Since a car's flooring is required to support heavy things, using filler material that won't compress much is best. Synthetic clothes/material works extremely well as a floor filler because it compresses little, is long-lived, and resists mold/mildew formation. In contrast, the sidewalls of a car's living area usually don't have heavy loading of their surfaces; therefore, high density, pink upholstery foam of the appropriate dimensions works well in filling in excessive sidewall indentations, such as side window indentations. If one can attain bubble-pack insulation of the correct thickness (use layers if necessary), bubble-pack insulation used to fill in window indentation will significantly increase insulation of a car's living area.

•CHOOSING THE CORRECT SIZE TUBE/SHELL INSULATING FOAM

FOAM THICKNESS CONSIDERATIONS The desired thickness of tube/shell insulating foam depends on: (1) what thickness will allow for sufficient insulation for the temperatures being parked in (cold weather consideration is more important), (2) the amount of car living area space that can be taken up by foam thickness, and (3) how well one wants the tube/shell foam covering to stay in place over the walls and ceiling without having to secure it. Lesser considerations are: (1) how soft one desires their car's living area to be, (2) the desired degree of soundproofing of the car living area, and (3) the thickness of any Mylar or metal roof bubble-pack insulation used as a 1st layer of insulation.

During sunny, hot weather, a car will naturally heat up to the outside ambient temperature. It will also take on additional heat provided by the outer surfaces of a car absorbing solar energy, converting it into heat (gloss/metallic white colored cars stay coolest). While parking in sunny hot climates, the thickness of tube/shell insulating foam determines how well a car's living area is insulated from the warmer car body. Because cooling a car's living area during sunny, hot weather is much more dependent on using the techniques discussed in Chapter 3, foam thickness can be less than what would be desired for use in cold weather.

When parking in cold temperatures, body heat is what mainly warms a car's living area, as solar heating is generally insignificant (example: 20°F car body solar heated to 25°F is insignificant). Thicker tube/shell insulating foam provides increased insulation and reduces the size of a car's living area, both of which decrease the amount of body heat required to warm a car's living area. During cold weather car living, the temperature difference between the car body and car living area can be extreme, thus using thicker foam is much more desirable when insulating a car that will be parked in cold climates. Also, I highly recommend placing Mylar laminated or metal roofing bubble-pack insulation sheeting behind the tube/shell foam to substantially increase insulation (the shiny silver side of metal roofing insulation should face the interior to help block in heat during cold weather).

INTERIOR SPACE LOST TO FOAM THICKNESS Interior space lost to foam thickness is another important consideration, especially for subcompact car owners. Completely wrapping a car's living area in foam that is X inches thick will decrease both the width and height of the car's living area by 2, times. Since high density, pink upholstery foam maintains its thickness very well, one should discount gaining any significant space from compression of the loaded floor foam.

SUPPORT REQUIRED IN SECURING TUBE/SHELL FOAM Because of high density, pink upholstery foam's natural tendency to lay flat, foam that is wrapped around the inside of a car's living area MAY stay in place against the side walls and ceiling area on its own. The thicker the foam is, the more it tends to stay in place on its own.

GENERAL FOAM THICKNESS RECOMMENDATIONS Depending on the climate, the size, shape, or color car being lived in, and the type of tube/shell being created, one will probably want to use high density, pink upholstery foam that has a thickness of 6-12 inches to insulate a car's living area. The exception to this thickness recommendation would be in insulating a car's trunk, which may require thinner foam and metal roofing bubble-pack insulation sheeting to save space (floor foam over bubble-pack insulation must be thick enough to prevent popping the bubble-pack--a 1" thick layer of foam between the floor and bubble-pack insulation will also be helpful in preventing popping of the bubble-pack. If parking in very cold temperatures, the thicker the foam is, the better (up to a point). If parking in warm climates, less thick foam may be sufficient.

FOAM THICKNESS CONSIDERATION FOR DIFFERENT TUBE/ SHELL INSULATING OPTIONS

As with most of the material described in this book, the tube/shell insulating option can be modified and/or enhanced in any number of ways to better meet one's needs. An option I've used to insulate subcompact cars is to use two layers of tube/shell foam during winter, and then remove the top layer during warm weather to create extra room. Using two pieces of foam, one piece of thick foam to cover just the floor, and a thinner piece to wrap around the sidewalls and ceiling, may be desirable. Another option is to wrap only the floor and sidewalls. Wrapping the floor and sidewalls with a single thick piece and using a thinner piece to cover the ceiling is another option. For better insulating qualities, placing Mylar laminated or metal roofing bubble-pack insulating sheeting underneath insulating foam is desirable.

FOAM LENGTH CONSIDERATIONS Tube/shell insulating foam's length should be the length of a car's living area. Generally, this is the distance extending from the back of a car to the backside of the front seats. To create a snug fit and to take into consideration slight curves along the length of a car's living area, adding an extra 8-12 inches of foam to the measured car living area length is a good idea. Any excess length of foam can be trimmed off from the front end of the tube/shell at a later date, preferably after the tube/shell has been completed, loaded, and lived in for a couple weeks.

FOAM WIDTH CONSIDERATIONS The width of tube/shell insulating foam will be the distance around a car's living area, which is the distance across the floor, sidewalls, and ceiling (if creating a full tube/shell). Adding an additional 10-20 inches to the measured width is a good idea. Any excess width can be trimmed off at a later date, preferably after the completed tube/shell has been loaded and lived in for a couple weeks.

WRAPPING A CAR'S LIVING AREA WITH TUBE/SHELL INSULATING FOAM

Tube/shell insulating foam can easily be wrapped around the car living area floor, sidewalls, and ceiling. If creating a full tube/shell, the center of the ceiling is an excellent location for the foam ends to meet because "no loading" of the ceiling foam helps prevent the foam ends from shifting or separating. The foam ends should press together firmly because of the foam being slightly wider than required.

NOTE: For cars that have more than one living area, such as cars that have the trunk separated from the back seat by a barrier wall, a tube/shell can be created separately in each area.

FILLING IN THE TWO CEILING-TO-SIDE WALL AND TWO FLOOR-TO-SIDE WALL SEAM AIR GAPS

Depending on the type of tube/shell being constructed, the thickness of the tube/shell insulating foam used, and the shape of a car's living area, there may be air gaps under the tube/shell foam along the two ceiling-to-side-wall seams and possibly along the two floor-to-side-wall seams. Unfortunately, condensation is likely to form on any non-insulated glass, metal, and/or plastic car interior surfaces in these seam air gap areas during cold weather car living. Therefore, if any exposed hard surfaces exist in these seam air gap areas, the air gap will need to be filled in with suitable insulating material, or eliminated in some way, to prevent undesirable condensation from forming.

EXTRA: Air gaps may also cause an unusual infrared signature to be emitted from the car when viewed with a thermal imager.

With hatchback type cars, one way to eliminate seam air gaps is to build a box frame that forces the tube/shell foam into the ceiling-to-side-wall and floor-to-side-wall seams. A box frame can be made of twelve pieces of 2 x 2-inch wood of the appropriate length: one piece positioned along each floor/side-wall and ceiling/side-wall seam, four pieces connecting the 2 x 2-inch wood ends at the front, and four pieces connecting the 2 x 2-inch wood ends at the rear. This type of box skeleton structure inside the tube/shell will force the tube/shell foam into the air gap seams, eliminating any air pockets.

Another way I've eliminated air gaps at the ceiling-to-side-wall and floor-to-side-wall seams is to fill in each of the seam air gaps with a triangular foam wedge placed behind the tube/shell insulating foam along the length of the seam. Cutting an appropriately sized rectangular block of foam through its diagonal along its entire length will provide two triangular wedge sections which can be used to fill in the two ceiling-to-side-wall seam air gaps. The same can be done with the floor-to-side wall seams, but using thinner foam wedges In fact, depending on how loaded the floor foam is and how thick the tube/shell foam is, floor-to-side wall foam wedges may not be needed.

SECURING TUBE/SHELL INSULATING FOAM Foam covering the car floor carpeting will stay in place with little or no shifting because of its high resistance to sliding on car floor carpet and because of the weight of things stored on top. Depending on the tube/shell foam thickness, the width of the side-wall and ceiling, whether foam wedges are being used to fill in ceiling-to-side wall seam air gaps, and whether a "full" tube/shell is being used, the tube/shell foam covering may or may not stay in place over the side walls and ceiling on its own. If securing the ceiling foam covering is necessary, a 1-3-inch diameter PVC tube can be roped in place along each side-wall to ceiling seam underneath the tube/shell foam for the purpose of pulling the foam in to fill the seam area. If using a thin foam or if covering an unusually wide ceiling, sagging/drooping ceiling foam can be held in place by installing a piece of PVC tubing stretched diagonally across the ceiling foam to hold the ceiling foam in place (Metal tubing can be placed inside the PVC tubing to increase its rigidity).

INSULATING THE REAR TUBE/SHELL OPENING The tube/shell created in a car's living area(s) has an opening at both the front and rear. The simplest way to insulate the rear tube/shell opening is to place an appropriately sized piece of high density, pink, upholstery foam in the opening. Using a slightly oversized (L x H) piece of foam that is 5-inch thick or more will generally allow it to stay in place on its own.

The rear tube/shell foam covering can be covered with carpet or some other suitable "breathable" covering. However, since high density, pink upholstery foam provides a soft, "breathable" covering that is moderately durable, and because covering the rear foam with carpet would be an unnecessary hassle, I generally have left the rear foam covering uncovered.

INSTALLING CARPET COVERING OVER TUBE/SHELL INSULATING FOAM

Carpet "breathes" well, helping to prevent condensation

formation and oxygen depletion problems, thus is a very suitable foam covering. Although the tube/shell insulating foam can be covered completely in carpet, for simplicity I've only covered the floor foam and lower portion of side wall foam, leaving much of the side wall and all ceiling foam uncovered.

To prevent the carpet covering from causing abrasion of the floor area foam, an anti-abrasive material covering should be placed in between the foam and carpet covering. Synthetic materials, such as a plastic tarp or synthetic sleeping bag, work well because of their long life, mildew/mold resistance, excellent anti-abrasion/wear quality, and their ability to prevent dirt and spills from reaching the foam.

Using a somewhat slick synthetic covering between the carpet and floor foam will require that the carpet covering be minimally secured to prevent it from sliding/shifting forward during car braking. Securing the aft corners of the carpet to the car body interior can be done using a couple C-clamps, safety wire or synthetic rope, and four 2 x 4-inch metal plates. Placing a metal plate below and above the carpet, then clamping the plates together using a C-clamp, and then tying the C-clamp to a suitable nearby car body fixture point will prevent the carpet from sliding forward while braking. Other tie-off points may be necessary, such as midway along both sides of the carpet, to keep the carpet stretched out.

*EXTRA: The C-clamps hold the metal plates more securely if points where the C-clamp contacts the plates are countersunk.

Modified "Tube/Shell" Insulating Option installed in hatchback type car.

1.4 CAR "PRIVACY/INSULATING PARTITION"

CREATING A PRIVACY/INSULATING PARTITION" TO COVER THE FRONT TUBE/SHELL OPENING

Creating a privacy/insulating partition at the front of the tube/shell insulating foam opening can be done by hanging a blanket, sleeping bag, etc. on a rope or removable car "clothes bar" suspended from side wall to side wall as close to the ceiling as possible, just behind the front seat(s). This type of privacy/insulating partition has several advantages: (1) It's easy to close or open by simply sliding the blanket/material to one side, (2) the covering material can be removed easily and washed whenever desired, (3) it's very comfortable to come in contact with, (4) its insulating properties are easily increased, and (5) it doesn't increase danger or damage during a possible car crash/accident.

WHY A PRIVACY INSULATING PARTITION IS NEEDED: PRIVACY AND PREVENTING CONDENSATION

As previously discussed, the three main benefits of using a "privacy insulating partition" are (1) to add privacy to a car's living area, (2) to minimize condensation from forming on the front-seat area cold hard surfaces during cold weather, and (3) to add insulation plus warmth to a car's living area(s) during cold weather car living. A privacy/insulating partition also helps to prevent outside light from bothering one's sleep, and it helps prevent interior light from being seen by anyone outside during nighttime.

What people don't see doesn't bother them, and thieves don't steal what they don't know exists. A privacy/insulating partition prevents anyone outside from seeing into a car's living area, such as when a front car door is opened, when a front door window is rolled down, and anytime a windshield shade isn't in place.

CUSTOM-MADE DASHBOARD COVERS

A custom-made dashboard cover is a specially designed, custom cut and sewn carpet or velour type of covering that covers a car's dashboard. Special material allows a dash cover to conform to the curves of the dashboard a short time after being in place. Dashboard covers contain air vent cutouts and a glove compartment flap covering that ensure proper operation of dashboard air vents and glove compartment door. Generally, the dashboard covering is held in place by Velcro tape strips stuck to the dash.

Custom-made dashboard covers add to the appearance of a car's interior (they look nice). They protect a car's dashboard from the sun's harmful UV rays and from being scratched. They reduce slippage of objects laid on top of the dash. Used in car living situations, dashboard covers minimize condensation formation on the dash during cold weather. Depending on the color, dashboard covers are generally much cooler than a bare dashboard would be during sunny weather, thus gas savings and less air-conditioner compressor wear during warm weather are likely benefits.

1.5 MINIMIZING A CAR'S "UNUSUAL" INFRARED SIGNATURE

Although the global police state isn't fully completed, it's just a matter of time before every patrol car, highway monitor, street light camera, etc. is equipped with infrared/thermal imaging equipment. No matter if using infrared imaging equipment that makes a black and white image in which cold is darker and hot is lighter and brighter, or if using infrared imaging equipment that uses a spectrum of colors to create an image of the hot to cold temperature objects in the image--both types will highlight temperature variations throughout a car's outer body, to what degree depends upon the sensitivity of the imager sensor. In addition to regular insulation used to make car outer surfaces appear more uniform in temperature, aluminum foil will need to be placed behind windows to prevent thermal radiation from easily passing through and seen by an infrared imager.

The main thing to remember about thermal imaging equipment is that the greater the temperature difference between areas/objects being viewed, the better the identifying image. For instance, if you're walking in a desert that is 98.6 degrees Fahrenheit, you're probably not going to be discernible in a thermal image. In car living situations, the cooler the ambient temperature (to a point), the easier it is to discern whether a car is possibly being occupied. Fortunately, there are things that can be done to make the thermal image of an occupied car appear more like the thermal image of an unoccupied car.

To get rid of "hot spots" on the outer car body, the car living area interior walls, ceiling, and floor, can be insulated as described in the preceding material. Doing so will allow the car living area outer car body to appear as a more uniform temperature to the infrared/thermal imager without any discernible hot spots, and it will also allow the car body temperature to remain closer to outside ambient temperature. The important thing is that all the car interior surfaces in a car's living area be covered with high density insulating foam (placing Mylar laminated or metal roofing bubble-pack insulating sheeting behind the foam increases insulation), as anything uncovered, such as a non-filled/non-insulated ceiling-to-side-wall seam, will saturate with warmer interior air causing hot spots and/or streaks to show up in the thermal image.

The next area to concentrate on is the front seat area. The least insulated area in the front seat area is the window area. 2 or 3-inch thick foam, aluminum foil, and a layer of Mylar laminated or metal roofing bubble-pack insulation sheeting can be placed against the tinted side windows and held in place with two thin backing boards and expandable, car clothes hanging bars. The better the foam, foil, and bubble-pack seals the window off from the car interior air, the better these areas will be camouflaged to infrared/thermal imaging equipment. In covering the windshield interior surface, placing a reflective synthetic windshield shade in front of the foam will be beneficial in camouflaging the foam, aluminum foil, and Mylar laminated or metal roofing bubble-pack insulating sheeting placed behind the shade (flexible piece of plastic sheeting of the appropriate thickness can be used to press the insulation materials in place, with two expandable clothes hanging bars pressed against the front seats and plastic sheeting backing the windshield insulation.

Because of the front seat area's being less insulated than the aft car's living area, it may be best to leave the air conditioning vents open to allow any heat to somewhat escape into the car engine area. If the car vent openings automatically close when the engine is turned off, pull the appropriate fuse before shutting down the engine to allow air vents to remain open; spring loaded vent doors can be held open by attaching a small vice-grip pliers to the door linkage, or by blocking the door open with an obstruction. In extreme situations, it may be desirable to create a vent directly from the car living area to the front seat area air vents, which can be done by using PVC pipe and flexible, insulated ducting, duct tape, and silicon sealant (a

12-volt DC brushless cooling fan can be placed inside the PVC to drive air in or out). Also, since non-circulating air in the car living area behind the privacy/insulating partition is an excellent insulator, suspending one's body in air as described in chapter 2 will also help minimize any unusual infrared signature being emitted from a car that is being lived in.

EXTRA: Black asphalt roads absorb and emit thermal radiation extremely well (a decent hiding place for a car that is being lived in). Bright, light-colored objects emit and absorb less thermal radiation as compared to dark-colored objects.

EXTRA: Diving under water will allow one to completely disappear from view of a infrared/thermal imager. (Carry a small scuba tank and regulator.)

EXTRA: To hide a person inside a car from border-crossing thermal imagers, the person can be placed inside a compartment whose inner walls are wrapped with an aluminum blanket. Body heat transfers throughout the entire blanket making the compartment appear as a uniformly heated rectangular area when viewed by a thermal imager, so it would be best located in an area near naturally warm area of a vehicle.

EXTRA: Ceramic paint may be another helpful tool to use in minimizing a car's unusual infrared signature to thermal/infrared imagers.

BLOWN IN FOAM OPTION A customer shared with me that her friend took the panels out of his mini-van and then had foam insulation blown onto the car living area surfaces. The foam was the type that quickly cures into a solid form.

1.6 CAR LIVING AREA LIGHTING

UNSUITABLE CAR LIVING AREA LIGHTING Because of possible oxygen depletion, fire/smoke hazards, excessive heat, and messiness--candles or any other type of oxygen depleting lighting equipment should not be used inside a car (waking up one winter night with a carpet fire raging next to my head permanently ended my desire to use candles inside my car). Also, I've never mounted any type of lighting fixture inside my cars, such as the 12-volt lamps used in recreational vehicles (RV). The reason being is that they give off too much light (breach of privacy concern), give off too much heat during warm weather, require too much 12-volt DC power, and could require car-damaging modifications that would eventually result in severe car body corrosion problems.

FLASHLIGHT LIGHTING OPTIONS Because of the limited space in a car's living area, minimal lighting is all that is required during the night. Using a small flashlight (1-2 AA batteries) has been the most suitable form of lighting in my car living/working situations. A small flashlight (and spare bulbs) is easy to use and store inside a car, as no mounting or electrical cord is required. A small flashlight uses little power causing no noticeable heating of a car's living area. In applications that require the use of both hands, a small flashlight can easily be (1) placed on one's chest while reading lying down, (2) held in one's mouth (wrap flashlight's aft section w/ duct tape), and (3) the flashlight can be held in a headband (headband generally available from the flashlight manufacturer). Since becoming readily available, I now mostly use headband flashlights.

Although using two rechargeable AA size batteries to power my flashlight allows it to operate about 70 percent as long as when using non-rechargeable batteries, using rechargeable batteries is extremely cost effective and is good for the environment. Rechargeable batteries provide slightly less light because of the rechargeable battery's 1.39 volt output as compared to 1.55-volt output of non-rechargeable AA size batteries (advantageous in car living situations).

Keeping spare batteries, spare bulbs, and a spare flashlight in an easily accessible location will be beneficial during nighttime use, such as when a flashlight bulb expires, batteries discharge, or the flashlight is temporarily lost.

TWELVE-VOLT POWER LIGHTING OPTION Another way to provide car living area lighting is to simply connect an extremely low-power 12-volt bulb to an auxiliary 12-volt battery (if used). However, if a 12-volt bulb is a low power type (1/4 amp or less), powering the bulb for two hours per night from a car's lead acid starting battery may be suitable if the car is driven at least 10 minutes each day or if a solar panel is being used to charge the car starting battery during the day.

Powering a low power bulb from a high capacity, 12-volt auxiliary battery has the advantage of having a power source that won't run out for an extremely long period before needing to be recharged. The disadvantage is having to transport a heavy 12-volt, totally sealed battery, and possibly getting things tangled in the bulb's power cord.

Instrument "press-in" type bulbs or bulb & fixture assemblies removed from instrument gauges are what I connect to auxiliary 12-volt batteries. Wrapping a bulb with electrical tape, or aluminum foil and electrical tape, allows for directing a bulb's light.

CHAPTER 2

SLEEPING/RELAXING COMFORTABLY INSIDE A CAR DURING EXTREME TEMPERATURE WEATHER

2.1 CHAPTER INTRODUCTION

There are many techniques and modifications discussed in other chapters that will help enhance one's comfort while living in a car, such as the material in Chapters 1 and 3. However, the information in this chapter is what I consider to be some of the most critical in allowing one to sleep and relax comfortably inside a car parked in most any temperature extreme. Although this material could easily be combined with Chapter 3 because of its similar subject matter, to stress this material's exclusiveness and importance, I've dedicated a single short chapter in presenting it.

Besides car living applications, the information in this chapter and in Chapter 3 will be extremely useful to anyone who sometimes sleeps somewhere other than on a conventional type bed located in a climate controlled residence (campers, hunters, hikers, campers, etc.). I just wish I had known about and understood the following information when I first began living in cars many years ago.

2.2 PROBLEMS WITH RELAXING/SLEEPING COMFORTABLY INSIDE A CAR DURING EXTREME TEMPERATURE WEATHER

When I first began living in a car, I didn't know the best way to stay comfortable in extremely cold or hot weather. I experienced significant discomfort while lying on my car's minimally insulated floor during warm weather and while using a mountain climbing sleeping bag during cold weather.

My discomfort came from excessively hot or cold car floor temperatures absorbing too much body heat during cold weather and adding too much heat during hot weather. Basically, if temperatures were below 45°F or above 85°F, my comfort level wasn't adequate enough to allow for a thoroughly good night's rest, and this can be fatiguing over time.

During this beginning car living period, I already knew a few temperature characteristics that should have led me in the right direction early on. From having taken a scuba diving class while a teenager, I knew that water takes away body heat 25 times faster than air of the same temperature (at least that is what I remember). I also knew from my hiking trips that temperature insulating properties of insulation decreases drastically as the insulation is compressed. Obviously, I knew that temperature conduction is very efficient in many types of solids, such as car body steel. And most important, I knew that the vacuum barrier in a thermos is an excellent insulating barrier. Even though I had this knowledge, it still took a year to figure out how to substantially enhance my comfort while parking in extremely hot and cold weather.

The main reason that I didn't figure out early on how to remain extremely comfortable during cold and hot weather temperature extremes was because I didn't want to try anything that would significantly use up my car's living area space. A lesser reason was that my young body could easily handle the slight discomfort caused by extreme car floor temperatures.

2.3 OVERCOMING DISCOMFORT DURING EXTREME TEMPERATURE WEATHER

CAR FLOOR INSULATING MATERIALS The obvious way to reduce temperature discomfort while lying on a cold or hot car floor is to increase insulation between oneself and the car floor. The first insulating material I tried was layers of cheap, 1-inch thick carpet foam, along with using a piece of carpet as a covering. Three layers of carpet foam did almost nothing in preventing the uncomfortably cold or hot car floor temperatures from making me a bit uncomfortable. Adding more layers of 1-inch thick carpet foam didn't help significantly either.

Since Styrofoam has excellent insulating qualities, I decided to modify the car floor insulation by adding a sheet of 1-inch thick Styrofoam building insulating material between layers of carpet foam. Unfortunately, it only got squashed into pieces, creating uncomfortable bumps. After removing the pieces of Styrofoam sheeting, I added a 1-inch thick sheet of corrugated cardboard type building material sandwiched in between layers of carpet foam. It didn't squish and break into pieces like the Styrofoam sheeting did, but it did almost nothing to increase the car floor insulation.

Since I liked the softness of the carpet foam, I thought that thickening the floor insulation with more layers might help; if not, at least it would be extremely soft to lie on. However, from my previous experience with carpet foam, I knew that to add any significant thickness to the floor insulation using 1-inch carpet foam would mean a dozen or more layers. So instead of adding more layers of carpet foam, I began to look around for a source of thicker, higher quality foam.

WHAT I FOUND AT UPHOLSTERY SHOPS Checking with upholstery shops, I learned that high density, pink upholstery foam could be purchased/ordered in most any size needed for insulating a car. Upholstery shops use high density, pink upholstery foam for replacing old foam in furniture being reupholstered. Being non-toxic, moisture resistant, extremely mold/mildew resistant, extremely soft, fairly durable and wear resistant, and extremely long lasting, I knew that it would be very suitable for use in car living situations.

I purchased a single piece of 6-inch thick, high-density, pink upholstery foam with length and width dimensions that covered my car's entire living area floor. To protect the foam, I placed a piece of carpet on top. This 6-inch thick foam covering provided significant benefit in increasing the insulation between my body and the car floor. However, during freezing temperatures, it still wasn't enough to prevent the cold car floor from absorbing significant amounts of body heat, making me slightly uncomfortable. It didn't matter how many covers I used to cover myself and sleeping bag with during freezing weather, the cold car floor still absorbed a bit too much of my body's heat to allow for a thoroughly good nights rest while parking in freezing temperatures.

Since the 6-inch thick high density, pink upholstery foam covering significantly increased the car floor insulation, I decided to lay down another 6-inch thick layer. With 12 inches of foam covering the car floor, the car living area's usable space was considerably reduced. Unfortunately, it still wasn't enough insulation to completely stop the minimally uncomfortable loss of body heat being absorbed into the cold car floor during freezing weather. However, since it significantly increased insulation and was extremely soft to lie on, I left it in place.

A FRIEND SUGGESTED USING A HAMMOCK INSIDE MY CAR

Sometime during my efforts in trying to find the ultimate way to limit uncomfortable car floor temperatures from making me slightly uncomfortable during extremely cold and hot weather, a friend mentioned that hanging a hammock in my car might be helpful in increasing my comfort during summer weather. However, from my experiences resting in outdoor hammocks, I knew that not lying flat while resting or relaxing would over time bring about cramps, stiff neck, backache, and problems with breathing. Also, there really wasn't anything inside my car that a hammock could be attached to and support my weight. Hanging a hammock in my car just wasn't a feasible option.

THE UNEXPECTED SURPRISE

One summer while parking in a sparsely populated wilderness area, I decided to purchase a sleeping cot to use outside at night while watching for shooting stars, hopefully preventing crawling bugs on the ground from reaching me. While lying on a cot, I knew that body heat build-up in the cot's thin material covering would be minimal. Nevertheless, I was extremely surprised at how much my body's cooling increased while lying on the cot.

With such an increase in cooling, I decided to see what using the cot inside my car would be like--no matter how much room it took up. I found it extremely comfortable to lie on inside my car during warm/hot weather as compared to lying on my car's insulated floor. Basically, lying on a cot with air surrounding my naked body inside a hot car provided increased insulation from the hot car floor, and it also allowed my body's perspiration evaporation cooling to function much more efficiently. Using a 12-volt DC computer cooling fan enhanced my body's cooling even more.

Up to that point in my life, I never would have thought that the cooling enhancement brought about from using a sleeping cot inside my car would be as extremely beneficial as it was in allowing me to remain cool during hot weather car living. I could now be comfortable inside my car in temperatures of up to 110 degrees Fahrenheit.

With the drastic increase in comfort gained by using a sleeping cot during hot weather, I soon began to wonder how the cot could be utilized to enhance my warmth during the coming winter. When cool temperatures came, I placed a 5-inch thick piece of high density, pink upholstery foam over my cot's surface for the purpose of trapping body heat. I found that this setup allowed me to remain much warmer as compared to sleeping on the heavily insulated car floor. Surprisingly, the main reason for my enhanced warmth was due to the extra insulation that the air barrier between the cot's surface and car floor provided. Basically, using a cot with a 5-inch thick foam covering inside my car during cold weather provided two insulating enhancements: (1) the foam covering trapped body heat keeping me warm, and (2) the air layer between the cot's surface and insulated car floor greatly increased the insulation between my body and the cold car floor (sort of like how a thermos or attic does).

EXTRA: Mylar laminated bubble-pack insulating sheeting or metal roof bubble-pack insulating sheeting can be placed behind insulating foam to substantially increase insulation with little loss in car living area space.

HOT/COLD WEATHER COT USAGE ENHANCEMENTS ARE DISCUSSED IN CHAPTER 3

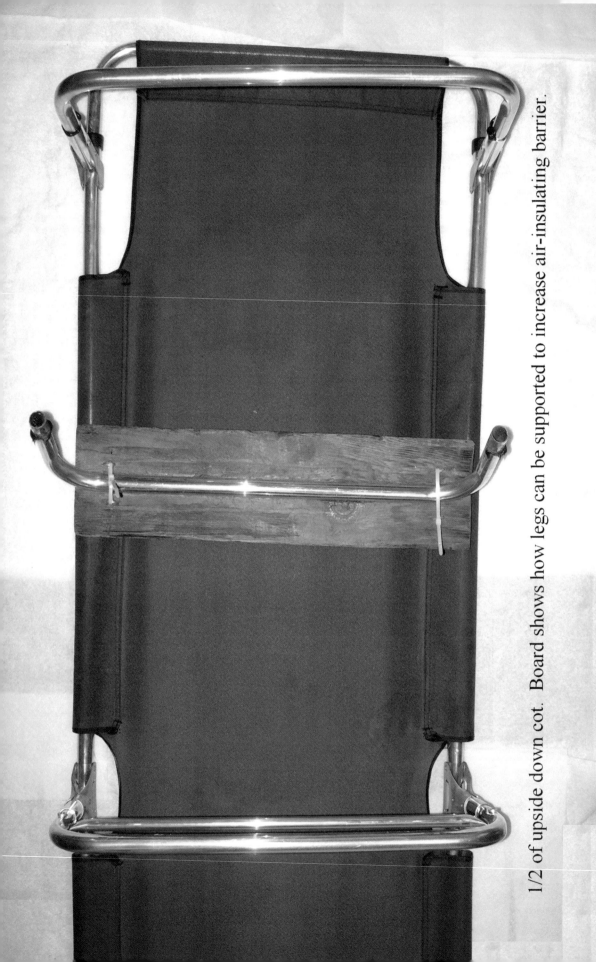

1/2 of upside down cot. Board shows how legs can be supported to increase air-insulating barrier.

2.4 EQUIPMENT RECOMMENDATIONS

• COT FEATURES MOST SUITABLE FOR CAR LIVING APPLICATIONS

TYPE MATERIAL COVERING With all the cots I've used in my car living/working applications, tearing of the cot material covering has been their greatest weakness. Since using a beaded car seat cover to lie on will prevent skin irritation, acquiring a cot that has the strongest, most tear-resistant synthetic material covering available should be one's goal. Unfortunately, cot manufacturers generally use a less expensive semi-synthetic blend that is more comfortable to one's skin, but is weaker and less tear resistant.
EXTRA: Small tears in semi-synthetic cot covering material may possibly be repaired using super glue. All material cot coverings degrade when exposed to UV rays (sunlight). Aircraft synthetic material covering is probably the strongest type material that could be used to re-cover a cot.

STRONGEST TYPE ATTACHMENT OF COT MATERIAL COVERING A cot material covering that wraps around the metal frame and is then sewn has always lasted longest in my applications. This type of attachment is very strong because it distributes the material loading throughout a greater area, and this is especially true if the cot frame is made of 1-inch diameter aluminum tubing.

BEWARE OF COT COVERINGS THAT ARE ATTACHED USING METAL SPRINGS I once purchased a worthless cot that came with a cheap removable cushion covering. Hidden under the cushion was a weak material covering that quickly came apart after minimal use. To top that off, the inferior material covering was attached to the cot's metal frame using dozens of small metal springs that would painfully pinch my body and pull out body hair anytime the cot was used without the cheap cushion cover, such as during warm/hot weather. Also, the cheap removable cushion cover was of no benefit because it trapped body heat during hot weather and was too thin to trap significant amounts of body heat during cool/cold weather.

DESIRABLE COT FRAME Collapsible cot frames assembled from several pieces of 1-inch diameter aluminum tubing have worked best in my car living/working situations. Smooth, hollow, 1-inch diameter aluminum tubing is extremely corrosion resistant, fairly strong, and lightweight. This type tubing is relatively comfortable to come in contact with because of its smoothness and because its hollowness allows for less temperature retention (lower thermal conductivity). Also, since these type cots can generally be folded in half while assembled, bending them around an opened car door makes them easy to install and remove.

One-inch diameter aluminum tubing "wrap around" type legs, which have straight portions of tubing the length of the cot's width contacting the floor, disperse the load over a larger area, thus minimize wear to the carpet and foam supporting the cot. If desired, the air barrier between the floor and cot covering can easily be increased by placing a piece of wood under each of the cot's three legs.

The 6-8 pieces of aluminum tubing, which press together forming my cot's frame, fit together securely and disassemble easily. Applying silicon adhesive sealant to the connecting points during assembly will allow them to stay together securely and still allow for easy disassembly. My disassembled cot stores in a small diameter, medium length bag that is easy to carry on a hiking trip.

EXTRA WIDE COT MAY NEED REINFORCING OF THE CENTER LEG

Depending on the type of cot, cot width, and the user's weight, the center leg's reinforcing bar (if applicable) may need to be reinforced to prevent it from bending and causing sagging of the cot covering. Since the center leg generally has a reinforcement bar built into it that is supposed to help maintain cot width by preventing the center leg from bending, all that needs to be done to reinforce the center leg is reinforce the center leg's reinforcing bar.

To reinforce the center leg's reinforcing bar, I cut in half lengthwise a piece of steel or aluminum tubing of the same diameter and length as the center leg's reinforcing bar (use hacksaw with 32 teeth/inch blade) and then secure the tubing halves over the center leg's reinforcing bar using plastic ties and/or small metal hose clamps. To prevent possible tearing of the cot covering material above, I wrap the reinforced bar with duct tape to cover the plastic ties and hose clamps' sharp edges.

•COT DIMENSIONS MOST SUITABLE FOR CAR LIVING APPLICATIONS

COT LENGTH AND WIDTH CONSIDERATION A sleeping cot needs to be a bit longer and wider than the person using it, so as to prevent one's head/feet and shoulder/arm from contacting the uncomfortably hard (cold in winter) cot frame. If car space permits, one will probably be comfortable with a cot length that is around 6-10 inches longer than one's height and that is 5-8 inches wider than one's width.

COT HEIGHT CONSIDERATION The larger the air barrier between a cot's surface and supporting floor, the greater one's comfort will be during both hot and cold weather. Fortunately, no matter what a cot's height is above the supporting floor, placing a piece of wood or other suitable material underneath a cot's supporting legs will increase the air barrier. Hook type nails and plastic ties can be used to secure the cot's supporting legs to the wood.

CHAPTER 3

EXTREME COLD AND HOT WEATHER CAR LIVING COMFORT ENHANCEMENTS

3.1 CHAPTER INTRODUCTION

Except for periods when performing surveillance in a privatized car parked in direct sunlight for days at a time not being able to significantly open any car windows or sunroof--I generally haven't had to deal with temperatures greater than 105 degrees Fahrenheit. The coldest climates I've lived in usually have had nighttime temperatures above -10 degrees Fahrenheit (exception: wind chill factor). Because of the severe temperature extremes encountered while living and working in cars, I've had to figure out ways to enhance my comfort. The information contained in Chapters 1, 2, and 3 is what has allowed me to remain comfortable while parking in most any temperature extreme.

3.2 COLD WEATHER (CW) AND HOT WEATHER (HW) COMFORT ENHANCEMENTS

HW AND CW ENHANCEMENT: CAR LIVING AREA TUBE/SHELL INSULATING OPTION (described in Ch. 1)

CW ENHANCEMENT: EXTRA TUBE/SHELL INSULATING FOAM
Depending on the shape of a car's living area and how much space exists, it may be beneficial to add another layer of high density, pink upholstery foam to partially or fully cover the existing tube/shell insulating foam during severe cold weather. Increasing insulation and making a car's living area smaller both help to allow one to stay warmer during cold weather.

HW AND CW ENHANCEMENT: BUBBLE-PACK INSULATING SHEETING Placing flexible Mylar laminated bubble-pack insulating sheeting or metal roof bubble-pack insulating sheeting behind car insulating foam will substantially increase insulation while using up very little space.

HW AND CW CONSIDERATION: CAR COLOR CONSIDERATIONS/ RECOMMENDATION Car color directly affects how much of the sun's solar energy will be absorbed by the car body and converted into heat. Temperature differences can easily be discerned by touching different colored cars parked on a parking lot during a sunny day. Darker colors, such as flat black, dark green, and navy blue, will absorb the most solar energy, becoming warmest, while light bright colors (gloss white) will absorb the least solar energy, remaining coolest. Bright light colors emit and absorb less thermal radiation as compared to dark colors.

It's much easier to insulate a car for comfortable cold weather living than it is to make a car cooler during hot sunny weather. Also, any solar heating of a car body during cold weather (less 35 degrees Fahrenheit) will be made insignificant because of the ambient cold temperature quickly absorbing away any solar heating generated. Therefore, a light bright colored car, such as metallic white, is much more desirable than a dark-colored car if living in climates that have both sunny hot and cold weather each year. In contrast, a dark-colored car would only be advantageous to own if living in cold climates where the warmest yearly temperatures seldom exceed 80 degrees Fahrenheit.

BEADED SEAT COVERS ENHANCE YOUR COMFORT
WHILE LYING ON ANY TEMPERATURE SURFACE.

BEADED SEAT COVERS WON'T IRRITATE SKIN.

HW AND CW ENHANCEMENT: CAR INTERIOR COLOR RECOMMENDATION The above also applies to car interior color, but with the exception that unlike a car body that is directly exposed to cold weather, solar heated, dark-colored car interiors can significantly add heat to a car's interior because of not being directly exposed to the cold outside temperature. In contrast, light-colored car interiors absorb and convert less solar energy into heat, and they absorb and emit less thermal radiation.

HW AND CW ENHANCEMENT: DASHBOARD COVER COLOR (described in Chapter 1)

• HW AND CW ENHANCEMENT: "PRIVATIZING" REAR WINDOWS FOR ENHANCED TEMPERATURES

SPRAY PAINTING INSIDE OF REAR CAR WINDOWS (isolated, wilderness car living)
   During warm/hot sunny weather, coating the inside of rear car windows with gloss white spray paint will allow the windows to remain much cooler. During cold weather, coating the inside of rear car windows with dark-colored spray paint will allow the windows to absorb maximum solar energy converting it into heat.

DARKENING REAR CAR WINDOWS WITH WINDOW TINT Except for mirror tint, which is legal to use on houses and buildings but illegal to use on cars, all the legal and almost legal car window tint I've used on my cars has heated up considerable when exposed to sunlight. When tinting rear car windows for warm/hot sunny weather car living, using only one layer of tint that has the highest heat rejection ratio and the lowest light transmissivity ratings that can be legally applied will allow for the coolest temperatures. Placing white poster board or white cloth behind a rear tinted car window may or may not help it remain cooler, but it will legally block out outside view into the car. In contrast, coating the inside of rear car windows with window tint that has a low heat rejection ratio rating will generate much solar heating. I've also found that using more than one layer of tint increases solar heating of the tint, no matter what type of tint or combinations of tint is used.
NOTE: Most U.S. cars have federal restrictions that limit the degree of darkness car windows can be tinted. If caught

driving a car with illegal window tint, the penalty can be very expensive. Interestingly, many ordinary vehicles that have illegal window tint are being used for some type of surveillance . . . I've found this to be true again and again.

HW AND CW ENHANCEMENT: WINDSHIELD SHADE COLOR

During hot sunny weather, a light-colored, reflective windshield shade enhances cooling by reflecting solar energy. During cool/cold weather, a dark-colored windshield shade will absorb maximum solar energy, converting it into heat. Not using a windshield shade during cool/cold weather will allow sunlight to shine on front-seat area surfaces generating more interior heat.

Electronic Equipment 12-V

DC COOLING FANS.

LivingInCars.com hosted by
WWW.CARTAMA.NET

HW AND CW ENHANCEMENT: LYING ON A WOODEN BEAD CAR SEAT COVER Wooden bead car seat covers are extremely comfortable to sit on while driving--they're also very comfortable to lie on when placed on a car floor, sleeping cot, or inside a sleeping bag. The air pockets within the wooden beads and in between the beads help to keep the user warmer in cool weather and cooler in hot weather. Also extremely beneficial is that wooden bead car seat covers won't irritate your skin.

HW ENHANCEMENT: USING A 12-VOLT DC FAN TO BLOW AIR OVER YOUR BODY During warm weather, a body cools itself by body heat being extracted by anything cooler contacting it. Additionally, during rigorous physical activity or while in hot weather, a body increases its cooling by giving off perspiration that extracts body heat as it evaporates. To speed up the evaporation, convection, and conduction cooling process, a small 12-volt DC fan can be used to blow air over your body (preferably naked body). The fan also benefits cooling by blowing away moisture-saturated air, replacing it with less moisture-saturated air.

FAN RECOMMENDATION: 12-VOLT DC BRUSH-LESS FAN Some electronic equipment, such as home computers, usually have a 12/24-volt DC or 120/240-volt AC brush-less cooling fan contained within their housing. During warm weather car living situations, a 12-volt DC brush-less cooling fan is well-suited for use in blowing air over your body. Twelve-volt DC brush-less electronic cooling fans are compact, thin, and lightweight, thus making them easy to hang or mount inside a car. They're offered in both square and circular housing designs. Because of having no motor brushes, the only thing to wear out on brush-less cooling fans are motor bearings--I've never worn out any of my 12-volt DC brush-less cooing fans. Their extremely low 12-volt DC power requirements (.125-.250 amps in my applications) and efficient, quiet operation also make them well suited for use inside a car.
EXTRA: Brush-less fans can be purchased from electronic supply businesses, mail-order catalogs, and the Internet.

HW ENHANCEMENT FOR SURVEILLANCE APPLICATIONS: DUCTING IN COOLER, DRYER OUTSIDE AIR WHILE EXPELLING MOISTURE-SATURATED, WARM CAR LIVING AREA AIR To gain maximum convection cooling of an enclosed area, it's best if cooler air/fluid enters the area directly opposite of where warmer air/fluid is expelled. For example, to gain maximum efficiency from a car radiator, car radiators are generally designed with an upper radiator hose connection at the top and near to one side and with the lower radiator hose connection at the bottom near the opposite side.

If all rear car interior surfaces have been covered with insulating foam, both cooling air enters and warmer air expels out the front seat driving area (a/c vents, opened windows/ sunroof)--and this is a very inefficient way to cool a car's living area while parked. To make matters more uncomfortable, during hot weather surveillance work, it may be necessary to keep the front seat area side windows and sunroof completely closed. During these extreme circumstances I've chosen to duct cooler dryer outside air from an opened front-seat area air vent to the rear of my car's living area using PVC pipe and a circular shaped 12-volt DC brush-less cooling fan installed inside the pipe, along with using flexible ducting material to attach the PVC pipe to the front-seat area air vent. The PVC pipe ducts cooler, dryer outside air to the rear of my car's living area while moisture-saturated car living area air is expelled out the other unused car air vent.

EXTRA: If your car's air vent closes when the engine is turned off, removing the appropriate fuse before turning off the engine may allow the vent to remain open. Spring loaded vent doors can be held open by attaching a small vise grip pliers to the door's linkage.

HW AND CW ENHANCEMENT: INSULATING FRONT SEAT AREA WINDOWS WITH 2-4" THICK FOAM During hot sunny weather, placing a piece of appropriately sized 2-4-inch thick foam behind the windshield's windshield shade and having the foam ends extend around to slightly opened side window(s) to expel trapped heat may considerably enhance a car's cooling during sunny weather. Installing a reflective windshield shade in front of the insulating foam almost eliminates the foam's solar absorption heating, it minimizes the foam's exposure to UV light that would otherwise cause foam deterioration, and it hides the foam, making the car appear normal looking. This heat dissipating method can also be used to dissipate heat generated by solar panels placed behind a car's windshield.

During cold weather, using 2-4-inch thick foam to cover the inner surface of front seat area windows will help insulate a car's front seat area. It also helps to lessen condensation formation on the inner surface of cold windows.

HW ENHANCEMENT: OPEN WINDOWS, SUNROOF, VENTS AND DOORS TO GAIN MAXIMUM COOLING

If living in an isolated private area, opening doors, sunroof, windows, and vents will substantially increase car living area cooling during hot weather, the main benefit being that warmer moisture-saturated interior air is more quickly replaced with cooler, dryer outside air.

If living in a populated area, hanging sheeting behind partially opened windows will help maintain privacy. Plastic shoehorns or cloths pin halves both work well in wedging sheeting in the upper door crevice.

HW ENHANCEMENT: PARKING FOR COOLER TEMPERATURES

Parking in a shaded area is the ultimate way to minimize a car's solar absorption heating--and this is especially true for dark-colored cars. Parking at a breezy location, such as the highest point in an area and/or away from large wind obstructing structures, can considerably enhance a car's living area cooling, too.

Light-colored parking surfaces absorb and transmit much less thermal radiation as compared to dark-colored surfaces-- park on a light-colored surface for much cooler temperatures.

Parking with the non-tinted windshield pointing towards the sun and using a reflective windshield shade will help minimize solar heating of a car's tinted side and/or rear windows.

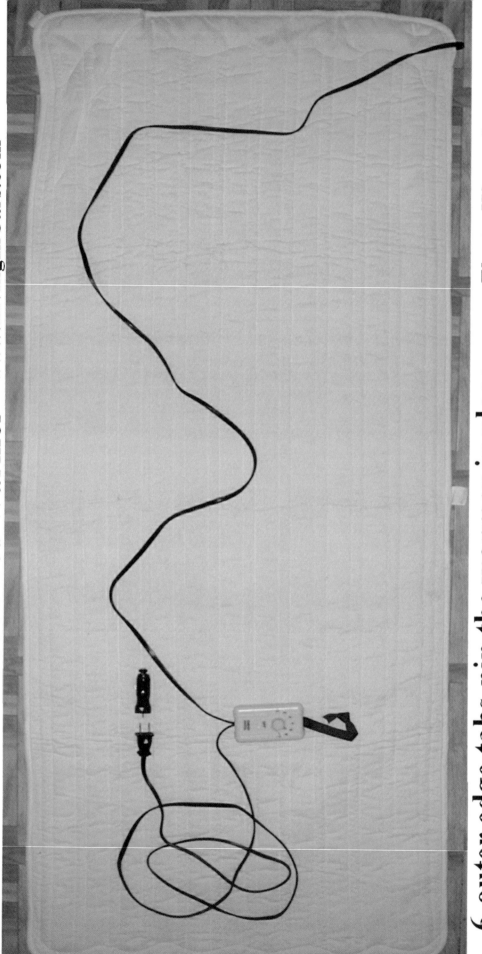

120V/12V Padded Bed Warmer -- www.LivingInCars.com

6 outer edge tabs pin the warmer in place -- www.ElectroWarmth.com

HW ENHANCEMENT: PROVIDING ARTIFICIAL SHADE BY SUSPENDING A TARP ABOVE CAR

While living in sparsely populated areas or when leaving the city for the weekend to camp somewhere beautiful, it has sometimes been beneficial to suspend a tarp above my car, creating artificial shade to enhance car cooling. Because of its light reflecting qualities, using a thick bright white 12x9-foot tarp has been most effective. Suspending two tarps above a car with a half-foot minimum space between the tarps will provide much more cooling, as compared to using only one tarp.

TARP SUSPENSION METHOD #1 Stretching an appropriately-sized tarp over the top of several 2.5 or 5 gallon empty plastic gas containers placed on top of my car and then using thin rope to tie off the tarp's front/rear ends to the sides of my car's front and rear bumper area has worked fairly well in suspending a tarp above my car. To make a tarp extend out beyond the sides of a car, a PVC pipe or board of the appropriate length can be placed in the front two gas container handles and another in the rear two gas container handles. The ends of the wood (or whatever is used) should be wrapped in something soft, such as a towel or piece of foam, to prevent the ends from rubbing through the tarp. Tying off the side of a tarp to a car's door handle, side mirror, or other suitable location, will prevent the tarp from flapping excessively while parking in windy weather. A gas container can be stabilized during windy conditions by partially filling it with water or sand; using silicon adhesive sealant to temporarily stick plastic gas containers to the top of a car without damaging the car paint is also possible.

To prevent bugs from gaining access to a car's interior by walking across some form of "bridge," make sure that the tarp, string/rope, and anything else used in the tarp suspension doesn't contact anything other than the car. If string/rope contacts the ground or nearby foliage, bugs will walk across it and enter the car.

TARP SUSPENSION METHOD #2 Tying off an appropriately-sized tarp above a car, securing it with rope and bungee cord to nearby trees or other suitable tie-off points, is another way of securing a tarp above a car. To prevent rain from accumulating in the center of the tarp, the tarp can be hung a bit slanted or hung in the shape of an A-frame. To prevent swaying trees from ripping apart an attached tarp, bungee cord can be used

with each securing rope. To prevent bugs from gaining access to the car, the tarp installation should not touch any part of the car. This tarp suspension option has the advantage of allowing a car to come and go without having to disassemble or reassemble the tarp installation._
*EXTRA: A large tarp placed over a non-privatized car is an easy way for a weekend camper to turn a car into a private camper.

HW ENHANCEMENT: 12-VOLT WATER MIST SYSTEM USED UNDER TARP/UMBRELLA

Although not for use inside a car, one can keep 30F+ degrees cooler by sitting under a large umbrella that sprays a water mist underneath. I've seen 12-volt water mist umbrella systems being used at outdoor motocross races and other sporting events . . . and they do work well if one doesn't mind getting damp by the water mist.

HW AND CW ENHANCEMENT: SKIN FUNGI RASH PREVENTION / ELIMINATION

I've had minimal trouble with skin fungus rash forming on my buttocks while living/working in cars during extremely hot, sunny, humid weather. Fortunately, a skin fungus rash can generally be cured by spraying the infected area with an anti-fungal spray, and by keeping the infected area dry. To keep one's buttock area dry during extremely hot humid weather, it may be necessary to position a 12-volt DC brush-less cooling fan beneath one's buttocks while lying on a wooden bead seat cover placed on top of a sleeping cot.

Because skin fungus rash is mainly caused by skin contacting bacteria infested moisture, a skin fungus rash can occur in cold weather, too. To prevent skin fungus rash from occurring in cold weather, it is most important that one not wear clothes against one's skin that easily saturate in moisture. Long underwear, ski mask liner, and sock liners made from a material that doesn't hold moisture, such as polypropylene, will allow skin to remain comfortably dry, thereby drastically reducing the chance of skin fungus rash from forming during cold weather car living.

• CW ENHANCEMENT: WEAR COLD WEATHER CLOTHING SKI-MASK LINER, SKI MASK, AND SKI CAP The head and neck area give off much body heat; therefore, while parking in severely cold weather, one will want to wear a ski mask to help stay warm. Wearing a ski mask liner will help prevent skin irritation and will allow a ski mask to stay clean longer (recommend polypropylene liner). To gain extra warmth, one can wear a ski cap over a ski mask.

WOOL / ELECTRIC SOCKS AND SOCK LINER Wearing warm socks, such as wool or electric socks, will be extremely beneficial in helping one stay warm and sleep more comfortably. Using sock liners, such as polypropylene socks, will enhance comfort by keeping feet dry and preventing skin irritation. Doing so will also increase the length between necessary washing of socks worn over the sock liners.

While taking trips in a compact car into Canada, I sleep in a sleeping bag on the driver's seat . . . a 12-volt pet warmer pad for my feet to rest on makes my sleeping very comfortable, otherwise, cold feet would become very fatiguing . . . I also place a 3-inch thick piece of foam over the adjacent driver's door to increase my comfort.

HIGH QUALITY LONG UNDERWEAR Wearing quality long underwear that "breathes" well and doesn't trap moisture, such as polypropylene underwear, will increase warmth and comfort, prevent skin irritation, and allow outer worn clothes to remain clean longer.

SKIING/MOTORCYCLING RIDING GLOVES Insulated gloves that cover hands, wrist, and beyond are the warmest gloves I've used.

Cold Weather Military Bunny Boots Encapsulate Feet In Air!

CW ENHANCEMENT: LIE ON 12-VOLT DC BED WARMER PAD – SOLD AT WWW.LIVINGINCARS.COM and WWW. ELECTROWARMTH.COM

The bed warmers I've used and sometimes sell at my www. LivingInCars.com web site and the manufacturer's www. ElectroWarmth.com web site are of very high quality. Their electronic thermostat operates noiselessly, and their thermostat control conserves much power. I especially like to place a small 12-volt pet warmer under my feet while sleeping during most any cool/cold weather car living.

CW ENHANCEMENT: "PRIVACY/INSULATING PARTITION" As disclosed in Chapter 1, a privacy/insulating partition is made by hanging a blanket, sleeping bag, or other suitable insulating material over a rope or tube installed just behind the front seats and as close to the ceiling as possible. During cold weather, the air gap between the top of the partition and ceiling above can be filled in with an appropriately sized piece of foam.

During cold weather, the purpose of a privacy/insulating partition is to separate the minimally insulated front-seat area from the heavily insulated aft car living area(s). This allows the minimally insulated front-seat area temperature to remain close to outside ambient temperature, thereby helping to prevent condensation from forming on non-insulated cold hard interior front-seat area surfaces, all while the insulated aft car living area is kept comfortably warm.

One way to increase the insulation of a privacy/insulating partition is to add another blanket, sleeping bag, etc. over what already exists. Another way is to place a 4-inch thick (or greater) piece of foam up against the back of the partition. If space and car design permit, a third way to increase insulation is to install a second privacy/insulating partition several inches behind the first, thus creating an air insulating barrier between the two partitions.

CW ENHANCEMENT: TEMPORARILY CREATING A SMALLER CAR LIVING AREA Since body heat is used to heat a car's living area, it only makes sense that as a car's living area is decreased in size by adding additional insulation, less body heat is required to warm the living space. Using thick, high density, pink upholstery foam cut to exact dimensions has been most effective to use in partitioning off a smaller car living/working area during certain cold weather situations, such as hunting, photography, etc.

If thick enough, high-density pink upholstery foam can be used as a partitioning wall with little or no support. Foam of the appropriate thickness can be cut to a desired size using a long fish fillet knife. Cutouts in the foam are easily made in which a rifle with scope or camera can easily be squeezed into, and an appropriately sized box placed on each side of the foam can make a sturdy equipment platform. After a rifle or camera is removed from the foam's cutout, the cutout hole can be plugged using the original foam that was removed to make the hole.

Thick, high density, pink upholstery foam has been the best material I've used in temporarily decreasing the size of a car's living area; however, other means, such as hanging a blanket, are suitable too. Using Mylar laminated bubble-pack insulating sheeting or metal roof bubble-pack insulation sheeting behind high-density pink upholstery foam will significantly increase insulation for most any application.

CW ENHANCEMENT: USING A "SUITABLE" COLD WEATHER SLEEPING BAG During freezing weather, I always use a sleeping bag on top of my cot's 6-8-inch thick foam covering. Sleeping bags that have a water/wind-proof synthetic plastic-like covering aren't well suited for use over long periods because they tend to trap body moisture instead of dissipating it. Therefore, when using a sleeping bag over long periods (1 or more months), it will be very beneficial to use a type that "breathes" well so that body moisture can dissipate easily, hopefully preventing skin irritation/rash.

To help prevent skin irritation and keep the sleeping bag cleaner longer, I generally lie on one or two wooden bead car-seat covers placed inside my sleeping bag.

CW ENHANCEMENT: SOLAR PANEL(S) PLACED BEHIND CAR WINDSHIELD Solar panels transform a small amount of the solar energy into electricity, while most of the solar energy received is either reflected or absorbed and converted into heat--solar panels can get quite hot. During cold weather car living, it may be beneficial to place a solar panel(s) behind the car windshield to generate extra heat (and 12-volt power).

CW/HW ENHANCEMENT: ELECTRONIC CLOCK/TEMPERATURE GAUGE USAGE While living in a privatized car, it will be beneficial to know both the time and the car living area temperature by simply glancing at a clock/temperature gauge. What typically happens in car living situations is that one quickly learns what comfort enhancements need to be implemented to remain comfortable in the temperature ranges encountered.

Knowing the time of day and what a car's living area temperature is, along with how fast the temperature is increasing/decreasing, will allow one to implement comfort enhancement(s) beforehand instead of waiting till discomfort forces one to make the necessary change. For instance, I'm comfortable lying on top of a wooden bead car seat cover placed on top of my insulated car floor when temperatures are between 60-80 degrees Fahrenheit. When temperatures go higher or lower, additional comfort enhancements, such as using a sleeping cot, will have to be implemented to remain comfortable. Simply looking at my temperature gauge at anytime to see whether any comfort enhancement needs to be implemented is much more productive than waiting till discomfort forces me to make the necessary changes.

Ski Mask, Artic Face Mask + Bib, Wool Sock, Mountain Climber's Stove, Polypropylene Sock + Ski Mask Liner, Wool Scarf, CW Extended Glove.

• HW/CW ENHANCEMENT: SLEEPING COT USAGE AND COT USAGE ENHANCEMENTS

HW ENHANCEMENT: LYING ON A SLEEPING COT .... A s disclosed in Chapter 2, lying naked on top of a sleeping cot inside a car basically surrounds one's body with air, and this allows for maximum convection and perspiration evaporation cooling.

CW ENHANCEMENT: PLACE 4-8-INCH THICK FOAM COVERING OVER SLEEPING COT Covering a cot with a piece of 4-8-inch thick foam will help trap body heat, keeping one much warmer during cold weather. Sizing the foam 6-inch wider and longer than the cot's frame will increase one's comfort by preventing possible body contact with the cold, hard cot frame. High density, pink upholstery foam is the best foam I've used in this application; it can be purchased/ordered from the manufacturer or from furniture upholstering shops in most any size.

HW/CW COT ENHANCEMENTS: MAXIMIZING A COT'S CRITICAL AIR BARRIER The air barrier between a cot's surface and underneath supporting floor substantially helps to insulate one from the uncomfortable car floor temperatures. Therefore, no matter whether a cot is being used to increase comfort in hot or cold weather, making sure the air barrier between the cot's surface and supporting floor is maximum will enhance one's comfort considerably.

To prevent a cot's legs from sinking into the supporting floor's tube/shell foam &carpet covering, the cot's legs can be supported by placing appropriately sized pieces of wood (also a decent insulator) underneath the cot's legs. Making a groove in the wood where the cot's leg contacts the board will aid in keeping the cot from sliding off (I drive u-shaped nails into the wood supports, and then strap the cot legs to the wood using plastic ties).

HW ENHANCEMENT: USE 12-VOLT DC COMPUTER COOLING FAN TO BLOW AIR OVER ONE'S BODY

SEVERE COLD WEATHER MASK + BIB

THERMAL POLYPROPYLENE SKI MASK LINER and

SKI MASK.   www.FreedomToFascism.com

CHAPTER 4

MEETING CAR LIVING ORGANIZATION AND STORAGE NEEDS

4.1 CHAPTER INTRODUCTION

Organizing personal possessions is a lifelong pursuit for just about everyone--and this is especially true for anyone living in a privatized car. In car living situations, organization mainly consists of storing necessary possessions in an organized and out-of-the-way fashion inside one's car while storing all non-essential and/or seldom used possessions at an external storage location.

An organized car interior provides the most usable living space and is easiest to keep clean. Using suitable storage containers for storing possessions (1) helps to organize a car's interior, (2) prevents anyone catching a glimpse of a car's interior from seeing any valuables/possessions, (3) helps protect possessions from possible damage caused by UV rays, moisture, abrasion, vibration, crushing, etc., and (4) allows for easy retrieval, storage, and inventorying of one's possessions.

4.2 SUITABLE STORAGE OPTIONS AND CONTAINERS FOR USE INSIDE A CAR

UNSUITABLE STORAGE OPTIONS The worst way to organize a car's living area would be to build metal or wooden structures/ cabinets, attaching them to a car's interior body. Permanent damaging modifications like these are unsuitable for a number of reasons: (1) They damage a car's body, possibly bringing about severe car body corrosion problems at some point; (2) they add unnecessary weight; (3) they make a car's living area less comfortable to live in by taking up valuable space unnecessarily and by allowing uncomfortable car body temperature faster conduction into the car living area; (4) they would cause condensation formation problems during cold weather; (5) they would make insulating a car's living area extremely difficult; (6) they would make a car more difficult to sell; and (7) they would make a car's interior more violent/lethal during a car crash/accident.

SUITABLE STORAGE OPTIONS   A much better way to organize a car's living area is to (1) store all "unsuitable," seldom used, and/or unnecessary possessions at an external storage location, such as at a family member's residence, rental storage room, bank box, etc., and (2) store necessary possessions inside suitable storage containers positioned at out-of-the-way car interior locations. I generally store my "car possessions" in plastic storage boxes positioned along one side of the car interior, and also in the front seat passenger area if necessary.

UNSUITABLE STORAGE CONTAINERS   Obviously, glass containers aren't suitable for use in car living storage applications--they're just too dangerous. Glass containers create excessive condensation problems during cool/cold weather car living. Their hardness and likely unpleasant temperatures make them uncomfortable to contact. Glass containers may not provide privacy of contents stored within, and they probably offer minimal protection from UV rays. After accidentally breaking a half-gallon glass urine storage container inside my car, I never allowed the use or transport of glass containers in my cars again (exception: jelly jar, chemical jar, etc. stored in protective container).

Metal storage containers aren't well suited for use in car living storage applications. Their heaviness and hardness makes them relatively dangerous to have inside a car during a possible car accident/crash. Their hardness and likely unpleasant temperature (high thermal conductivity) make them uncomfortable to come in contact with in the small confines of a car during any temperature weather. Condensation will easily form on metal containers used in cold weather car living storage applications. Unless finely finished inside and out, metal containers can easily cause abrasion to anything they contact.

Wooden storage containers are heavy and bulky. As compared to other types of storage containers, they generally take up more space for a given volume of storage space. The high humidity of a car living environment could eventually cause wooden storage containers to rot. If used in vibrating environments, wooden containers will eventually cause abrasion to anything they contact, including contents stored inside.

STORAGE CONTAINERS SUITABLE FOR USE IN CAR LIVING STORAGE APPLICATIONS Plastic storage containers are inexpensive and readily available. They are lightweight, non-corrosive, durable, long lasting, and minimally abrasive. Because plastic is a better temperature insulator, having a much lower thermal conductivity rating than glass or metal, plastic containers cause minimal condensation problems during cool/cold weather car living and are much more comfortable to come in contact with during any temperature weather.

PLASTIC HUNTING BOXES AND PLASTIC FILE BOXES Plastic file and hunting boxes have been some of the best storage containers I've used for storing and organizing possessions carried in my privatized cars and for storing possessions at my external storage location. Against a sidewall or in the front passenger's floor area are two out-of-the-way locations I place them. Lining the inside of a plastic file/hunting box with a layer of 1-inch thick foam will provide extra protection of fragile contents.

Plastic file boxes generally have ideal dimensions for storing paper documents; however, they are quite useful in storing most anything that will fit inside them. Typical inside L x H x W dimensions are 12 x 10 x 9 inches or 12 x 9.75 x 9.5 inches. They're often sold containing removable file folders that are very useful in organizing/separating paper documents. Plastic file boxes are inexpensive and readily available for purchase most anywhere office/school supplies are sold.

Plastic hunting boxes are generally much stronger and more durable than plastic file boxes because of being made of a higher quality plastic. Many have removable o-ring sealed lids that make these containers suitable for applications where airtight storage is needed, such as in a humid car living environment. Many are designed so their lids can be locked with a pad lock. The inside L x H x W dimensions of the two type hunting storage boxes I use are 13 x 7 x 7.5 inches and 12 x 10 x 7 inches. Because they are strong, durable, airtight, and have suitable dimensions for use in car living storage applications, plastic hunting boxes are what I use most for organizing and storing possessions kept inside my car and at my external storage location. Plastic hunting boxes are generally available for purchase at locations where sporting goods are sold, especially during hunting season.

Plastic boxes w/ files + foam wrapped equip., Re-sealable bags, VHS case, Anhydrous Calcium Sulfate on cloth and tied off in cloth.

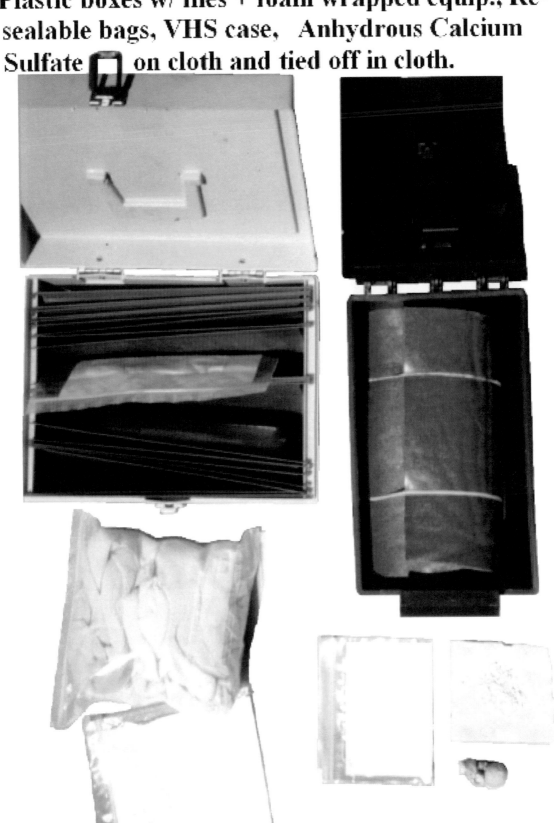

PLASTIC BOAT BATTERY STORAGE BOXES Plastic boat battery storage boxes generally come in two sizes: a large size for storing a medium-large size 12-volt battery, and a medium size for storing a small-medium size 12-volt battery. Typical inside L x H x W dimensions are 13 x 8 x 7.5 inches (large box) and 10 x 8 x 7.5 inches (small box). Generally, the top removable lid/cover is held in place by a strap that wraps around the center section of the box and lid. The battery box cover contains two small holes, one positioned above a battery's positive terminal and the other positioned above the negative terminal, in which the battery positive and negative wires can conveniently pass through. Plastic boat battery storage boxes are available from automotive and sporting goods suppliers.

PLASTIC VHS VIDEO STORAGE CONTAINERS Although they're becoming harder to find, plastic VHS tape storage containers work well in organizing, protecting, storing, and preventing loss of small items/possessions. Wrapping the VHS case with a rubber band prevents it from opening. Storing a mini-computer, pager, TV remote, etc., each individually inside a sock and then placed inside a plastic VHS storage container, are a few applications that come to mind.
*EXTRA: A single edge razor blade can be used to remove the two molded VHS tape guides located on the bottom inside of a plastic VHS storage box, thus making the bottom flat.

PLASTIC FOOD STORAGE CONTAINERS Airtight plastic food storage containers are inexpensive and readily available in many sizes. Storage of mailing envelopes, stamps, and any other small items that need to be sealed off from a humid car living environment are applications well suited for food storage containers.

BAR SOAP PLASTIC STORAGE CONTAINERS I use bar soap plastic storage containers for storing bar soap and for storing film containers containing shampoo.

FILM CONTAINERS Storing four plastic film containers full of shampoo inside a bar soap plastic storage container is one application for using film containers. Storing vitamins and medications is another application.

VITAMIN / MEDICINE CONTAINERS

RESEALABLE FREEZER BAGS Resealable freezer bags come in many sizes: tiny sizes, pint, quart, half-gallon, 1-gallon, and 2-gallon sizes. They're excellent to use for storing, organizing, protecting, and preserving many things, such as receipts/invoices, documents, tax records, books/magazines, money/change, small batteries, sockets (wrench set), hardware (nuts/bolts), first aid supplies, equipment manuals, tire repair kit, spare car parts, wire soldering supplies, toilet paper roll, DC and AC adapters, dc-to-ac inverter, camera equipment, food, printer paper, out-of-season clothes, etc. Eliminating dust and moisture, and minimizing abrasion are a few benefits resealable storage bags provide.

5-6" DIAMETER PLASTIC CYLINDER TYPE FLUID DISPENSER COOLER As described in Chapter 5, a plastic 5-6-inch diameter fluid dispenser cooler can be helpful in meeting bathroom and waste storage needs.

5-1 GALLON-SIZE AIRTIGHT PLASTIC FRUIT JUICE/DRINK CONTAINER   As disclosed in Chapter Five, a .5-1 gallon-size, airtight, plastic, fruit juice/drink container works well in helping to meet urination and urine storage needs.

4.3 SPECIALIZED STORAGE CONTAINERS

FRAGILE MOISTURE-SENSITIVE STORAGE Depending on the size and type of equipment, I generally store fragile equipment inside either a plastic hunting storage box lined with 1-2-inch thick, high density, pink upholstery foam, or I store it in plastic, airtight Pelican or SKB case. If using an o-ring sealed hunting storage box, extra fragile equipment can first be wrapped in foam and then placed inside a resealable bag before being placed inside a foam-lined plastic hunting box. The plastic hunting storage boxes I use each have a removable o-ring sealed lid that provides for airtight seal. Placing a pouch of drying agent, silica gel desiccant or anhydrous calcium sulfate, in a hunting storage box or Pelican/SKB case is all that is required to remove moisture.

Foam (and leather) attracts moisture, so some type of drying agent needs to be placed inside the case or storage box. The foam lined case or box needs to be o-ring sealed and airtight, otherwise the foam would continually attract moisture and quickly saturate any drying agent stored within the case.

OXYGEN SENSITIVE STORAGE   Oxygen is an ingredient required for many types of corrosion and spoilage to take place. To preserve certain types of metals, foods, equipment, etc. over extremely long periods, a storage container that can be totally sealed with the oxygen removed is best; also, it's generally best if the storage container remain cool wherever it is placed.

In oxygen sensitive storage applications, I've chosen to use PVC tubing in which a metal motorcycle valve stem (.301-inch diameter dirt bike valve stem, such as #VS-1218R) can be screwed into a hole drilled (9/32-inch drill bit) into each of the two PVC end caps/plugs before sealing the end caps onto each end of the PVC tube. To remove the oxygen, the tube can be purged with nitrogen by applying nitrogen of very low pressure into one motorcycle valve stem while holding the other motorcycle valve stem open. Nitrogen tank, regulator, air hose, and air chuck may be rented from oxygen/welding supply businesses.
CAUTION: The purging process can be extremely dangerous if too high pressure is applied!
EXTRA: Using a PVC adapter end and screw-on lid will make the tube reusable. Using rubber plugs will also make a tube reusable.

BURYING YOUR TREASURE Government instruments that are pulled over the ground can identify your treasure down to 10 feet and much more, depending on the instrument, so you have to figure ways to camouflage your treasure, such as burying your treasure under structures that government instruments can't pass over easily.

Nitrogen-Purged PVC Storage Tube with Motorcycle Valve Stems screwed into PVC End Caps. Black Silicon Sealant covering base of Chrome Valve Stems isn't necessary. www.GiveMeLiberty.org www.FreedomToFacism.com www.PrisonPlanet.com PrisonPlanet.tv www.InfoWars.com

4.4 CLOTHES STORAGE OPTIONS FOR CAR LIVING

Some of the locations I've stored my clothes at while living in cars include (1) inside my car, (2) family/friend's residence, (3) rental storage room, (4) health club locker, and (5) college athletic facility locker. Clothes storage containers I've used include (1) pillow case, (2) military duffel bag, (3) 1-2 gallon-size resealable freezer bags, (4) hanging suit bag, (5) plastic storage box, and (6) suitcase.

PLASTIC HUNTING STORAGE BOX Using a plastic hunting storage box for storing folded clothes offers the benefits of airtight storage, keeping clothes fresh smelling, dry, well protected, and minimally wrinkled. Its disadvantage is that minimal storage capacity requires that most clothes be stored folded.

PILLOW CASE CLOTHES STORAGE OPTION Pillowcases can be used to store clothes that can be stored wrinkled, such as socks, underwear, dirty clothes, etc. Tying off a pillow case opening with a rubber band is easy. Pillow case clothes storage advantages include medium capacity and softness. Disadvantages include weak storage, wrinkling of clothes, clothes taking on car living area smell, and clothes being susceptible to humidity and accidental spills, possibly causing mold/mildew.
*EXTRA: Line pillowcase with garbage bag and seal to keep clothes fresh smelling and better protected.

USING A HANGING CLOTHES BAR INSIDE CAR .... (self-explanatory)

HANGING SUIT BAG FOR DRESS CLOTHES STORAGE When needing to store dress clothes wrinkle-free inside a car, I usually have used a hanging suit bag. Its disadvantage is that it must be laid flat, taking up much car space, thus requiring it be moved to gain access to the area of the car it covers. Even with this disadvantage, using a hanging suit bag is an excellent way to store suits and other dress clothes wrinkle free inside a car.

It is possible to hang a half-length suit bag from a car clothes bar inside a car, but not a full-length suit bag.
MILITARY DUFFEL BAG CLOTHES STORAGE OPTION   I

sometimes have used military duffel bags for storing (1) dirty clothes, (2) out-of-season clothes that have been sealed in resealable freezer bags, and (3) clean clothes that can be stored wrinkled. Because of their high strength and large capacity, military duffel bags are excellent for use in transporting clothes. Other advantages include softness, water resistance, and sunlight blockage. Their main disadvantage is clothes wrinkling.

ONE TO TWO GALLON-SIZE RESEALABLE FREEZER BAG: LONG-TERM CLOTHES STORAGE If used in a suitable climate controlled environment or if clothes are cleaned as often as necessary to prevent mildew/mold from possibly forming, any of the previously mentioned clothes storage options can be used for long-term clothes storage. However, the best way I've found to protect clothes that will be stored in adverse environments (extreme temperatures, humidity, chemical fumes) over long periods is to place dry, clean clothes inside a 1-2 gallon-size resealable freezer bag, and then press out the air before sealing it by singeing about 3/16-inch of the resealable end with flame while the end (less 3/16-inch end portion) is squeezed between a horizontal flat surface and a thin vertical surface. The flame sealed resealable bag of clothes can then be sealed inside another resealable bag, thus creating double-bag protection.

To prevent condensation from forming inside a resealable bag and to prevent UV ray degradation of a resealable bag, resealable bags of clothes should be stored somewhere dark, such as inside a military duffel bag or other suitable container in which significant amounts of sunlight won't pass through. If kept away from sunlight, clothes stored in this way can be stored for many years (if not decades) without adverse effects.

EXTRA: Including a pouch of drying agent (silica gel desiccant, anhydrous calcium sulfate, etc.) in with the clothes may be beneficial.

4" dia. PVC Pipe, Two Rubber Plugs, and Two End Caps make a Reusable Airtight Storage Container. www.LivingInCars.com is hosted by www.CARTAMA.NET

CHAPTER 5

STAYING CLEAN AND MEETING BATHROOM NEEDS WHILE LIVING IN CARS

5.1 CAR LIVING AREA CLEANLINESS AND BUG ELIMINATION CONCERNS

DO BUGS LIVE IN CARS? For over a decade I've lived and worked in privatized cars at various locations throughout the U.S., mainly in populated areas but sometimes in sparsely populated wilderness areas. A nice aspect of car living is that a car's interior is practically a bug-free, pesticide-free environment. The exception to this is when parking in areas that have flies and mosquitoes that can enter any opened car windows not covered with sheeting or mosquito netting (during hot weather). Unlike most conventional homes that are easily accessible to crawling bugs, such as fleas, tics, spiders, roaches, ants, etc., car interiors don't seem to be accessible to crawling bugs, probably because the trip over tires, chassis/frame, and car body is too long and complicated.

• CONDITIONS THAT MAY ALLOW CERTAIN TYPES OF BUGS TO ENTER A CAR

BUGS CAN BE UNINTENTIONALLY TRANSPORTED INTO A CAR Fleas can be transported into a car by allowing a cat or dog inside a car during warm weather. Transporting bags of livestock feed and pet food that contains bugs may allow bug entry. Fortunately, bugs contained within livestock feed can be prevented from escaping by first placing the bag of feed inside a large plastic trash bag before transporting it inside a car. Momentarily leaving a bag/backpack on the ground or floor with an opened food container inside, such as an opened bag of chips, and then placing it inside a car may allow bugs

67

to unintentionally be brought into a car.

BUGS CAN ENTER BY TRAVELING ACROSS AN UNINTENTIONALLY MADE BRIDGE I've found that if a short "bridge" from the ground to a car's body is unintentionally created, ants and possibly spiders may walk across it to enter a car. A "bridge" can be created in a number of ways: (1) parking near tall grass, foliage, or tree branches that touch the car body, (2) using a power cord that travels along the ground and into one's car, (3) using a rope/string to tie something to a car in which excess rope/string dangles to the ground, and (4) parking under overhanging branches or structures from which spiders can lower themselves. Eliminating any unintentionally made bridges should prevent any type of crawling bug from entering a car (exception: spiders from overhead structures).

PREVENTING BUG ENTRY ACROSS CORD/ROPE BRIDGES During wilderness/isolated car living situations where bridges couldn't be eliminated, such as when using a power cord that extends from my car interior to nearby solar panels, I've developed two different approaches in preventing bug access. Applying petroleum jelly or automotive grease to a 4-inch portion of the suspended cord at a point just before where it enters the car will prevent bugs from passing over the greased portion. Unfortunately, this option can easily become very messy if one unintentionally makes contact with the grease.

A second way to prevent bug access over a power cord extending from a car is to implement what I refer to as the "moat" option. It consists of using a jack stand placed inside a 5-gallon-size bucket filled with water. The power cord enters over the side of the bucket, travels down underneath the jack stand, and then travels back over the top of the jack stand's support and into a nearby car. With the moat method, bugs would have to swim across the water to get to the power cord exiting over the top of the jack stand's vertical supporting arm, which isn't likely.

PREVENTING FLYING BUGS FROM ENTERING A CAR About the only time flies and mosquitoes have entered my car has been during warm/hot weather when car windows, doors, sunroofs and/or air vents were opened for cooling purposes while parking in wet wilderness areas where quantities of mosquitoes and flies reside. In wilderness parking situations with front car doors left open, I've also had a few visits from grasshoppers, wasps, bees, moths, and small birds. Except for flies and mosquitoes, most other type flying bugs want nothing to do with being inside an occupied car, and they will leave quickly once finding that a car is occupied. Fortunately, there are several options that prevent flying type bugs from entering a car.

In helping to prevent fly and mosquito entry, urine should be disposed far away from one's parking location, as the smell of urine does attract flies. Any car openings that allow flying bugs access into a car can be covered with mosquito netting or sheeting using masking/duct tape or silicon adhesive sealant to hold it in place. Under dashboard air duct openings can be covered with mosquito netting held in place with a rubber band, duct tape, and/or silicon adhesive sealant.

If parking in an isolated wilderness area where flies and mosquitoes are thick, and where hot temperatures make it desirable to leave a car's front doors opened to allow for maximum cooling--instead of trying to cover the door opening with mosquito netting or sheeting, it may be easier to make a car's privacy/insulating partition (Ch. 1) out of mosquito netting, so as to prevent mosquitoes and flies from gaining access to a car's living area. To make a sleeping cot fly/mosquito-proof, a mosquito netting cot tent covering can be placed over and around a sleeping cot by suspending it from a car's ceiling (military mosquito netting cot-covering tents are specifically made for this).

CAR INTERIOR CLEANING EXTRAS Vacuuming carpet/ upholstery along with dusting and cleaning glass, plastic, vinyl, and metal interior surfaces is the usual way to clean a car interior. An addition to cleaning a car being lived in is to put a bit more effort into killing bacteria that causes odor. Spray disinfectants that can be sprayed on any surface (foam, carpet, plastic, vinyl, etc.) to kill bacteria and then evaporate have worked well in allowing my car interiors to stay clean smelling.

If one has allergies or eye problems caused by dust, pollen, etc., it may be beneficial to carry a small powerful hand-held vacuum and a dc-to-ac inverter for powering the vacuum cleaner whenever desired. The car engine should be operating when powering a vacuum cleaner from an inverter that is connected to a car's electrical system, so as to provide enough power to the inverter and to keep the car starting battery from being damaged/discharged. Use of small vacuum cleaner attachments when cleaning computer keyboards, mobile phone, and like equipment may be very useful/beneficial.

Although I never used one during my first ten years of living/working in cars, I do presently own an electronic air-cleaning machine. I operate it for about 30 minutes before going to sleep. It is beneficial to people who wear contacts, have allergy problems, or simply desire cleaner air.

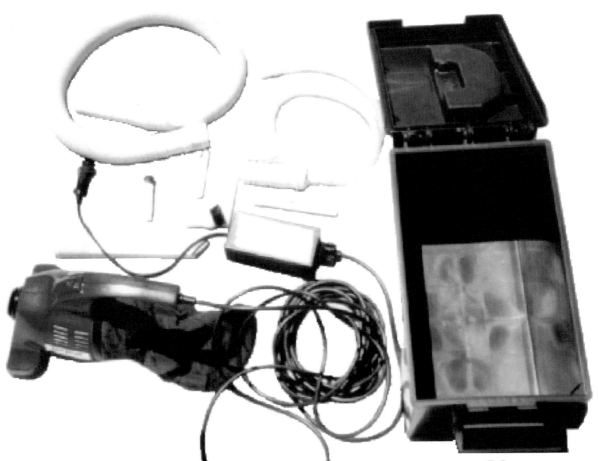

Handheld Vacuum, 400-Watt Inverter, Vacuum Attachments, Plastic Hunting Box with O-ring Sealed Lid.

5.2 CLOTHES WASHING OPTIONS, CONSIDERATIONS, AND RECOMMENDATIONS

• CLOTHES WASHING/DRYING OPTIONS

FRIEND/RELATIVE'S WASHER AND DRYER I prefer washing my clothes at a friend's or relative/family member's residence for the benefits of privacy, minimal expense, cleanliness of equipment, and good overall atmosphere.

APARTMENT COMMUNITY LAUNDROMATS As a benefit for tenants, apartment community Laundromats are generally inexpensive, well maintained, and have nice atmospheres. While washing clothes at an apartment community, one may be able to swim and charge rechargeable equipment.

BUSINESS LAUNDROMATS OPENED TO THE PUBLIC Washing clothes at public Laundromats can be a dull, dreary, gloomy experience. However, I have used a few Laundromats located in resort areas or next to entertainment type businesses that have had pleasing atmospheres and clean machines, both of which helped make these businesses fairly satisfying to use.

HOTEL/MOTEL LAUNDROMATS Hotel/motel Laundromats usually are small with few machines, and they generally are relatively expensive to use.

• CLOTHES WASHING CONSIDERATIONS/ RECOMMENDATIONS

PREVENTING STAINS DURING CLOTHES WASHING It can be extremely disappointing to use some washer and have nice clothes come out stained. Fortunately, there are a couple ways to prevent this from happening. One can simply wait until someone washing his or her nice clothes is finished and then use that same washing machine. A faster way would be to use any washing machine to first wash a load of inexpensive hidden type clothes (towels, underwear, etc.) to make sure that they come out stain-free before washing valuable outer clothes.

ELIMINATING BACTERIA DURING CLOTHES WASHING Bacteria in clothes cause them to smell quickly after donning them. It's easy to kill bacteria when washing clothes by simply including a tablespoon of suitable disinfectant or by using detergent that contains bleach. The same disinfectant I spray on my car's interior surfaces to kill bacteria and help make my car smell clean is what I add to my wash. Disinfectant is best added to the wash cycle after the washer has filled with water.

PREVENTING STAINS DURING CLOTHES DRYING Wiping the inside of a dryer (cage) with a clean white rag, cloth, or paper towel to see if any undesirable discoloring of the rag occurs is one way to ensure that a dryer is clean. Drying less valuable clothes first to farther ensure a dryer's cleanliness may be beneficial.

DISCREETLY CHARGING RECHARGEABLE EQUIPMENT WHILE WASHING/DRYING CLOTHES Charging rechargeable equipment from a 120-volt AC wall outlet is convenient to do while washing clothes. Carrying a bag with rechargeable equipment inside in which all equipment cords are plugged into a multiple AC outlet adapter that is connected to a short extension cord that extends out of the bag to a nearby 120-volt AC wall outlet is a fairly discreet way of charging rechargeable equipment while washing clothes.

5.3 CAR LIVING BATHING OPTIONS

There are many places to bath while living in a privatized car, such as at lakes, friends/family's/acquaintances' residence, truck stops, privately-owned campgrounds, health clubs, college dormitories and athletic facilities, etc. However, when not parking close to a location that has convenient to use private showering facilities, having to drive a moderate distance to shower each time a shower is needed may be time consuming, wasteful, expensive, and/or very inconvenient. Being able to shower at wherever one is parked or very nearby may be much more satisfying. Fortunately, bathing inside one's car or just outside is easy to do.

• TWO JUGS OF WATER SHOWERING OPTION
During my U.S. travels, which is when I first really began living in cars, I initially tried to satisfy my showering needs by finding a suitable body of water (lake, stream, river, pond)

to bath in, or by finding a water hose in a private location to shower with. Obviously, this wasted much time, energy, and gasoline, so it didn't take but a week or less before figuring out a much more suitable way to satisfy my showering needs. I soon began storing a few gallons of water inside my car to use in a quick, thorough, efficient bathing option I call the "two jugs of water" showering option. Since one is always parked nearby a private location in which one can quickly drive to and then quickly shower at just outside one's car, such as behind a shopping center or business, a secluded road, etc., the two jugs of water showering option quickly became and still is today the fastest option I use in my car living bathing applications when conventional showering options aren't readily available.

PERFORMING THE TWO JUGS OF WATER SHOWERING OPTION Performing the two jugs of water showering option requires a bar of soap, shampoo, washcloth, towel, and one or two gallon-size plastic jugs (milk jugs work well) filled with comfortable temperature water. Although any combination of steps can be used, I've found the following steps to be quickest using the least amount of water: (1) After driving to a suitable semi-private/private location in which you can bath comfortably just outside your car, begin by pouring comfortable temperature water over your head allowing the water to wet your naked body (wear bathing suit if necessary); (2) apply shampoo to your hair and lather; (3) before rinsing the shampoo from your hair, use a washcloth and bar of soap to clean your body; (4) rinse the shampoo from your hair allowing the water to drain over your body rinsing it too; (5) finish rinsing any body part that needs additional rinsing; and (6) repeat all or part of the preceding steps if desired/necessary.

TWO JUGS OF WATER SHOWERING OPTION ADVANTAGES The two jugs of water showering option is extremely thorough and fast, taking only 45-90 seconds for a male to complete. Wearing a bathing suit in populated areas, one can hop out of his car at a semi-private or private location for a quick 45-90 second shower, such as behind shopping centers/businesses, a secluded road, etc. Basically, anywhere one can hop out of a car for 45-90 seconds and not be in view of anyone is suitable.

Although I use the two jugs of water showering option just outside my car door, there are other places well suited for this type showering, such as in any rest room where the floor has water drainage provisions.

As long as one has suitable temperature water and a warm car to climb back into after a 45-90 second shower, cold adverse weather isn't a problem when performing the two jugs of water showering option (0 degree weather with steam pouring off my body--no problem).

DISADVANTAGES OF THE TWO JUGS OF WATER SHOWERING OPTION Because bathing water is applied fully to one's body, using water of suitable temperature is necessary if one is to remain comfortable, especially during cold weather bathing.

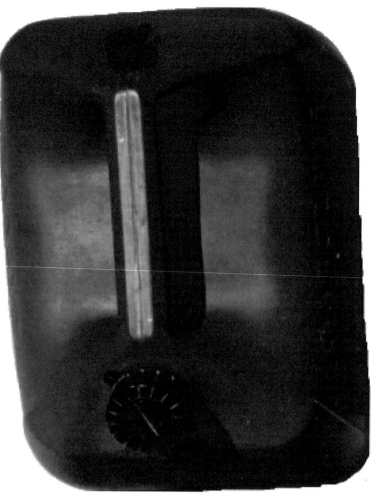

www.PrisonPlanet.com

www.INFOWARS.COM

www.PrisonPlanet.tv

www.JonesReport.com

www.FreedomToFascism.com

www.GiveMeLiberty.org

ONE-HALF, ONE and TWO GALLON WATER STORAGE CONTAINERS.

• THE CAR PRIVACY BATHING OPTION

The two jugs of water showering option can work extremely well in satisfying bathing needs while living in a privatized car. However, when parked in extremely populated areas, or during surveillance work when one can't leave one's parked privatized car for several days or more, or when warm water isn't conveniently obtainable while parking in severe cold weather, it will be necessary to be able to bathe privately inside a privatized car. Fortunately, bathing inside a car is easily accomplished by performing what I refer to as the "car privacy" bathing option.

PERFORMING THE CAR PRIVACY BATHING OPTION The car privacy bathing option requires the following bathing supplies: bar soap, shampoo, soaping washcloth, 1-2 rinsing washcloths, towel, and gallon jug of water. In addition, a large pan/container, such as a large plastic engine oil drain container, and an extra towel are required.

Inside a car's living area, place the extra towel on the floor, and then place the large drain pan/container on top. While in a kneeling position, lean over and hang your head as close to the inside of the container as possible so that all water applied to your head will drain into the container. Next, pour water from a gallon-size jug over your head and upper neck area to thoroughly wet your hair. Staying in the kneeling, bent-over position, shampoo your hair and wash your face and neck. Use the gallon jug of water to rinse your hair, head, and neck. After cleaning the head area, sit up and clean the rest of your body in sections using bar soap, soaping washcloth, and rinsing washcloth(s). Although you can clean and rinse the rest of your body by applying soap to your body with the soaping washcloth and then rinse with the rinsing washcloth(s) using only two steps, I've found that washing and rinsing different areas of my body separately is easiest, very comfortable to do, and allows for a more thorough cleaning. After applying soap and scrubbing an area of your body, rinse the area by using a thoroughly moistened rinsing washcloth to wipe away soap. To remove the soap from your body sufficiently, you will need to perform 2-3 rinses, rinsing out the soap gathered in the rinsing washcloth after each body section rinsing. This process can be repeated for each section of your body until completely clean.

GENITAL AREA CLEANING The genital area is easily cleaned by squatting over the plastic drain pan/container with one's genital and buttocks positioned as far inside the plastic container as possible. Water from the gallon-size jug can be poured onto one's lower stomach and lower back area that will run over one's genital and buttock area draining into the container beneath. One's moistened genitals and buttocks can now be washed with a bar of soap and then rinsed clean by again pouring water over one's lower back and lower stomach area.

CAR PRIVACY BATHING OPTION ADVANTAGES The car privacy bathing option is an excellent backup option to use when it is necessary to bath inside a privatized car or when needing to conserve water (I've never had to use more than a gallon). Because water isn't poured directly against the body (exception: head and genital areas), and because bathing and rinsing is done to different body sections one at a time, and because a car's interior can be climate controlled with the car's heater or air conditioner (exception: surveillance/secret parking)--bathing water temperature isn't critical to one's comfort. The car privacy bathing option can be performed inside a privatized car parked anywhere--and without anyone outside knowing what is taking place.

CAR PRIVACY BATHING OPTION DISADVANTAGE As compared to the two jugs of water showering option, the car privacy bathing option requires more setup, bathing supplies, and work, and therefore takes much longer to complete.

DISCREETLY GETTING RID OF WASH WATER Wash water can simply be thrown out onto the ground; however, for discreet disposal the wash water can be poured into a funnel and hose assembly that deposits it directly underneath the car or car door crevice, or the wash water can be stored in a suitable storage container until reaching a private location where it can be poured out.

DRYING USED TOWELS AND WASHCLOTHS While parked, hanging towels over the inside of a front side window or "privacy/insulating partition's" support; or laying them over the dashboard may be good places to dry towels and washcloths, depending on the temperature, amount of sunlight available, color of towels/washcloths, color of dashboard, and color of front seat area car interior. During driving, placing towels and washcloths over a car's dashboard defrost vent will allow hot defrost air to dry them extremely fast.

TRUCK STOP SHOWERS MAY BE AVAILABLE--AND THEY MAY BE FREE
PRIVATELY OWNED CAMPGROUNDS MAY HAVE SHOWERS (pay to use)
HEALTH AND FITNESS CENTER SHOWER FACILITIES

5.4 BATHING WATER SOURCES, RETRIEVAL, AND STORAGE OPTIONS

There are unlimited places to retrieve bathing water; there are many ways to retrieve bathing water; there are many types of containers suitable for use in retrieving and storing bathing water; there are many ways of heating bathing water. Since water storage containers are used in retrieval, transfer, and storage of both bathing and drinking water, the first thing to consider is what type water storage container(s) will be most suitable for use in car living situations. Type of material a water storage container is made of is the first thing to consider.

• BATHING/DRINKING WATER STORAGE CONTAINERS

UNSUITABLE WATER STORAGE CONTAINERS: Glass storage containers aren't suitable for use in car living situations: (1) They're too dangerous, (2) they would create condensation formation problems during cool/cold weather car living, and (3) because of their hardness and moderate thermal conductivity, a glass container is uncomfortable to contact in the confines of a car during any temperature weather.

PLASTIC IS THE BEST MATERIAL FOR WATER STORAGE CONTAINERS
Plastic containers are the best containers I've used in storing both bathing and drinking water inside a car. They're inexpensive, readily available, lightweight, non-toxic, durable, and long lasting. As compared to glass and metal containers, plastic containers are much safer to use inside a car. Because plastic is a better temperature insulator, having a lower thermal

conductivity than glass or metal, plastic containers cause less condensation formation during cool/cold weather car living, and they are more comfortable to come in contact with during any temperature weather. Being somewhat flexible also makes plastic containers more comfortable to use inside a car.

EXTRA: If stored in sunlight, plastic containers can be painted to help protect them from damaging UV rays.

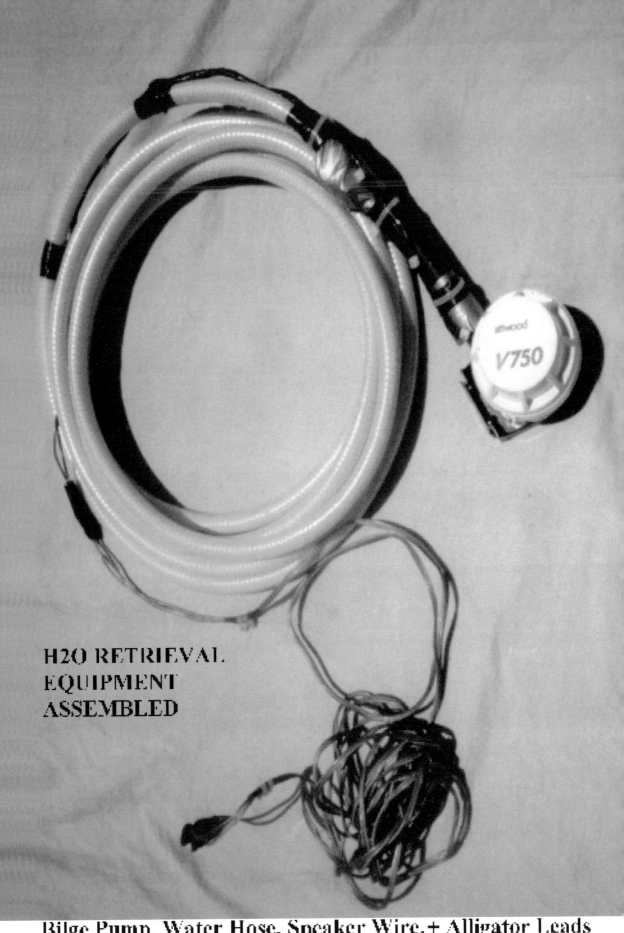

H2O RETRIEVAL
EQUIPMENT
ASSEMBLED

Bilge Pump, Water Hose, Speaker Wire,+ Alligator Leads

• PLASTIC CONTAINERS SUITABLE FOR STORING BATHING AND DRINKING WATER

PORTABLE RECREATIONAL VEHICLES (RV) WASTE STORAGE TANKS – NOT MY FIRST CHOICE Many recreational vehicle (RV) suppliers sell rectangular-shaped, plastic, portable RV waste storage tanks that are suitable for use in storing both bathing and drinking water. Five to thirty gallon-size waste storage tanks are what I've seen offered. The large capacity tanks may come with two wheels that allow the tank to be pulled around easily. The narrow shape and the location of their carry handle make them easy to carry, sort of like carrying a briefcase. Their narrow rectangular shape makes them extremely stable while being transported inside a car, if laid flat.

Plastic RV portable waste storage tanks' narrow rectangular shape takes up much useable car space, storing a relatively small amount of water. They aren't suitable for stacking inside a car. The location of the cap, vent, and carry handle makes them extremely difficult to pour from. The RV waste storage tanks I've seen marketed are relatively expensive (five times as much as plastic gas containers) and aren't readily available. Although rectangular-shaped RV waste storage tanks could be used for storing water, they're not what I consider an ideal water storage container for use in car living situations.

THIN-WALL PLASTIC GALLON-SIZE JUGS AREN'T SUITABLE FOR STORING QUANTITIES OF WATER

Thin-wall plastic gallon-size jugs, the type that milk and bottled water comes in, are extremely easy to handle and pour from, and therefore have a few car living application uses. However, their suitable uses don't include storing quantities of water inside a car.

ADVANTAGES OF THIN-WALL PLASTIC GALLON JUGS Ease in handling make thin-wall plastic gallon-size jugs a pleasure to use in performing the two jugs of water and car privacy bathing options. They can be used in automotive oil/fluid replacement, storage, and recycling applications. Cutting out the top portion of a thin-wall gallon jug can make a homemade funnel and drain pan. Because heat easily transfers to water contained within a thin-wall gallon jug, they are suitable to use in bathing water-heating applications. They can be used to obtain purified water from water dispensing machines, and if desired, transfer the purified water into a larger, stronger water storage container. Storing a day's supply of drinking water in a thin-wall gallon jug to pour from during the day is easy and convenient.

DISADVANTAGES OF THIN-WALL PLASTIC GALLON JUGS

Several undesirable characteristics make thin-wall plastic gallon-size jugs unsuitable for storing quantities of water inside a car. Their capacity being only one gallon would require that many of these containers be used. Because of their thin, cheap plastic construction, thin-wall plastic gallon-size jugs rupture, crack, puncture, and leak water very easily; their life span is generally very short if transported inside a car. Their press/screw-on caps don't seal well or stay on securely. Because of their unstable shape, they easily tip over and leak water while being transported in a car. They are very susceptible to deterioration caused by exposure to UV rays--I've seen them shatter like glass after only a couple months of direct exposure to sunlight.

PLASTIC GAS CONTAINERS ARE EXCELLENT WATER STORAGE CONTAINERS

The best containers I've used for storing both bathing and drinking water are inexpensive red-plastic gasoline storage containers. These containers are very rugged and long lasting. They're readily available almost anywhere automotive and/or hardware supplies are sold. The 2.5 and 5-gallon-size gas containers are the ones I've mainly used, but they are available in other sizes, too.

STABLE RECTANGULAR SHAPE Their stable rectangular shape makes it difficult for them to tip over inside a moving car. The location of the carry handle, vent, and dispenser spout, along with their rectangular shape make these containers very easy to handle and pour from. The gas container's rectangular shape allows for maximum water storage while taking up the least amount of space inside a car.

SMOOTH SHAPE The smoothness and flexibility of plastic gas containers along with optimal placement of the spout and vent makes these containers comfortable to contact in the close confines of a car. Plastic being a better temperature insulator (low thermal conductivity) than glass or metal allows plastic gas containers to produce less condensation during cool/cold weather car living, and it makes them more comfortable to contact during any temperature weather--they're even comfortable enough to sleep in contact with for the purpose of warming bathing water.

NO LEAKAGE PROBLEMS   The removable dispenser spout and air vent both seal extremely well, thus these containers generally won't leak or spill water if tipped over on their sides.

REMOVABLE/RETRACTABLE DISPENSER NOZZLE BENEFITS The removable/retractable dispenser spout is especially suited for use in filling a thin wall plastic gallon-size jug. Likewise, with the dispenser spout removed, a thin-wall gallon-size jug's opening mates well to the gas container's opening. Therefore, a gallon-size jug can be used to fill plastic gas containers with water, such as when retrieving drinking water from a drinking water dispensing machine and then transfer it into a 2.5 or 5 gallon-size plastic gas container.

PLASTIC GAS CONTAINER DISADVANTAGE Exposure of non-painted plastic to UV rays causes it to fade in color and become extremely weak and brittle. A plastic gas container should be painted if it will be stored exposed to direct sunlight.

55-GALLON PLASTIC BARREL In isolated car living situations, storing water in a 55-gallon plastic barrel may be convenient. 55-gallon capacity allows obtaining maximum amounts of water during water retrieval trips (if applicable). Siphoning water from a 55-gallon barrel to another barrel/container allows for easy transferring of water. Either of the 55-gallon barrel's two plastic screw caps can be fitted with a faucet/valve.
EXTRA: If stored in direct sunlight, plastic containers should be painted to lessen exposure to UV rays.

• BATHING WATER SOURCES AND RETRIEVAL OPTIONS

WATER HOSE HYDRANT While living in a privatized car, it's easy to drive up next to any suitable water hydrant, such as hydrants located at gas stations, convenience stores, businesses, restaurants, apartment buildings, etc., and connect a water hose to it and then retrieve large quantities of water quickly. The equipment needed is a short water hose, on/off spray nozzle, and suitable water storage container(s).
    After parking next to a suitable hydrant, I install a windshield

shade to prevent anyone outside from seeing into my privatized car. Next, with the water hose nozzle turned off and attached to the water hose, I run the other hose end outside my car, attach it to the hydrant, and then turn on the hydrant. Climbing back into my car I partially close the car door, barely being able to latch and lock it, to prevent anyone outside from seeing inside my car while I fill up water storage container(s). After filling up the last container, I turn off the spray nozzle and slip back outside to turn off the water hydrant and disconnect the water hose, and then I slip back into my car pulling the hose inside. ADVANTAGES If a car is completely privatized with windshield shade in place, the stealthiness and discreetness of this water retrieval option allows one to quickly fill up water storage container(s) without anyone seeing how much water is being transferred. It is an extremely fast method of acquiring as much bathing water as desired. There are unlimited water hydrants available to use.

SINK FAUCET WATER RETRIEVAL OPTION

Like water hose hydrants, there are unlimited sink faucets to retrieve bathing water from, but with the added benefit of any temperature water generally being available. Two pieces of equipment are needed for retrieving water from a sink faucet: (1) a suitable water container(s), and (2) a three to five foot length of five-eighths-inch or three-fourths-inch diameter automotive hose. To obtain water, place the hose end over the faucet head, and while squeezing the hose and faucet connection together with one hand, turn on the faucet and direct faucet water into a water storage container. For discreetness, the hose and water container(s) can be transported inside a backpack or carry bag. ADVANTAGES AND DISADVANTAGES Unlimited sink faucets to retrieve water from, the availability of any temperature water, and the ability to retrieve water somewhat discreetly are some advantages associated with the sink faucet water retrieval option. The obvious disadvantage of this water retrieval option is the limited amount of water that one can physically carry.

HIGH-CAPACITY BILGE PUMP WATER RETRIEVAL OPTION

The high capacity bilge pump water retrieval option can be performed at locations where one can drive within 25-50 feet of a suitable body of water, such as a stream, lake, river, swimming pool, pond, etc., to acquire bathing water from. My main application in using this water retrieval option has been while living in sparsely populated wilderness areas in which a clean body of water was located within easy driving distance.

Obtaining bathing water using the bilge pump water retrieval option requires an assembly of several pieces of equipment: (1) a 12-volt DC boat bilge pump (impeller feed design) with 3-amp or larger motor, (2) 15-foot or longer water hose (hose's hydrant connector end may need to be cut off), (3) 20-22 gauge speaker wire with alligator lead connectors soldered to all four wire ends (wire should be 5' longer than the water hose), (4) 2x2' of metal window screen to wrap around the bilge pump and act as a pre-filter, and (5) a hose adapter and hose clamp to connect the hose to the bilge pump. Both ends of the speaker wire should have insulated alligator clip leads (two red, two black) soldered to them so that one end of the speaker wire can be attached to the bilge pump motor wires, and the other end attached to a car's electrical system (fuse box, cigarette lighter, battery, etc.). The speaker wire can be secured along the hose using duct tape at 1-3' intervals. The window screen can be wrapped around the bilge pump and tied off around the hose connection using string, plastic ties, and/or duct tape.

After parking close to a suitable body of water, simply throw the bilge pump assembly into the water while holding on to the end of the attached hose and wire assembly. Connect the speaker wire's alligator leads to a suitable point in the car's electrical system, and then direct the water into a water storage container. When finished filling water storage containers, reverse the electrical connections so that the bilge pump will empty the hose of water while the assembly is being pulled back inside one's car.

PURCHASE DRINKING WATER AND USE IT FOR BATHING
RETRIEVE BATHING WATER FROM A BUSINESS SWIMMING POOL (You're getting it for your overheated car.)

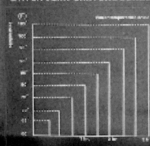

5.5 BATHING WATER HEATING OPTIONS

During cold weather it is desirable to have bathing water that is warm and comfortable to bath with. Fortunately, there are dozens of ways to heat bathing water while living in a car.

WATER TEMPERATURE ISN'T CRITICAL WHEN PERFORMING THE CAR PRIVACY BATHING OPTION
Using warm bathing water may not be necessary while performing the car privacy bathing option in an operating climate-controlled privatized car. An operating car can be cooled or heated to a point in which one may be able to bath with uncomfortable temperature water, experiencing only minimal discomfort. More importantly, when performing the "car privacy" showering option, bathing water isn't poured directly onto one's body (exception: head and near genital area). Also, because of cleaning one's body in sections instead of all at once, using uncomfortable temperature bathing water is felt only by the body section being cleaned, thus minimizing one's discomfort.

CAR HEATER OPTION IN WARMING BATHING WATER When a car engine is operating, a container of water can be placed below a car heater air outlet so that warm air will be blown onto the container, warming it. This option works best if a car will be operating 30 minutes or more, as 30 minutes or longer may be required to adequately warm 1-2 gallons of cold bathing water. An enhancement that allows for faster water heating is to shroud the water container(s) and heater air outlet with a blanket, so as to better direct the heated air onto the bathing water container(s).
Plastic gallon-size jugs or plastic gas containers work well in this bathing water heating option. Metal water storage containers may also work well if they are insulated from the cold car floor.

SLEEPING OPTION IN WARMING BATHING WATER In certain situations it may be convenient to simply sleep with a container of water pressed against or very close to one's body so that it will be at or near body temperature upon wakening. A 1.5 or 2.5-gallon plastic gas container is what I use most in this option, mainly because of the container's smoothness, and because the container's relatively thick-walled plastic construction allows body heat transfer at a slower rate, minimizing discomfort.

CAR DASHBOARD SOLAR HEATING OPTION IN WARMING BATHING WATER Depending on the amount of sunlight available and the color of the car dashboard, a car's dashboard might heat up enough to warm container(s) of water placed on top. Painting the water container with flat black colored paint will enhance the container's solar absorption heating.

THERMOS OPTION IN WARMING BATHING WATER The vacuum barrier inside a thermos container forms an excellent insulating barrier that allows for cold or hot fluids to maintain near constant temperature over long periods. Also, increasing insulation is the thermos' inner mirror like surface, which helps prevent thermal radiation from being transferred to or from the fluid held within the thermos.

Filling a one liter thermos with hot water before leaving work, and then mixing it with cool/cold bathing water the next morning, or whenever needing to bathe, can work out extremely well in providing warm bathing water. This is a very discreet way of obtaining warm bathing water during cool/cold weather, as filling a thermos with hot water looks normal.

SOLAR SHOWER BAG OPTION IN WARMING BATHING WATER Using the Solar Shower Bag to heat bathing water from sunlight has been perfect for my summer trips to northern wilderness locations where fuel conservation is critical. Just fill the solar shower bag with bathing water and suspend it from an open car hood, tree branch, etc.--anywhere it will receive the most sunlight to cause maximum heating of the water. It works best when there is no wind, but if much wind is present, the bag can be placed on a Styrofoam lid on a car dash.

CAR ENGINE BATHING WATER HEATING OPTION IS POTENTIALLY DANGEROUS/DAMAGING!

A suitable container of water placed on or against exhaust system components (tailpipe, catalytic converter, and muffler) or hot engine areas (intake/exhaust manifold, radiator, radiator hoses, heater hoses, valve cover, etc.) can heat bathing water-- BUT IS POTENTIALLY DANGEROUS AND DAMAGING. Because certain components of an operating engine can easily grab hold of clothing, hair, hand, and arm, I only place or remove container(s) of water when my car's engine isn't operating.

When removing a water container with the engine turned off, one still has to be concerned with not contacting hot surfaces. Water containers placed where they could vibrate around and get caught in externally moving engine components may cause engine/component damage.

There are plenty of surfaces in the engine compartment that will puncture thin-wall plastic gallon-size jugs or gallon-size resealable bags of water. If using a metal container to heat bathing water, the vibrating metal container will cause abrasion to any surface it contacts.

CHARCOAL GRILL OPTION IN HEATING BATHING WATER
Placing a thin-wall plastic gallon-size jug or metal container inside or on top of a wood/charcoal burning grill may be convenient to do during one's regular cooking.

FOUR-CYCLE, AIR-COOLED ENGINE EXHAUST OPTION IN HEATING BATHING WATER
Four-cycle, air-cooled engine's exhaust can get quite hot, especially when the engine is operating near its peak power rpm range. While living in sparsely populated wilderness areas during cold weather, it has sometimes been easy to quickly (<5 min.) heat bathing water by placing gallon-size jugs or a 2.5-gallon plastic gas container of water in front of and within 10" of an air-cooled, 4-cycle engine's exhaust stream outlet.

MICROWAVE OVEN WATER HEATING OPTION..............
Using a microwave oven to heat a plastic container full of bathing water is very fast. Using a car's electrical system to power a microwave oven requires (1) an inverter with high enough wattage capacity to power a microwave oven, (2) the inverter be wired directly to the car starting battery, and (3) the car engine be operating at fast idle during use of the microwave oven.

THERMOELECTRIC WARMER USED TO WARM CONTAINER(S) OF BATHING WATER IS EXTREMELY SLOW

PORTABLE THREE-WAY REFRIGERATOR/FREEZER OPTION IN HEATING BATHING WATER
OPTION #1: Water container suspended 4-10 inches above an operating three-way refrigerator/freezer's heat exhaust stack.
OPTION #2: Water container minimally set over heat exhaust stack.

DISADVANTAGE OF OPTION #1 and #2: Potentially damaging--covering the heat stack may cause excessive heating of the refrigerator's boiler section, possibly ruining the cooling unit.

5.6 SATISFYING TOLET NEEDS

Except for surveillance work and possibly a few other jobs, and only part of the time, living in a car isn't a 24-hour activity. Most people have jobs and other daily activities that take place outside their cars at locations where toilet needs can be satisfied. However, many times it will be much more convenient to be able to take care of toilet needs while inside a privatized car, such as when parking at night. Fortunately, satisfying toilet needs inside a privatized car is fairly easy.

UNSUITABLE CAR LIVING AREA REST ROOMS Installing any type of toilet inside a car, such as the type used in RV's, would be impractical and nearly impossible because of minimal space, and because permanent car damaging modifications, would possibly cause severe car body corrosion problems. Using a self-contained portable toilet really isn't suitable either, as it would smell bad, take up too much space, require water and chemicals, require dumping at limited locations, and might possibly devastate one's living area if it ever tipped over and leaked. Since having a conventional or semi-conventional toilet inside a privatized car isn't feasible, one really needs a simple alternative way of satisfying toilet needs while living inside a privatized car.

• MEETING URINATION AND URINE STORAGE NEEDS INSIDE A PRIVATIZED CAR

MALE URINATION AND URINE STORAGE After receiving my driver's license as a teenager, it wasn't long before I figured out how easy it is to urinate into a container, such as a paper cup, soda can, etc., while driving, and then pour the urine onto the street whenever traveling slow or when stopped. However, there were problems in using non-resealable small containers, such as spillage problems or problems in filling a small container to the point of overflow before finishing urinating. To prevent spillage and overflow problems, I soon started using .5-1 gallon-size, resealable, plastic juice/drink containers.

URINE STORAGE CONTAINER: .5-1 GALLON-SIZE, RESEALABLE, PLASTIC JUICE/DRINK CONTAINER

One-half to one gallon-size, resealable, plastic juice/drink containers are well suited for short and long-term urine storage. The rubber seal in these containers' lids creates an airtight seal that prevents any odor or urine from escaping. Surprisingly, these plastic containers don't appear to deteriorate from long-term contact with urine, as I have used a single container in excess of 4 years before replacing it. Other container benefits include: (1) They are extremely durable; (2) unlike glass containers, plastic containers are safe to use inside a car; and (3) plastic having a low thermal conductivity makes plastic containers relatively comfortable to contact during any temperature weather. One-half to one gallon-size, resealable, plastic juice/drink containers have been the best containers I've used in satisfying my urination and urine storage needs while living/working in privatized cars.

FEMALE URINATION A cylinder shaped plastic fluid dispensing cooler that has a 5 to 6-inch diameter removable lid is fairly easy for females to squat over and urinate into. Afterwards, the urine can be poured onto the ground or poured into a .5-1 gallon-size, resealable, plastic, juice/drink container for storing as long as necessary.

URINE DISPOSAL CONSIDERATIONS Urine spilled inside a car could create severe car body corrosion problems--don't let it happen. Since urine attracts flies and creates a lasting smell that is noticeable to anyone passing nearby, urine shouldn't be poured out onto the ground within a 150 feet of one's parking location. In choosing a suitable location to dispose of urine, keep in mind that urine can kill most any plant whose roots it saturates--especially old urine that has been stored for days.

RESTROOM EQUIPMENT: Half-gallon Size Plastic Fruit Juice Container, Toilet Paper Roll inside quart size Resealable Bag, 6" diameter Fluid Dispenser Cooler and Lid.

www.InfoWars.com

www.JonesReport.com

www.GiveMeLiberty.org

www.FreedomToFascism.com

- MEETING DEFECATION AND BOWEL MOVEMENT STORAGE NEEDS

While inside a privatized car, a male or female can defecate by squatting over a quart size resealable freezer bag held open directly beneath one's anus. Used toilet paper can be placed inside the resealable freezer bag. A suitable urination container, such as an oil drain pan or a cylinder shaped fluid dispenser cooler with a 5-6-inch diameter lid, can be urinated into while defecating. With a little practice, males can urinate into a half-gallon-size plastic fruit juice/drink container while defecating. Since hand-washing facilities are limited inside a car, using disposable rubber gloves is desirable.

BOWEL MOVEMENT STORAGE There is something about the smell of human waste that is incredibly irritating to be around--even the slightest odor will be intolerable for any substantial period.   Therefore, human waste that can't be disposed of immediately will have to be stored in an airtight storage container until disposal is possible.

In storing bowel movement, first place the resealable bag of waste and used toilet paper inside another resealable bag to give added strength and to farther limit release of odor. The double-bagged waste can then be placed in a suitable airtight container, such as a cylinder shaped plastic fluid dispensing cooler having a 5-6-inch diameter lid. To prevent the slightest amount of odor from escaping the fluid dispenser cooler, silicon adhesive sealant can be placed on the lid's threads before screwing the lid onto the container. Any fluid dispenser valve/nozzle can be filled with silicon adhesive sealant by momentarily opening the valve and then forcing sealant into it. Silicon adhesive sealant dries to a rubbery state that is fairly easy to peel off a plastic container's lid threads and reapplied whenever necessary, such as when emptying the container or adding more waste to the container.

- MAKESHIFT OUTDOOR TOILET FOR USE AT SPARSELY POPULATED WILDERNESS AREAS
URINE DISPOSAL CONSIDERATIONS When convenient, it's best to store urine until it can be disposed into a conventional toilet. If a toilet is not available, take care to dispose of urine in an area where it won't find its way into bodies of water (streams, ponds, rivers, lakes, etc.). Since urine attracts flies, it should be disposed of at least 150 feet or more from where one is parked. As previously disclosed, urine, especially old

urine, may possibly kill any plants whose roots it saturates.

WILDERNESS AREA BOWEL MOVEMENT DISPOSAL RECOMMENDATIONS It's disappointing to find human waste and toilet paper strewn on the ground while walking in sparsely populated areas--especially since it's very easy to take care of one's bowel movement needs, leaving no evidence to spoil an area's natural beauty.

CAT OPTION While at wilderness areas, one can simply dig a small hole in the ground to defecate into and then cover it back over. Carrying a small digging/entrenchment tool, such as a small plastic spade, will be necessary.

MEETING LONG-TERM DEFECATING NEEDS When living at a sparsely populated wilderness location, one will need to create a simple way to satisfy human waste disposal needs. Using a posthole digger to dig a 4-5' deep hole in the ground, which can then be defecated into for a number of months before having to dig another hole, has worked out well in my wilderness car living situations. Burning used toilet paper inside the hole allows the hole to fill less quickly--be very careful to not start a forest fire.

Because flies that gain access to human waste can easily spread disease, it is critical that a human waste hole be covered over at all times except when being defecated into. Covering the hole with a piece of plywood and rock is sufficient.

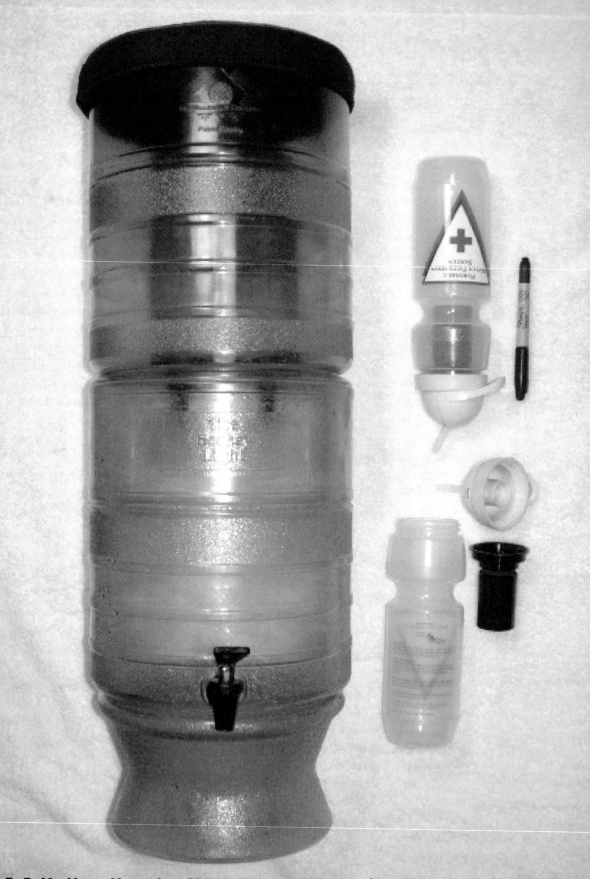

2.5 Gallon Gravity H2O Filter + Two Camping H2O Filters

CHAPTER 6

MEETING FOOD AND DRINKING WATER NEEDS WHILE LIVING IN CARS

6.1 DRINKING WATER SOURCES, RETRIEVAL, AND STORAGE

A very important requirement in staying healthy is having clean drinking water. Although water can be obtained from almost any source and then filtered to make it safe to consume, because of the availability and minimal cost of commercially available, quality drinking water, I've generally chosen to purchase quality drinking water when living in locations where it was inexpensively available. Fortunately, whatever the situation, they're a lot of ways to meet drinking water needs.

Drinking water storage containers are covered at the beginning of section 5.4 in Chapter 5.

• DRINKING WATER SOURCES AND RETRIEVAL OPTIONS

There are many locations and a variety of ways to use in obtaining both drinking and bathing water; some are disclosed in Chapter 5. The following material discusses some of the drinking water sources I've used while living/working in cars.

MELTED ICE WATER REMOVED FROM A "DOUBLE COOLER ICE CHEST" Before drinking ice water removed from a "double cooler ice chest," the water should be filtered through some type of water filter/purifier.

FAUCET TAP WATER Faucet tap water should be at least minimally filtered to remove lead, copper, other minerals, biological, and chemical contaminants before drinking. Public rest room faucets, in which people bump their hands against and splash biological and chemical contaminated water into the faucet head, should not be used as a drinking water source unless the water is filtered using filtering/purifying equipment capable of removing a broad range of biological, mineral, and chemical contaminants.

*EXTRA: Discrete method in retrieving faucet tap water is disclosed in Chapter 5.

PURIFIED WATER DISPENSING MACHINES One of the least expensive sources of quality drinking water are purified water dispensing machines located around grocery stores and other businesses. To retrieve purified water, simply place a gallon plastic jug below the fill nozzle, feed the machine the correct amount of change/money, and then press the appropriate button.

A dispensing machine's water quality mainly depends on if the machine's filters are being replaced/cleaned on schedule. Also, depending on the location, children may touch a machine's dispensing nozzle and leave behind biological and chemical contaminants to contaminate the purified water as it is dispensed.

Since thin-wall gallon-size jugs have minimal capacity and aren't suitable for use in storing quantities of drinking water inside a car, one will probably want to store drinking water in a more suitable storage container, such as 2.5 or 5-gallon-size plastic gas containers. If a water-dispensing machine only has room to fill a gallon-size jug, to speed up the process one can fill a 2.5 or 5-gallon gas container using two 1-gallon-size jugs. While the water-dispensing machine fills a gallon-size jug, the other jug can be emptied into a 2.5 or 5-gallon-size plastic gas container. A thin-wall gallon-size jug's opening mates well to the opening of a plastic gas container, thus allows for easy transferring of water with minimal spillage.

PURCHASING PURIFIED/DISTILLED BOTTLED WATER If one doesn't mind paying a little more as compared to purchasing purified water from water dispensing machines, purified/distilled bottled water can be purchased just about anywhere.

OTHER DRINKING WATER SOURCES
(1) Water fountain. (2) Water hose hydrants (recommend filtering). (3) Streams, rivers, lakes (should filter through very thorough water filtering/purifying equipment).

6.2 FOOD EATING/PREPARATION UTENSILS AND STORAGE CONTAINERS

Essentially the same foods one would eat while living in a conventional residence can also be consumed while living in cars. However, since refrigeration and cooking options are somewhat limited and because certain foods spoil much faster than others, one may wish to choose foods that are easier to store and prepare while living in cars.

MINIMIZE FOOD SPOILAGE ACCELERATORS/CONTAMINANTS Car living environments are generally abundant with food spoilage accelerators like heat, moisture/humidity, and biologicals. Therefore, food storage containers generally should be airtight and as sterile as possible.

To help minimize introducing spoilage contaminants into food, one should never drink or eat from a food storage container. It's also best to remove food portions from a food storage container using sterile utensils, such as a new disposable plastic spoon. Also, wearing disposable rubber gloves will help prevent introducing food contaminants during certain food retrieval, preparation, processing applications.

• FOOD PREPARATION/PROCESSING/EATING UTENSILS
Because hot water is in short supply inside a car, using a new inexpensive disposable clean eating utensil, such as disposable plastic spoons/forks, to retrieve portions of food from food storage containers may have an advantage over using non-disposable utensils that need to be cleaned in hot water or sterilized with flame or alcohol.

While living in cars, my eating and food preparation utensils have mainly been disposable rubber gloves, hard plastic cups, disposable resealable freezer bags, wax paper, plastic food wrap, aluminum foil, disposable plastic spoons, metal fork, hunting knife, can opener, vegetable peeler, plastic food storage containers, and scissors. Besides using disposable rubber gloves, I also use an evaporative alcohol-based hand sanitizer.

DISPOSABLE RUBBER GLOVES Using disposable rubber gloves while cooking/preparing food, processing game/fish, and while eating food will minimize introducing food spoilage contaminants, minimize the need/use of eating utensils, and minimize the need for hand-washing water. Car maintenance/

repair applications (Ch. 13) and rest room applications (Ch. 5) are other applications in which using disposable rubber gloves are very beneficial.

Quantities of 50-200 pair of inexpensive disposable rubber gloves are what I commonly find available most anywhere pharmacy/bathroom supplies are sold, such as at grocery stores, discount stores, department stores, pharmacies.

HARD PLASTIC CUP(S) Hard plastic cups can be used both as a bowl or cup in fulfilling a number of food preparation and eating needs, such as in mixing powdered milk, mixing orange juice concentrate, mixing oatmeal, eating cereal, drinking beverages, etc. Lining the inside of a hard plastic cup with plastic food wrap prevents dirtying the cup during usage. Hard plastic cups generally last much longer than easily cracked flexible plastic cups.

DISPOSABLE RESEALABLE FREEZER BAGS Resealable freezer bags are inexpensive and are readily available in a variety of sizes (pint, quart, half-gallon-sizes). The inside of new resealable freezer bags being very clean and airtight makes them excellent disposable food storage containers. I use them for storing dry, perishable, and frozen foods, many times saving space by eliminating bulky food boxes. Resealable freezer bags are excellent to use in mixing/preparing certain foods, such as in breading of meat/fish/poultry. A pint or quart size resealable freezer bag makes a usable disposable cup. Resealable freezer bags work well in food heating applications, such as when heating food in boiling water or in a microwave oven.

In storing a four days' supply of meat inside a double cooler ice chest, in which bacteria introduced into the meat storage container could easily spread throughout and cause premature food spoilage, it will be beneficial to store a day's portion of meat individually wrapped in aluminum foil and stored individually in a small resealable freezer bag.

ALUMINUM FOIL Wrapping food in aluminum foil allows it to be heated/cooked by placing it near a suitable heat source (fire, engine/exhaust component, etc.). Meat can be wrapped in aluminum foil to make it last longer while stored in a freezer or when placed in a resealable freezer bag stored in a "double cooler ice chest." Lining a pan with aluminum foil prevents the pan from being dirtied when heating/cooking certain foods, thus helps to conserve wash water.

PLASTIC FOOD WRAP AND WAX PAPER Lining a cup, bowl, or plate with disposable plastic food wrap or wax paper will help conserve wash water. Wax paper is also useful in certain gluing and sealing applications.

DISPOSABLE PLASTIC SPOONS Using a new disposable spoon to retrieve food from a food storage container will limit bacteria entry, thus helping to prevent premature food spoilage. Removing portions of jelly from a jelly container is one beneficial application that comes to mind.
EXTRA: Metal utensils can be sterilized with flame or by wiping with alcohol.

METAL FORK Since disposable plastic forks tend to break very easily, I prefer using a metal fork.

HUNTING KNIFE I've found that high chromium steel blades and 440C stainless steel blades retain their sharpness longest.
CAUTION: Non-folding knives may be illegal to transport in a car except under certain conditions. Therefore, carrying a legal folding lock-blade knife of legal dimensions is desirable. (To verify legality, check with Joseph Stalin)

PLASTIC FOOD STORAGE CONTAINERS I seldom use plastic food storage containers for storing perishable and frozen food. The reason being is that they would take up excessive space in my double cooler ice chest and externally stored portable three-way freezer. I generally store perishable and frozen foods in resealable freezer bags to save room.

My main use of plastic food storage containers has been for storing and organizing small personal possessions. They are also well suited for use in airtight storage applications, such as in storing mailing envelopes sealed off from the humid car living area.
SCISSORS
CAN OPENER
VEGETABLE PEELER
CLOTHESPINS Used to close off opened food bags.
ALCOHOL Used for sterilizing eating utensils.
ALCOHOL-BASED EVAPORATIVE HAND CLEANER

Super Lightweight, Fast-burning TRIOXANE is an excellent Campfire Starter.

Slower burning STERNO is suitable for cooking with.

6.3 HEATING/COOKING FOOD WHILE LIVING IN CARS

I've found it easiest to cook meat at a suitable location once or twice per month and then store it in my externally stored portable three-way freezer. Removing a 3-5-day supply of pre-cooked frozen food and block ice from my externally stored freezer and then storing it in my car's double cooler ice chest has allowed me to eat high quality food inexpensively while living in cars. Fortunately, one has many options in meeting their food cooking/heating needs.

MICROWAVE OVEN POWERED BY AN INVERTER CONNECTED TO A CAR'S STARTING BATTERY Using a microwave oven to quickly cook food and heat bathing water can be very convenient, especially during freezing weather. Its advantages are speed and cleanliness. Its disadvantages are (1) large size, heavy weight, and high power requirement, and (2) the need to use a high wattage 12-volt DC to 120-volt AC inverter that must be electrically connected to or very near to a car's starting battery, and (3) the car engine must be operating at a fast idle rpm while powering the microwave oven. Since certain foods taste so much better heated, and since heating bathing water with a microwave oven is extremely fast, I've found that a microwave oven's use benefits may outweigh its disadvantages in car living situations--especially during cold, freezing weather.

USING A STORE'S MICROWAVE OVEN MAY BE CONVENIENT Purchasing a microwave oven entree and then heating it in the store's microwave oven may be convenient to do, especially when traveling.

LP-POWERED CAMPING STOVE/BURNER For those desiring to cook gourmet meals inside a car, there are a variety of LP powered, small camping stoves/burners available along with small-sized fuel canisters to power them with. Their main advantage is that their small size makes them easy to store inside a car. Their disadvantages include high humidity and the possibility of oxygen depletion, fire, and toxic fuel vapor hazards when used inside a car. Some small LP fuel canisters are very expensive; fortunately, many small camping stoves can be inexpensively powered from a refillable 5 lb. propane bottle using an adapter hose (see picture).
EXTRA: A useful accessory I've seen marketed is an adapter

that allows refilling of certain small LP fuel canisters from a regular size propane bottle, thus allowing for certain small expensive LP fuel canisters to be reused inexpensively over and over again.

SMOKER/GRILL
    A. ADVANTAGES
    1. POSSIBLE FUELS: Charcoal, wood, LP, electricity, etc.
    2. Propane may already exist at external storage location if powering a three-way freezer from propane.
    3. Propane power advantage: Connects directly to a regular propane bottle via a hose, regulator, and adapter (inexpensive operation).
    B. STORAGE OPTION: Stored with freezer at external storage location.
    C. COOKING "TIP": Water container placed inside smoker mustn't run dry if meat is to cook moist and tender.
    D. PROPANE FUEL HAZARDS: Oxygen depletion, toxic gas, explosion, fire.

ELECTRIC ROASTER
    A. USE ADVANTAGE: Little or no smoke--just aroma (possibly suitable for use at external storage location).
    B. EXTERNAL STORAGE LOCATION POWER OPTION: (1) Screw in light bulb plug adapter; or (2) temporarily wire in 120-volt outlet to a light fixture's wiring.
    C. STORAGE: Stored with freezer at external storage location.

HEATING FOOD WRAPPED IN ALUMINUM FOIL PLACED NEAR A SUITABLE HEAT SOURCE (fire, grill, smoker, car engine, etc.)

SINGLE/DOUBLE BURNER LP STOVE
STERNO FUEL AND BURNER PLATFORM
KEROSENE BURNER CAMPING STOVE
TRIOXANE FUEL – Used to quickly start a campfire.

HEATING UNOPENED CANNED FOOD PLACED NEAR A HEAT SOURCE IS DANGEROUS! A very dangerous way of heating unopened canned food is to place it near a source of heat--I've seen brick and metal grills severely damaged by exploding cans of food. I've sometimes heated canned food by placing it near a warm/hot engine surface while driving for 15-30 minutes.

Obviously, a can of food that dislodges or explodes in a car's engine compartment can be damaging. Puncturing a warm/hot can of food with a can opener will allow hot gases and juices to spew, thus one should put the can in a bowl/container and cover it with plastic food wrap before puncturing/opening it--you can be severely injured if the can explodes during this process!

Camping Stove powered by 5 lb. Propane Bottle via Adapter Hose.

6.4 FOOD REFRIGERATION/FREEZER STORAGE OPTIONS

Canning food is an inexpensive option that can eliminate the need for a refrigerator/freezer; however, canned food will spoil given enough time and/or heat. Because canning really needs to be done in as sterile an environment as possible, canning really needs to be performed in a very clean kitchen. One could do away with the need for refrigeration by simply eating non-perishable and canned food, but doing so would be much less satisfying and much more expensive. Therefore, food refrigeration is the main problem to overcome in meeting food storage needs in car living situations.

"DOUBLE COOLER ICE CHEST"
The best way I've found to keep perishable food cold inside a parked car is to store the food inside a "double cooler ice chest." A double cooler ice chest is made by placing a smaller cooler inside a larger cooler, and installing some sort of spacer between the two coolers to create an air-insulating barrier (1" PVC pipe is a good spacer). The air-insulating barrier considerably increases insulation, thus allowing for ice held within the inner cooler to last much longer. In creating a spacer between the inner and outer coolers, I've generally stuck wood or plastic strips to the inner bottom and inner sides of the larger cooler using black silicon adhesive sealant (rope or cord also works). Using a double cooler ice chest inside my car for storing perishable food, and using an externally stored freezer to retrieve a 3-4 day portion of frozen food and block ice from when needing to replenish my double cooler ice chest has allowed me to eat extremely well while living/working in cars. ADVANTAGES OF THE DOUBLE COOLER ICE CHEST Many of the problems and hazards associated with using other type refrigerators inside a car aren't a part of using a double cooler ice chest, such as (1) electricity/fuel requirement, (2) oxygen depletion hazard, (3) fire hazard, (4) toxic fumes hazard, (5) heat, (6) noise, (7) off-level operating problems, (8) ambient temperature operating restrictions, (9) repairs.

A double cooler ice chest offers fast cool-down capabilities and stable compartment temperatures. The drastic increase in insulation due to the air-insulating barrier has increased inner cooler ice' life span threefold in my applications. Using an externally stored freezer to make block ice in, which can then be used in a "double cooler ice chest," is inexpensive and allows one to produce colder ice--the colder the block ice is when first placed inside a cooler, the longer it lasts. A double cooler ice chest can easily be made into a freezer by simply adding "dry ice."

A double cooler ice chest's ice water can be consumed, or used in other applications. Pieces of ice taken from a double cooler ice chest can be used to cool a glass of one's favorite beverage. Any space between the inner and outer cooler can be used to store items that store best away from sunlight in temperatures below 80°F, such as vitamins, medicines, jelly, canned meat, etc.

DOUBLE COOLER ICE CHEST DISADVANTAGES Although a double cooler ice chest has the hassles of having to replenish ice and remove melted ice water, it has been the best type of refrigeration I've used inside my cars.

PORTABLE, 12-VOLT DC-POWERED, COMPRESSOR-TYPE CAMPING REFRIGERATOR/FREEZER
Portable, 12-volt DC-powered, compressor-type camping refrigerator/freezers are generally ruggedly built and look similar to a well-made metal ice chest cooler. The cooling unit operates much like a household refrigerator's cooling unit, but is designed for operation in a broader range of temperatures (at least on the low temp. end). They're generally designed to operate on 12-volt dc, but they can also be powered with 120-volt AC electricity by using an adapter.
ADVANTAGES Portable, 12-volt DC-powered, compressor-type camping refrigerator/freezers are generally well made, providing much protection of the cooling unit. They operate as both a refrigerator and freezer by changing the thermostat setting. Because of their very efficient method of cooling, they generally have the best cool-down capabilities of any type of portable camping refrigerator/freezer (exception: ice chest), thus making them very suitable to use in freezing freshly processed game. They can be operated off-level (up to 30 degrees for the unit I own) and in vibrating environments. Being thermostatically controlled allows for compartment temperature stability, minimal power consumption, and minimal cooling unit wear. Since they don't deplete oxygen, they're safe to use inside an enclosed car (exception: if coolant leaks).
DISADVANTAGES Excessive power requirements (12-volt DC @ 3.5 to 6-amps typical), noise, and excessive car interior heating have made portable, 12-volt, compressor-type camping

refrigerator/freezers unsuitable for use in most of my car living/working situations (exceptions: when traveling or when transporting freshly processed game). The electric motor and compressor assemblies are susceptible to increased wear and/or damage from contact with dust/dirt/sand (all mechanical assemblies wear out eventually). These refrigerator/freezers usually aren't designed for frost-free operation. Portable, 12-volt DC-powered, compressor-type camping refrigerator/freezers are fairly expensive.

PURCHASING CONSIDERATIONS/RECOMMENDATIONS Make sure all desired features are part of the unit before purchasing it. For instance, the unit needs to be thermostatically controlled to conserve power, minimize compressor and motor wear, and to minimize refrigeration compartment temperature variations. Because all mechanical assemblies wear out eventually, purchasing extended warranty coverage (if available) may be a good investment for this type refrigerator/freezer. Purchasing the manufacturer's repair/service manual will be useful in helping one better understand and maintain their unit.

DOUBLE COOLER ICE CHEST

The electrical cord is used as a spacer between
the coolers--the air barrier created drastically
increases insulation! 1" dia. PVC--good spacer.

12-VOLT DC THERMOELECTRIC COOLER/WARMER

Thermoelectric cooler/warmers are unique in that they can be operated as both a cooler and warmer by simply reversing the direction of DC current flow through the cooling unit. The cooling/warming unit consists of two dissimilar materials fused together, such as silicon and metal, in which a 12-volt DC current runs through creating cooling on one side and heating on the other side of the fused dissimilar materials. The thermoelectric cooler/warmers I've owned warm to around 125°F, and cool to around 40°F below ambient air temperature.

ADVANTAGES OF THERMOELECTRIC COOLER/WARMERS

Thermoelectric cooler/warmers are very lightweight and relatively rugged. They can be operated in almost any position as long as the cooling/warming unit's venting area isn't obstructed. They're relatively inexpensive and are readily available at many locations where ice coolers are sold. Except for a cooling unit fan, thermoelectric refrigerators have no moving parts, thus they're long-lived by design and operate practically maintenance-free. Twelve-volt DC-powered thermoelectric cooler/warmers can be powered from a car's cigarette lighter; using an adapter allows powering from a 120-volt AC wall outlet. Thermoelectric coolers offer a high degree of safety in that they operate without depleting oxygen and without the use of chemicals. Using the thermoelectric cooler/warmer to heat a container of water or precooked food may be a useful application.

DISADVANTAGES OF THERMOELECTRIC COOLER/WARMERS

The main disadvantages associated with the thermoelectric cooler/warmers I've owned are continuous fan noise, continuous power draw and excessive temperature variations with changes in ambient temperature, excessive power requirements (2.5 to 4-amps), inadequate cooling when used in hot ambient temperatures, extremely slow cool-down capabilities, excessive heating of car interior when parking in temperatures above 70°F, and an inefficient cooling process that provides minimal cooling for the relatively high amount of power consumed. My thermoelectric cooler/warmers' cooling ability has decreased substantially when the 12-volt power source has dropped below 12.5 volts. Although thermoelectric coolers are generally supposed to stay 40°F cooler than ambient temperatures, mine have only done so under ideal conditions.

PURCHASING CONSIDERATIONS/RECOMMENDATIONS

If available, ordering a slightly cosmetically flawed thermoelectric cooler/warmer direct from the manufacturer can be well worth the savings if the unit comes with the regular warranty. Purchasing a 120-volt AC to 12-volt DC adapter for use in powering the cooler from any 120-volt AC wall outlet may be beneficial.

120-VOLT AC-POWERED HOUSEHOLD REFRIGERATOR/ FREEZER

120-volt AC-powered household refrigerator/freezers (r/f) generally aren't suitable for use inside a car, but they can be stored at an external storage location and used for making ice and storing food.

HOUSEHOLD REFRIGERATOR ADVANTAGES 120-volt AC-powered household refrigerators/freezers are available in many different sizes, are relatively inexpensive, and are readily available most anywhere household appliances are sold. They have excellent cool-down and cold temperature capabilities. Being thermostatically controlled and having a very efficient cooling process allows for constant compartment temperature while using minimal power. Household refrigerator/freezers generally operate frost-free. They're available as refrigerators, freezers, or combination refrigerator and freezer. They can maintain very cold temperatures--the colder ice is made, the longer it lasts after being placed inside a cooler.

**EXTRA: If desiring to store and use a household refrigerator at a rental storage room that has a light but no 120-volt AC wall outlet, installing a "light bulb plug adapter" into a light fixture socket may allow for powering of a refrigerator. If refrigerator power requirements exceed the light bulb socket adapter's maximum continuous power limit (600 watts typical), temporarily removing the light fixture and wiring in a 120-volt AC outlet in its place may be possible.

HOUSEHOLD REFRIGERATOR DISADVANTAGES 120-volt AC-powered household refrigerator/freezers are designed for stationary use; they are relatively easy to damage when being moved/transported. Being designed for operation in climate-controlled environments, a household refrigerators/ freezer's (r/f's) compressor unit may seize up if operated in cold temperatures. Household r/f''s are usually designed to operate only on 120-volt AC electricity, thus their operating locations are limited. Household refrigerator/freezers make a little bit of noise that might attract unwanted attention when used secretly at certain locations, such as at a rental storage room.

THERMOELECTRIC COOLER

12 volt d.c.

Warms nearly to 125F--Cools nearly 40F below
Ambient Temperature.

PORTABLE THREE-WAY REFRIGERATOR/FREEZERS

Three-way refrigerators/freezers, sometimes referred to as dual-energy absorption refrigerators, are used almost exclusively in recreational vehicles (RV), such as motorhomes and travel trailers. The reasons for this are that three-way refrigerator/freezers (1) can operate in an extremely broad temperature range, and (2) they usually can be powered from any of three sources: 12-volt DC electricity, 120-volt AC electricity, and either propane gas or kerosene.

Portable three-way refrigerator/freezers generally aren't suitable for use inside a car that is being lived in. However, if stored at an external storage location, such as at a rental storage room or friend's residence, a portable three-way refrigerator/freezer can be extremely beneficial in helping one meet their food and ice needs while living in a car.

• ADVANTAGES OF PORTABLE THREE-WAY REFRIGERATOR/ FREEZERS

MANY POWER OPTIONS Three-way refrigerator/freezers use a source of power to heat the cooling unit's boiler section a specified amount, thus many forms of power may be suitable. They're generally equipped to be powered from 12-volt DC electricity, 120-volt AC electricity, and propane gas or kerosene (one power source at a time).

COOLING UNIT CAN OPERATE IN A BROAD TEMPERATURE RANGE The "absorption" type cooling unit used in three-way refrigerators/freezers can operate in a relatively broad temperature range without adverse effects. Three-way refrigerator/freezer cooling units can be designed to have a very high temperature differential capability: my portable three-way refrigerator/freezer can maintain a 90°F temperature differential, thus it can keep food frozen even when the ambient temperature reaches 110°F.

COOLING UNIT HAS NO MOVING PARTS A three-way refrigerator/freezer's cooling unit having no moving parts and being completely sealed makes three-way refrigerator/freezers suitable for use in dusty, sandy, and/or humid environments. Three-way refrigerator/freezers operate practically maintenance free, and they have an extremely long lifespan if operated properly (typically 15 years). Noiseless operation makes them comfortable to sleep near. Both noiseless operation and portable power capability (propane bottle or kerosene) makes portable three-way refrigerator/freezers very suitable for use at noise sensitive and/or remote locations, such as hunting leases, rental storage rooms, etc.

HIGHLY EFFICIENT OPERATION Three-way refrigerator/freezers operate very efficiently, returning much cooling for the power consumed. Thermostatically controlled units maintain their compartment temperature very well in varying temperature environments--thermostatic control also helps to minimize power consumption.

• DISADVANTAGES OF PORTABLE THREE-WAY REFRIGERATOR /FREEZERS

Portable three-way refrigerator/freezers are relatively expensive. They're not readily available, thus they will probably have to be ordered through a camping supplier, RV dealer, or camping supply mail-order business—or they can be easily found and ordered on the Internet.

EASILY DAMAGED COOLING UNIT Because of relatively weak construction and operating deficits, three-way refrigerator/ freezers are probably the most easily damaged portable camping refrigerator/freezer available. Their main operating vulnerability is accidental overheating of the cooling unit boiler section's internal chemicals, which can be caused by off-level operation or by obstructing the heat release vent/stack area. If operated off level, the chemicals inside the boiler section could puddle and possibly cause overheating and undesirable chemical changes that will ruin the unit. The cooling unit's heat release area (chimney stack and vent area) must never be covered, as overheating of the boiler section will cause undesirable chemical changes to the chemicals held within, thus ruining the cooling unit.

OPERATING DEFICITS Three-way refrigerator/freezers (r/f) won't cool properly if operated off level or while operating in vibrating environments. Three-way r/f generally have fairly slow cool-down capabilities; cooling ambient temperature food, freshly processed game, or making ice probably takes four to eight times as long as a household r/f takes. Three-way r/f generally don't operate frost-free. Although most three-way r/f are thermostatically controlled, there are a few on the market that aren't--non-thermostatically controlled three-way r/f waste power, probably have poor temperature differential capabilities, and have compartment temperatures that vary with ambient temperature changes.

POSSIBLE PROPANE OPERATING HAZARDS The tiny flame produced while operating on propane can easily ignite nearby flammable chemicals and/or possibly deplete oxygen when used in a small enclosed area. A small propane leak while operating in an enclosed area could create a toxic and/or explosive environment (use LP detector/alarm). Accidentally covering the burner's "chimney" stack could easily catch on fire the covering object, and it could also overheat the boiler section and ruin the unit.

PURCHASING CONSIDERATIONS/RECOMMENDATIONS

When considering purchasing a portable three-way refrigerator/freezer, there are a number of desirable features that one will probably want a unit to have. Having the compartment's door/lid on top and opening upward will allow for the least amount of cooling loss when retrieving/adding food. Three-way r/f having a cooling unit that can maintain up to a 90 degrees Fahrenheit temperature differential will allow frozen food to stay frozen even when ambient temperatures reach 110 degrees Fahrenheit. Having a high temperature differential capability allows for block ice to be produced at colder temperatures—the colder the ice is made, the longer it lasts when used inside a cooler. To have maximum compartment temperature stability and minimal fuel/power consumption, the cooling unit MUST be thermostatically controlled. Because of having no moving parts, three-way refrigerator/freezers generally last 15 years, and they have very few things that can break or be repaired; therefore, purchasing a manufacturer's extended warranty, in my opinion, is a waste of money.

Absorption Type 3-WAY FREEZER

3-way freezer can be powered by 12-Volt D.C. 12-Volt A.C. or Propane.

CHAPTER 7

USEFUL EQUIPMENT TO HAVE WHILE LIVING IN CARS

7.1 CHAPTER INTRODUCTION

Part of the enjoyment of living in cars comes from being able to satisfy all one's needs while inside a car. In part, this self-sufficiency is possible due to the capabilities, small size, and low power requirements of modern equipment.

This chapter discloses the equipment and useful possessions I use while living in cars, much of which is discussed in other chapters. For simplicity and easy reference, I've categorized the equipment/possession into the following four sections: (1) non-electrical equipment/possessions, (2) battery powered equipment (small size batteries), (3) 12-volt DC-powered equipment, and (4) 120-volt AC-powered equipment. Keep in mind that some of my equipment and possessions are stored at external storage locations, such as at a residence, bank box, rental storage room, etc. Also, only equipment/possessions used to enhance my car living, in some way or another, are disclosed in this chapter.

12-VOLT DC-POWERED EQUIPMENT RECOMMENDATION
Because of a car's ability to supply ample 12-volt DC electricity, and because of the ease in which an additional auxiliary 12-volt power source can be used inside a car, and because of the potential problems associated with powering 120-volt AC-powered equipment from a 12-volt DC to 120-volt AC modified sine wave inverter--it just makes good sense to use 12-volt DC-powered electrical equipment whenever possible while living in cars. Fortunately, almost any 110-volt AC-powered equipment is available in a 12-volt DC-powered version.

ELECTRIC/ELECTRONIC EQUIPMENT CONSIDERATION: WATER-RESISTANT VERSION IS BEST Water-resistant electrical/electronic equipment is much more suitable to use in car living situations because it usually has rubber seals that keep out moisture, humidity, water, dust, sand, dirt, debris which would otherwise shorten their life if allowed entry--life span is substantially increased.

7.2 USEFUL NON-ELECTRIC EQUIPMENT

• AUTOMOTIVE SPARE PARTS: Non-electrical and electrical (Ch. 13).
• AUTOMOTIVE REPAIR TOOLS (Ch. 13).
• BODY ARMOR—Wear while hiking around extremely dangerous wildlife.
• CAR MAINTENANCE/REPAIR MANUALS (Ch. 13).
• CAR MAINTENANCE/REPAIR RECORDS LOGS (Ch. 13).
• CAR SEAT COVER: wooden bead car seat cover (Ch. 3).
• CHAIN SAW—Remote wilderness tree on dirt road applications (tree removal).
• CLOTHES PINS.
    Hanging sheeting or mosquito netting behind car interior openings (Ch. 3).
    Temporarily closing off non-sealable plastic food storage bags (Ch. 6).
    Temporarily hanging a 12-volt DC brush-less cooling fan.
• COLD WEATHER CLOTHING (Ch. 3).
• CYLINDER-SHAPED FLUID DISPENSING COOLER.
    Bowel movement storage (Ch. 5).
    Female urination (Ch. 5).
• DISPOSABLE RUBBER GLOVES.
    Car maintenance/repair applications (Ch. 13).
    Gun cleaning applications.
    Processing/preparing/eating food (Ch. 6).
    Rest room applications (Ch. 5).
• DRYING AGENT: Silica Gel Desiccant, Anhydrous Calcium Sulfate, etc.
    Humidity/moisture sensitive storage applications (Ch. 4).
• EAR PLUGS (washable, soft, spongy type)--noise reduction applications.

- EAR MUFFS--noise reduction applications.
- ENGINE OIL DRAIN VALVE (Ch. 13).
- FOAM (pink, high density upholstery foam).
    Car insulating applications (Ch. 1).
    Cold weather car living comfort enhancements (Ch. 2 and 3).
    Equipment storage applications (Ch. 4 and 13).
- Food   Processing/Preparation/Cooking/Heating/Eating Utensils & Equipment (Ch. 6).
- HAIR STYLIST'S SCISSORS.
- INFLATABLE RAFT.
- "JIG" TYPE KNIFE SHARPENING KIT & LEATHER WEIGHT LIFTING BELT.
- LIGHTER.
    Flame sealing resealable freezer bags (Ch. 4).
    Flame sterilizing metal eating utensils (Ch. 6).
- MAGNIFYING GLASS.
- MECHANIX GLOVES.
- METAL ROOF BUBBLE-PACK INSULATING SHEETING/ROLL (Ch.1, 3).
- MILITARY DUFFEL BAG--clothes storage applications (Ch. 4).
- MYLAR LAMINATED BUBBLE-PACK INSULATING SHEETING (Ch.1, 3).
- NITROGEN TANK W/ REGULATOR & AIR CHUCK.
- PILLOW CASE--clothes storage applications (Ch. 4).
- PLASTIC .5-1 GALLON SIZE FRUIT JUICE/DRINK BOTTLE.
    Urine storage (Ch. 5).
    Male urination (Ch. 5).
- PLASTIC 2.5 OR 5-GALLON SIZE GASOLINE CONTAINER.
    Tarp suspension (Ch. 3).
    Bathing water storage (Ch. 5).
    Drinking water storage (Ch. 6).
- PLASTIC BOAT BATTERY STORAGE BOX.
    Storage/organization (Ch. 4).
    Storage/protection of auxiliary 12-volt battery (Ch. 8).
- PLASTIC FOAM-LINED PORTABLE COMPUTER CARRYING CASE.
- PLASTIC FOOD STORAGE CONTAINERS.
    Airtight storage of mailing envelopes, stamps, CDs, memory cards, etc. (Ch. 4).
- PLASTIC SHOEHORN--Hanging sheeting or mosquito netting from car door crevice (Ch. 3).
- PLASTIC STORAGE CONTAINERS/BOXES/CASES (Ch. 4).

- PLASTIC TIES--Tying off electrical wire, electrical tape, trash bags, etc.
- RAIN PONCHO.
- REFRIGERATOR/FREEZERS.
    Food storage applications (Ch. 6 and 11).
    Double cooler ice chest (Ch. 6).
    Portable 12-volt DC-powered compressor-type camping refrigerator/freezer (Ch. 6).
    Portable three-way freezer (Ch. 6).
    Household refrigerator/freezer (Ch. 6).
    Thermoelectric cooler/warmer (Ch. 6).
- RESEALABLE FREEZER BAGS.
    Storage/organization applications (Ch. 4, 11, 13).
    Rest room applications (Ch. 5).
    Bathing water-heating applications (Ch. 5).
    Food storage/preparation/cooking applications (Ch. 6).
    Book storage applications (Ch. 11).
    Car maintenance applications (Ch. 13).
- SILICON ADHESIVE SEALANT.
    Cot assembly (Ch. 2).
    Securing sheeting or mosquito netting over car vents/openings (Ch. 3).
    Sealing plastic storage containers; key storage applications (Ch. 4).
    Bowel movement storage applications (Ch. 5).
    Car maintenance/repair applications (Ch. 13).
- SINGLE EDGE RAZOR BLADES.
- SLEEPING COT (Ch. 2 & 3).
- SMALL SCUBA TANK & REGULATOR (Ch.1).
- SPECIALIZED STORAGE CONTAINERS (Ch. 4).
- SPRAY-PAINTING MASK, DUST MASK, GAS MASK, RESPIRATOR.
- TAPE: electrical, duct, masking, and transparent tape (Ch. 3, 8).
- TIRE AIR PRESSURE GAUGE.
- TIRE PUNCTURE REPAIR KITS (Ch. 13).
- TOILET PAPER ROLL(S) individually stored inside quart size resealable freezer bags (Ch. 5).
- TORQUE WRENCH (Ch. 13).
- WATER HOSE (short) and SPRAY NOZZLE--use: water retrieval/transfer applications (Ch. 5).
- WATER FILTERING/PURIFYING EQUIPMENT (Ch.6).
- WET SUIT.

**6V BATTERY, 25-OHM POTENTIOMETER,
and SHAVER with Internal Batteries Removed.**

7.3 USEFUL BATTERY POWERED EQUIPMENT

The useful equipment disclosed in this section is equipment that is powered by AAA, AA, C, D, 9-volt, and/or smaller size batteries.

BATTERY RECOMMENDATION Using rechargeable batteries saves lots of money and helps preserve the environment. The small nickel metal hydride rechargeable batteries I've used have worked extremely well and have had a fairly long life span if charged from a suitable power source--they're also mercury-free. Rechargeable Lithium Ion/Polymer batteries have even higher capacity, no cell memory effect problems, and they are becoming available in a plethora of sizes. No matter the type battery, all batteries really need to be disposed through proper channels for recycling; fortunately, many battery retailers offer recycling for the type batteries sold in their stores.

INVERTER USE CAUTION: If the adapter used in charging rechargeable equipment/batteries must be powered from a 120-volt AC source, I recommend connecting it only to a 120-volt AC wall outlet (don't connect it to a modified sine wave type inverter). I quit using my 12-volt DC to 120-volt AC modified sine wave inverter to charge rechargeable equipment/ batteries after ruining charging circuit rectifying diodes and substantially increasing cell memory effect problems in applicable rechargeable batteries.
UPDATE: Pure sine wave inverters that digitally build their 120-volt a.c. sine wave output are safe to use if their 12-volt d.c. input is continuously above 12.5 volts--otherwise their use is likely to increase cell memory effect problems while recharging applicable batteries.

BATTERY POWERED EQUIPMENT LIST
• AUTOMOTIVE DIAGNOSTICS SCANNER.
• CAMERA & VIDEO EQUIPMENT (w/ optional 12-Volt d.c. adapters).
• CARBON MONIXIDE DETECTOR (non-rechargeable batteries last much longer in this equipment).
• CELL PHONE.
• COMPUTER (portable).
• DIGITAL MULTI-METER (non-rechargeable batteries last much longer in this equipment).

Uses: Polarity checks; electrical measurements: voltage, resistance, current, etc. (Ch:8).
- EAREPHONES—use with applicable equipment to help prevent breach of privacy.
- ELECTRIC SOCKS.
- ELECTRONIC CLOCK/TEMPERATURE GAUGE (Ch. 3).
- ELECTRONIC ENTERTAINMENT EQUIPMENT.
    Recommendation: water-resistant version will last much longer than non-water-resistant version (best if stored in airtight storage container).
- FIRE EXTINGUISHER: Small chemical type unit suitable for extinguishing any type of car fire.
- FIRE/SMOKE ALARM (Ch: 9). Non-rechargeable batteries last much longer in this equipment.
- FLASHLIGHTS (Ch. 1).
- GPS (Global Positioning Satellite System).
- LP GAS DETECTOR. (Non-rechargeable batteries last much longer in this equipment).
- REMOTE CONTROLS for associated equip. (Non-rechargeable batteries last much longer in this equip).
- SATELLITE PHONE.
- SHORTWAVE RADIO.
- SONAR (HAND-HELD).

7.4 USEFUL 12-VOLT D.C. POWERED ELECTRICAL EQUIPMENT

- 12-Volt DC ADAPTERS for powering applicable equipment.
- 12-VOLT HIGH CAPACITY BATTERIES (Ch. 8).
- 12-VOLT BED WARMERS (Ch. 3). **sold at LivingInCars. com & ElectroWarmth.com**
- 12-VOLT BOAT BILGE PUMP (Ch. 5—water retrieval applications).
- Multiple or Dual 12-VOLT CIGARETTE/ACCESSORY PLUG ADAPTER (turns one 12-volt outlet into two or more).
- 12-VOLT FAN: BRUSH-LESS ELECTRONIC COOLING FAN (Ch. 3).
- 12-VOLT MOBILE PHONE (Ch. 9).
- 12-VOLT PORTABLE COMPUTER.
- 12-VOLT SATELLITE PHONE—a must have for those who like to explore remote wilderness locations.
- 12-VOLT SOLAR PANELS (Ch. 8).

- 12-VOLT TIMING LIGHT (inductive pickup)--ignition system checks (Ch. 13).
- 12-VOLT TIRE AIR PUMP (Ch: 13).
- 12-VOLT SWITCH MODE POWER SUPPLY–allows constant 12-volt output from a varying d.c. voltage imput..
- 12-VOLT PET WARMING PAD to keep feet warm. *Sold at LivingInCars.com & ElectroWarmth.com*

- 12-VOLT D.C. TO 120-VOLT A.C. INVERTER
   While living in cars, it's best to use 12-volt DC powered electrical equipment because of the abundant availability of 12-volt DC power. However, 120-volt AC-powered equipment isn't always available in a 12-volt DC-powered version, so there probably will be instances when 120-volt AC-powered equipment will need to be used when a 120-volt AC wall outlet isn't available. Fortunately, there is a simple way to power 120-volt AC-powered equipment while inside a car.
   An inverter is a complex electronic device that transforms 12-volt DC electricity into a form of 120-volt AC electricity, either a modified sine wave or a desired pure sine wave. Small wattage inverters (<400 watts) usually can be plugged into a car's cigarette lighter receptacle, while larger wattage inverters need to be connected directly to a car's starting battery, or at the car's starter. Being small in size, extremely rugged, 12-volt DC-powered, water resistant, shock resistant, dust resistant, and being available in a variety of power sizes (wattage), an inverter is well suited for use inside a car.

POSSIBLE INVERTER USE PROBLEMS PERTAINING TO "MODIFIED SINE WAVE" TYPE INVERTORS Before discussing problems I've had with using a modified sine wave inverter, I need to state that an inverter is a very useful electronic device that I use, at least minimally, everyday. Also, expensive invertors that digitally build a pure sine wave have, for the most part, overcome the electrical problems associated with modified sine wave inverters. The following material is provided to help the user identify and minimize potential inverter use problems, mainly pertaining to modified sine wave inverters.
   Most problems associated with using a modified sine wave inverter come from two conditions: (1) the inverter's inability to exactly duplicate the pure sine wave produced by electric companies, and (2) an inverter's inability to provide itself with a constant 12-volt DC voltage level when being powered from a varying voltage level type 12-volt battery (this second issue

is still a problem with both type inverters, but at least the pure sine wave inverters generally cut off when input gets too low).

MODIFIED SINE WAVE PROBLEMS   The modified sine wave inverters I've owned produce what their manufacture describes as a "modified" sine wave, which, in my opinion, on an oscilloscope looks more like a 120-volt AC square wave (definitely not ideal). The two deficits produced in an inverter's modified sine wave are (1) an extremely fast voltage rise and fall rate, and (2) voltage spikes. The extremely fast voltage rise and fall rate causes extra heating of inductive loads, such as motors, transformers, inductors, etc., and this extra heating can shorten the lifespan and even ruin certain types of electrical/ electronic equipment. Voltage spikes produced in the modified sine wave can damage or ruin certain unprotected voltage sensitive electronic components, such as cheap rectifying diodes.

INVERTER OUTPUT VOLTAGE/POWER MAY VARY WHEN 12-VOLT DC INPUT VARIES As a varying voltage type battery's 12-volt output powering an inverter decreases, an inverter's power output generally decreases too (expensive pure sine wave inverters generally cut off when input voltage goes below a certain level, which is good). An improper varying output from a modified sine wave inverter can become damaging to certain types of electrical/electronic equipment...in my applications, the main problem has been quickly increasing applicable batteries' cell memory effect problem, thus quickly shortening the battery lifespan (example: internal Ni-cad and Ni-MH batteries used in certain rechargeable equipment).

INVERTER CAN BE DAMAGED BY TOO MUCH AC RIPPLE VOLTAGE If powering an inverter from a 12-volt power source that, for some reason, has excessive AC ripple voltage riding on the 12-volt dc, such as possibly from a car's electrical system (defective voltage regulation of some sort) or from a cheap battery charger--excessive AC ripple voltage can damage an inverter, and this damage probably won't be covered by the inverter manufacturer's warranty.

120-VOLT AC-POWERED EQUIPMENT I WOULDN'T POWER FROM A MODIFIED SINE WAVE INVERTER Unlike the modified sine wave produced by applicable inverters, the 120-volt AC electricity produced by electric companies is very distortion free--it is the best source to use in powering 120-volt AC-powered rechargeable equipment/batteries, although the expensive pure sine wave inverters are safe to use if connected to a constant level 12-volt power source.

Because of the problem I've had with my modified sine wave inverter's voltage spikes ruining some of my rechargeable equipment's internal rectifying diodes (electric shavers, flashlights, etc.), and because of the problems I've had in quickly increasing applicable batteries' cell memory effect problem when powering a modified sine wave inverter from a varying voltage 12-volt power source--I try not to use an inverter to power any type of rechargeable equipment (exception: pure sine wave inverters are safe to use if connected to a constant 12-volt power source).

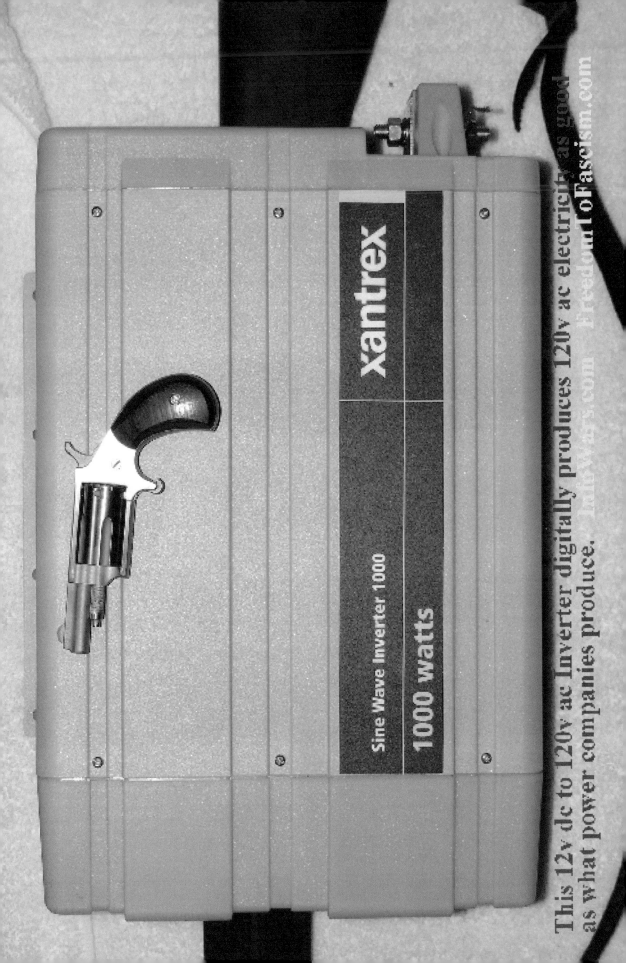

This 12v dc to 120v ac Inverter digitally produces 120v ac electricity as good as what power companies produce.   InfoWars.com   FreedomToFascism.com

7.5 USEFUL 120-VOLT AC-POWERED EQUIPMENT

- AIR FILTERING MACHING (run for 15-30 minutes before going to sleep).
- PORTABLE 3-WAY REFRIGERATOR/FREEZER (Ch. 6 & 11).
- AC ADAPTERS for use w/ applicable equipment.
- BATTERY CHARGERS for 12-volt & other size batteries (Ch. 8).
- RECHARGABLE EQUIPMENT: power tools, entertainment/ business equipment, etc.
  RECOMMENDATION: Rechargeable equipment/batteries are best charged from a 120-volt AC wall outlet (see previous section on inverters); however, equipment using a 12-volt DC adapter that utilizes an internal switch-mode power supply is OK to use with a 12-volt DC power source.
- VARIABLE SPEED 1/2" DRILL.
  Power Option: using a cheap modified sine wave inverter of large enough wattage has worked out satisfactorily in powering my electric drill, but with extra heating of the drill motor--car engine generally needs to be running when powering an inverter from a car's electrical system, so the voltage powering the inverter remains high.
- PRINTER & SCANNER.
  Power Option: powering my printer from an inexpensive modified sine wave inverter has worked out OK in my applications, but with extra heating and noise being emitted from the printer's power transformer (12-volt d.c. adapter may be available from equip. mfg.).
- VACUUM CLEANER (Ch. 6).
  Power Option: powering an inexpensive modified sine wave inverter from my car's electrical system with car engine operating has worked out satisfactory in powering my powerful hand-held vacuum cleaner, but with extra heating of the vacuum cleaner motor.
- "WATER-PIK" MACHINE.
  Use: Cleaning gums + teeth with jets of water & baking soda mixture.
  Power option: powering from an inverter for less than two minutes per day has been OK.
- WIRE SOLDERING SUPPLIES: solder iron, solder, tip, electrical tape, wire strippers, flux, alligator leads, heat sinks.
  STORAGE: Stores easily in quart size resealable bag.
  POWER OPTION: Powering soldering iron from an inexpensive modified sine wave inverter has worked out satisfactorily in my applications.

CHAPTER 8

MEETING 12-VOLT DC AND 120-VOLT AC ELECTRICAL POWER NEEDS INSIDE A CAR

8.1 CHAPTER INTRODUCTION

Since a car's electrical system can supply plenty of 12-volt DC power while the car engine is operating, using 12-volt DC-powered equipment, instead of 120-volt AC-powered equipment, whenever possible is desirable. 120-volt AC-powered equipment can possibly be powered by a car's electrical system via a 12-volt DC to 120-volt AC inverter, but generally with deficits. Unfortunately, powering any type of equipment from a car's 12-volt lead acid starting battery while the car engine is off will probably discharge and quickly ruin the battery, thus an auxiliary 12-volt power source may be necessary.

Depending on the car living/working situation, electrical power needs may or may not be minimal while parked (engine off). Using internal battery powered equipment (rechargeable batteries) and rechargeable equipment, which can be charged during one's daily work/activities away from one's car or at one's external storage location, may eliminate the need of having a 12-volt auxiliary power source. However, in car living/working situations in which substantial amounts of 12-volt DC electricity is needed while parked, having an auxiliary 12-volt power source may be necessary.

There are a few requirements that an auxiliary 12-volt power source should meet if it is to be used inside a car. First, since there generally isn't much room underneath a car or in a car's engine compartment, the auxiliary power source needs to be of a type that can be used and stored inside a car, thus it needs to be a clean, non-toxic source of 12-volt DC power. It needs to be able to meet one's power needs anytime the car engine isn't running. To prevent breach of privacy, a 12-volt DC auxiliary power source should supply power with little or no noise.

This chapter explores several 12-volt DC auxiliary power source options and gives recommendations as to what will be most suitable to use inside a car.

8.2 TWELVE-VOLT AUXILIARY POWER SOURCE OPTIONS

TWELVE-VOLT LEAD ACID CAR STARTING BATTERY ISN'T SUITABLE TO USE AS AN AUXILIARY POWER SOURCE Lead acid car-starting batteries are easily ruined if left in a partially/fully discharged state; they are only suitable for applications in which they will be maintained in a near fully charged state at all times. Severely discharging a lead-acid battery or leaving it in a partially discharge state causes its internal resistance to increase, and this effect is cumulative and eventually causes much of a battery's voltage to be dropped internally as the battery approaches the end of its life. Therefore, to allow a lead acid car starting battery the longest possible life, significant amounts of power should not be drawn from it while the car engine isn't operating.

TWELVE-VOLT CAR ALTERNATOR: NOT A SUITABLE AUXILIARY POWER SOURCE A car's alternator can supply plenty of electrical power while the car engine is operating (generally 60-120A @ 14V). However, wasting gas, adding excessive engine wear, and breaching one's privacy by starting a car's engine each time power is needed isn't practical. However, starting a car and using alternator power may be the only option in high power applications, such as when using an inverter to power a microwave oven, vacuum cleaner, power tools, etc.

USING A 120-VOLT AC POWERED 12-VOLT BATTERY CHARGER AS AN AUXILLIARY POWER SOURCE USUALLY ISN'T POSSIBLE While living/working in cars, my parking locations generally haven't had a 120-volt AC outlet nearby in which I could plug a battery charger into. At parking location where there was an outlet nearby, plugging into it would have caused breach of privacy of my secret living/working situation. However, in the few situations when parked near a 120-volt

AC outlet in which breach of privacy wasn't a concern, using a 12-volt battery charger to charge my car's starting battery has worked out well in making my car's electrical system a suitable 12-volt auxiliary power source.

PORTABLE GENERATORS GENERALLY AREN'T SUITABLE FOR USE AS AN AUXILIARY 12-VOLT POWER SOURCE Simplicity is a large part of the enjoyment that comes with living in a privatized car. Although I once used a portable generator to help satisfy my 12-volt electrical power needs while parking in a sparsely populated, severely cold wilderness location, because of the hassles involved and the minimal benefits received, I probably wouldn't consider doing so again.

SOLAR PANELS: NOT A SUITABLE 12-VOLT AUXILIARY POWER SOURCE

Solar panels supply relatively small amounts of power and only during daylight, thus they're probably not a suitable stand-alone 12-volt auxiliary power source for car living/working situations.

8.3 CERTAIN TYPES OF HIGH-CAPACITY, RECHARGEABLE, 12-VOLT BATTERIES MAY BE SUITABLE TO USE AS AN AUXILLIARY 12-VOLT POWER SOURCE INSIDE A CAR

Totally sealed, 12-volt, high-capacity batteries can be a noise-less, clean, non-toxic source of 12-volt DC power whenever needed, and therefore may be suitable for use inside a car. If placed inside a sealable, vented battery box, non-totally sealed batteries may also be used. Some 12-volt batteries can be charged from a number of sources, such as from a battery charger, generator, solar panel, and most importantly, from a car's 12-volt electrical system during driving.

The main factors in deciding what type of 12-volt battery would be most suitable to use as an auxiliary power source in car living/working situations are (1) battery construction—sealed or non-sealed, (2) charge/discharge characteristics and requirements, (3) cost, and (4) toxicity of gases that may be emitted during overcharging.

BATTERY CONSTRUCTION Most cars don't have enough

room underneath the car or inside the engine compartment to store any auxiliary 12-volt batteries; therefore, I've usually stored them on the front passenger seat floor area. This area allows for easy access to a car's fuse box for charging when driving as well as easy battery removal from a car whenever necessary.

Totally sealed, rechargeable 12-volt batteries that emit no gases/fumes (exception: during excessive overcharging) have worked well because of their being able to be stored and used inside my cars without the use of a sealed + vented battery box. However, in certain power applications when expensive constant voltage level type 12-volt batteries are needed, using serviceable batteries that can be serviced and repaired whenever necessary will be much more cost effective and well worth the hassle of having to store them in sealable vented battery storage boxes. Fortunately, batteries are constantly being improved, so you'll continue to have more and more options in meeting your auxiliary power needs for just about any situation.

• BATTERY CHARGE/DISCHARGE CHARACTERISTICS
INTERMITTENT CHARGE/DISCHARGE CAPABILITY Batteries susceptible to significant cell memory effect (cell imbalance) problems generally require that their charging cycle be uninterrupted from start to finish if they are to provide long life. Unfortunately, intermittent battery charging and discharging is what is abundantly available from a car's electrical system. Therefore, except in specialized work applications, I've generally used 12-volt batteries that can be charged/discharged intermittently without adversely affecting the battery's life span, which are generally the type that have a varying output voltage level. During the times I've used 12-volt batteries susceptible to cell memory effect problems (generally, constant level output voltage type batteries), I've fully met their charging needs by charging them uninterrupted at my external storage location using a 120-volt AC-powered, constant current type battery charger.

Some types of batteries have both a max voltage and max current charging level that requires a specialized charger that monitors battery temperature and limits the charging current to within safe limits for different temperatures.

FULL CHARGE VOLTAGE LEVEL CONSIDERATION If a varying voltage level type auxiliary battery's fully charge voltage level is within .5 volts of a lead acid car starting battery's fully charged voltage level, the auxiliary battery may be able to be charged directly from a car's electrical system while driving, and an auxiliary charging regulator/filter may not be necessary. Basically, if a car's electrical system won't supply too much voltage, current, and AC ripple voltage when charging auxiliary batteries, a charging regulator may not be needed (pertains to varying voltage level type 12-volt batteries only, not constant voltage level type batteries).

BATTERY'S IMMUNITY FROM AC RIPPLE VOLTAGE As with most rectifying circuits, car alternators produce a small amount of AC ripple voltage that rides on the 12-volt DC voltage. Certain types of rechargeable batteries will be adversely affected by significant amounts of AC ripple voltage, thus use of an auxiliary regulator/filter may be necessary when charging from a car's electrical system. To prevent from having to use an auxiliary charging regulator/filter, using a varying voltage type 12-volt battery that can handle the AC ripple voltage produced in a car's electrical system may be desirable.

PORTION OF CHARGE THAT CAN BE USED W/O ADVERSELY AFFECTING BATTERY LIFESPAN How far a 12-volt auxiliary battery can be discharged without adversely affecting its lifespan is one determining factor in how many batteries will be required to satisfy an application. The more of a battery's charge that can be used without adverse effects, the less number of batteries required for a given application.

HOW A BATTERY'S VOLTAGE LEVEL DECREASES DURING DISCHARGING How a battery's voltage decreases as it discharges may be an important consideration depending on the application. 12-volt batteries whose internal resistance increases during discharging provide a voltage level output that decreases continuously (very slowly) as the battery discharges, thus using only a portion of the battery's charge is possible (exception: using a switch-mode power supply can allow much more of the battery's charge to be used, but with adverse effects to battery lifespan). In contrast, 12-volt batteries that exhibit almost no internal resistance provide a near constant voltage level during discharging of the battery until almost completely discharged. There are advantages and disadvantages to both types of batteries.

BATTERY COST CONSIDERATION Since all batteries eventually expire (exception: serviceable/repairable batteries with individual cells that can be continuously rebuilt/replaced as needed), purchasing the least expensive battery that will adequately satisfy the application is desirable.

BATTERY FUMES POSSIBLY EMITTED DURING OVERCHARGING Most totally sealed 12-volt batteries are completely sealed at all times except during prolonged periods of overcharging in which internal gas pressure may rise to the point of momentarily opening an internal pressure relief valve. Depending on how and where a battery is being charged, knowing what type fumes a battery can emit during periods of overcharging may be useful information to know.

Two things one can implement so as not to have to be concerned with battery fumes are (1) place battery(s) in sealed battery box(s) that are vented to the outside, or (2) use specialized charging equipment that eliminates the possibility of overcharging, (3) use a type battery that utilizes Recombinant Gas technology that practically eliminates the release of internal gases.

BATTERY ELECTROLYTE One could be doused with battery electrolyte from batteries carried inside a car during a possibly car accident. Therefore, carrying a battery electrolyte neutralizer inside one's car may be desirable.

BATTERIES POSSIBLY SUITABLE FOR USE AS AN AUXILIARY 12-VOLT POWER SOURCE

The batteries discussed in this section are the one's I'm most familiar with (I've owned and used each type).

LEAD ACID CAR STARTING BATTERY IS UNSUITABLE TO USE AS AN AUXILIARY POWER SOURCE

As previously disclosed, 12-volt lead acid car-starting batteries aren't suitable for use in applications where they won't be maintained in a fully charged state, as leaving them in a fully/partially discharge state drastically shortens their life because of the cumulative effect of increasing internal resistance. Also, the toxicity and corrosiveness of lead acid battery electrolyte makes vented lead acid batteries undesirable to use in car living/working power applications. Keep in mind that a lead acid car starting battery is the cheapest form of 12-volt lead acid battery . . . more advanced types of lead acid batteries are manufactured for Marine, RV, and Aircraft applications, and they are constantly being improved.

LITHIUM ION or LITHIUM POLYMER BATTERY: Depending on what is being powered, Lithium Ion or Lithium Polymer batteries may be suitable to use as an auxiliary power source in car living power applications. Powering portable electronics, such as cell phones, portable computers, digital cameras, RC electric cars and planes is where Lithium Ion and Lithium Polymer batteries are often used – the RC model planes and cars generally use lithium Polymer batteries because the cells are flat (allowing more charge per volume) and very safe concerning cell rupture, whereas Lithium Ion cells are cylinder in shape and can emit shards of aluminum during a cell rupture. The advances in Lithium Ion/Poly battery technology, along with the sophisticated electronics used in their charge and discharge cycle, has finally allowed high-capacity 12 & 24 volt Lithium Ion batteries to be used in modern applications— especially in low weight applications.

Lithium Ion/Polymer batteries have many desirable characteristics, such as light weight, high energy density, high capacity and long cycle life. Having no significant cell memory effect problems allows lithium Ion/polymer batteries to be used in applications where they may be intermittently charged/discharged – they also charge relatively fast. Because of having almost no internal resistance, they maintain a high voltage level until almost fully discharged. Since most of the charge can be utilized, fewer batteries will be required to satisfy an application. Keep in mind that constant voltage level type batteries have only so many charge discharge cycles in their lifespan -- 300 charge/discharge cycles is typical.

Charging, discharging, and temperature limitations have traditionally limited Lithium Ion/Polymer batteries to more "stable" applications. Fortunately, their charging and discharging vulnerabilities have largely been overcome with internal improvements, along with the use of sophisticated electronics that limit/control charging and discharging of the battery. Charging current and battery temperature limitations require that specialized chargers be used for charging Lithium Ion/Polymer batteries– a good charger will have battery temperature monitoring capability (some Lithium Ion/Polymer batteries have one or more internal temperature sensors that relay battery temperature to the charger). Exceeding max current output and battery temperature limits will quickly ruin Lithium Ion/Polymer batteries, fortunately, sophisticated electronics now take care of Lithium Ion/Polymer batteries very well, allowing their use in more and more applications.

Lithium Ion/Polymer batteries and the sophisticated electronics that keep operating parameters within limits have undergone continuous improvement and advancement. It's because of these advancements that we're now starting to see high capacity 24-volt Lithium Ion/Polymer batteries being used in aircraft applications – they've always had the lightweight, high energy density, high capacity and long cycle life.

NICKEL METAL HYDRIDE & NICKEL CADMIUM 12-VOLT BATTERIES

Nickel Metal Hydride (Ni-MH) and Nickel Cadmium (Ni-Cd) batteries are constant voltage level type batteries with characteristics similar to Lithium Ion/Polymer batteries, but have less capacity. Unlike Lithium Ion/Polymer batteries, Ni-Cd and Ni-MH have significant cell memory effect problems. Ni-MH batteries generally have a bit more capacity than Ni-Cd batteries. Although I'm discussing Ni-MH and Ni-Cd batteries together because of their similar characteristics, I'm not suggesting that more than one type of battery be used to make up an auxiliary power source--IT'S BEST IF ONLY ONE TYPE OF BATTERY BE USED TO MAKE UP AN AUXILIARY POWER SOURCE, no matter if using varying or non-varying output voltage level type batteries. Differences in electrical parameters/characteristics, electrolyte, charging requirements, capacity, etc. really require that only one type of battery be used to make up an auxiliary power source, no matter how many batteries are used.

Nickel metal hydride (NI-MH) and nickel cadmium (Ni-Cd) batteries are susceptible to cell memory effect (cell imbalance) problems, and even though the Ni-MH battery cell memory effect problem has been significantly reduced by internal advances over time, it hasn't been eliminated. To avoid cell imbalance problems, they are best charged uninterrupted, sometimes deep-cycled, as specified by their manufacture. Cell memory effect problems make NI-MH and Ni-Cd batteries a bad choice for applications where much intermittent charging and discharging occurs--deep-cycling often helps to counter the cell memory effect problem. The recommended ambient temperature range for charging NI-MH and Ni-Cd batteries is generally between 60 degrees and 86 degrees Fahrenheit-- like Lithium Ion/Polymer batteries, exceeding internal battery temperature limits will quickly ruin NI-MH and Ni-Cd batteries.

Serviceable/repairable high capacity 24-volt Ni-Cd aircraft batteries have been available for decades, but are now receiving quite a bit of competition from Absorbed Glass Mat (AGM) lead acid batteries that have a few really nice features: (1) the AGM keeps electrolyte against the cell plates under almost any condition, which prevents cell burn during charging -- the AGM lead acid battery can work in any position and under high G loads; (2) if utilizing recombinant gas technology, their pressurized cells cause the hydrogen and oxygen gases generated during charging to recombine into water–almost no loss of electrolyte during the life of the battery makes for a truly maintenance free battery; (3) no temperature monitoring or other sophisticated charging/discharging electronics are needed for the lead acid battery (they are functionally and physically rugged). The traditional high capacity 24-volt Ni-Cd aircraft battery now has plenty of competition from AGM lead acid and Lithium Ion/Polymer batteries – lightweight powerful high-capacity 24-volt Lithium Ion/Polymer batteries will probably reign in the near future as king of the aircraft battery, at least until something better displaces it.

For car living applications, a serviceable/repairable 24-volt Ni-Cd aircraft battery that can be physically configured to 12-volts by making changes to how the cells connect to each other, and that can be continuously repaired (change out bad cell), may be fairly economical for those that want to properly maintain it, and store it in a sealed vented battery storage box inside their car

Having a near constant voltage level until almost fully discharged makes Ni-Cd and Ni-MH (and Lithium Ion/Polymer) batteries a pleasure to use in applications where a constant voltage source is needed. Since most of the battery's charge can be utilized without adversely affecting the battery's normal life span, fewer batteries are required to satisfy an application; however, keep in mind that constant voltage level type batteries have only so many charge discharge cycles in their lifespan (300+ charge/discharge cycles is typical).

EXTRA: The AAA, AA, C, D, 9V size rechargeable Nickel Metal Hydride batteries I use are mercury free and offer a much higher capacity than Ni-Cd batteries. Using a battery charger that allows Ni-MH and Ni-Cd batteries to be fully discharged in the charger and then charged at a 5-hour rate will allow for maximum battery lifespan. The AAA, AA, C, D, 9V size batteries are slowly being offered in rechargeable Lithium Ion versions.

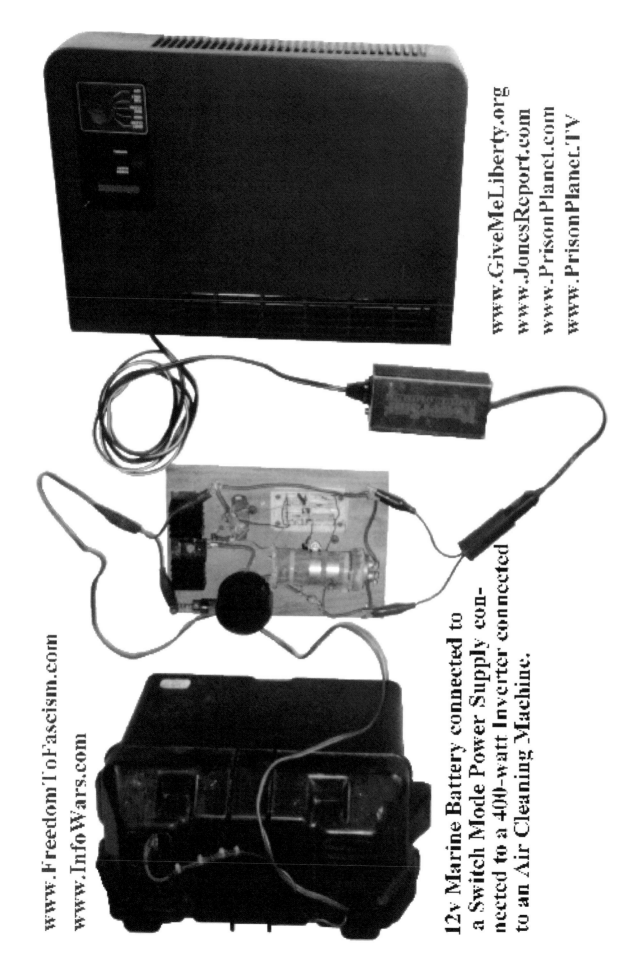

www.FreedomToFascism.com

www.InfoWars.com

www.GiveMeLiberty.org
www.JonesReport.com
www.PrisonPlanet1.com
www.PrisonPlanet.TV

12v Marine Battery connected to a Switch Mode Power Supply connected to a 400-watt Inverter connected to an Air Cleaning Machine.

TWELVE-VOLT MARINE/RV BATTERY -- A GOOD CHOICE

Totally sealed 12-volt marine/RV batteries have worked well in satisfying my 12-volt DC electrical needs (exception: when constant voltage level type battery is needed). I've always chosen to purchase totally sealed units that can be stored in a car without having to use a sealable vented battery box.

Marine batteries have no cell imbalance problems, thus charging and discharging them intermittently is OK. Being able to charge/discharge marine batteries intermittently makes them suitable for charging from a car's electrical system while driving--a car electrical system's AC ripple voltage isn't a problem either. The general rule for marine batteries is not to discharge them more than 50%, and to keep them fully charged when not in use so as to maximize battery lifespan. Like a car lead acid starting battery, deep-cycle marine batteries last longer if kept near a fully charged state. Discharging a lead acid marine battery continually below 50% of its capacity leads to a much shorter battery life, mainly due to cumulative amounts of lead sulfate building up on the battery cell plates that can't be removed during charging (a chemical reaction inside the battery that increases internal resistance and limits its ability to hold a charge).

Three types of marine batteries are the (1) flooded cell, (2) gel cell, and (3) absorbed glass mat cell. Absorbed Glass Mat (AGM) marine batteries that utilize recombinant gas (RG) technology are truly maintenance-free, having very little loss of electrolyte throughout their lifespan. AGM marine batteries have lead plates packed between glass mats, which hold electrolytes in suspension. The glass mat capillary action qualities provide abundant acid contact to the lead plates under extreme vibration, g loads, inverted installations, etc. Compared to flooded cell and gel cell marine batteries, AGM marine batteries charge faster, last longer, and they supply temporary high current loads more efficiently with a higher voltage.

The marine batteries I've owned have had full charge voltage levels within .4 volts of a lead acid car starting battery's fully charged voltage level. I've had no problems charging marine batteries directly from a car's electrical system without the use of an auxiliary charging regulator while driving. However, since a marine battery's fully charged voltage level is slightly less than that of a lead acid car starting battery, it must be disconnected from a car's electrical system whenever the car engine isn't operating (a battery isolator will do this automatically), so as to prevent minimally discharging and shortening the life of the lead acid car starting battery. If available, using the battery manufacturer's 12-volt car charging equipment is highly recommended.

Note: any type of lead acid battery is a varying voltage level type battery.

8.4 AUXILLIARY POWER SOURCE RECOMMENDATIONS/ CONSIDERATIONS

I enjoy living in privatized cars not using an auxiliary 12-volt DC power source whenever possible; however, this isn't always possible. The following information is recommendations and considerations pertaining to creating an auxiliary power supply.

SINGLE BATTERY TYPE IS ABSOLUTELY NECESSARY Different type batteries generally have different fully charged voltage levels, different charging needs, different electrolyte, different capacity, etc. Connecting different type batteries together in "parallel" (positive to positive, negative to negative) generally adversely affects battery lifespan. Therefore, it is most important that all batteries used to make up an auxiliary power source be of the same type and same capacity. Also, it is very important that the same type batteries connected in parallel all have good/similar internal condition (more later).

Note: One could build a computer-controlled electronic wiring harness/grid that could allow multiple types of 12-volt batteries to be connected in "parallel" for use as an auxiliary power source without adverse effects. I'm sure applications with large banks of batteries, such as large solar power generation fields or large battery backup applications for electronic communications hardware, use a sophisticated battery monitoring and battery adjustment grid.

BATTERY STORAGE I generally store totally sealed, high capacity 12-volt marine/RV batteries individually in plastic boat battery boxes (lined with 1" foam) located in the front seat passenger floor area, as this area allows for easy connection to the car's fuse box as well as easy battery removal. The plastic boat battery box lid covers the battery terminals, thus prevents shorting of a battery terminals against anything metal nearby. Plastic boat battery boxes have two holes cutout in their lid in which the battery positive wire and negative wire can protrude through.

When using serviceable/repairable constant voltage level type batteries, I store them inside sealable vented battery storage boxes positioned in the front passenger seat floor area with the vent hoses extending out the passenger door crevice or through climate control vents and into the lower engine compartment area.

BATTERY TYPE   I use high capacity constant voltage level batteries (Ni-Cd, Ni-MH, Lithium-ion, Li-Poly) for powering expensive equipment that requires a constant level power source. Since high-capacity constant-voltage level type 12-volt batteries are very expensive, I've sometimes used serviceable/repairable units (24-volt Ni-Cd aircraft starting batteries reconfigured for 12-volts). To gain maximum battery life, I've chosen to properly charge, service, and repair them at my external storage locations strictly adhering to the battery manufacturer's guidelines, or purchase and use the battery manufacturer's 12-volt charging equipment when traveling long enough to fully charge the battery (intermittent charge/ discharge is unacceptable).

For general car living situations, I usually use totally sealed marine/RV batteries to satisfy my 12-volt DC auxiliary power needs. Although not repairable, totally sealed marine batteries are relatively inexpensive and will last a fairly long time if used and cared for properly (don't discharge more than 50%, and keep them fully charged when possible). Using varying voltage type batteries with a boost switch-mode power supply will provide a constant voltage level output, but one needs to be careful and monitor battery discharge, not letting it go below a 50% discharge level (pertains to marine/RV batteries).

CREATING FUSE PROTECTED BATTERY LEADS   I generally make fuse protected battery leads out of 18-gauge speaker wire, a splice-in type wire fuse assembly, and two alligator leads. As compared to using two separate wires, speaker wire has the advantage of being more tangle-free. Splicing in an in-line fuse assembly and soldering it into the positive wire close to a battery's positive terminal will protect the battery and down circuit equipment/wiring/etc. from a variety of electrical hazards. Soldering a red and black alligator lead to the speaker wire makes exceptional lead ends that can easily clip to a car fuse box, power-bus, 12-volt DC adapter, switch-mode power supply, etc.

* CONNECTING VARYING VOLTAGE LEVEL TYPE 12-VOLT BATTERIES IN "PARALLEL" *
BATTERIES CONNECTED IN "PARALLEL" NEED TO BE IN GOOD CONDITION, AND THEY NEED TO BE OF THE SAME TYPE Different varying voltage level type 12-volt batteries generally have slightly different fully charged voltage levels. Also, a battery in poor condition has a lower fully charged voltage level than a same type battery that is in good condition. When two or more fully charged batteries are connected in parallel (pos. terminal to pos. terminal, neg. terminal to neg. terminal), the higher voltage level battery(s) will quickly discharge to the voltage level of the lowest voltage level battery in the group- -and this can shorten the life of all the batteries connected in parallel, especially the higher voltage level good condition batteries. Therefore, batteries connected in parallel must be of the same type, have the same capacity, and have similar good internal condition if battery lifespan is to be maximized.

DETERMINING THE CONDITION OF A CONSTANT VOLTAGE LEVEL TYPE 12-VOLT BATTERY (serviceable type) Constant voltage level type batteries are batteries whose output voltage and extremely low internal resistance remain nearly constant until the battery is almost fully discharged: Nickel Cadmium, Nickel Metal Hydride, Lithium Ion, Lithium Polymer, etc. The Nickel Cadmium aircraft starting battery is the only serviceable/ repairable type battery I've owned, as most other constant voltage level type batteries aren't serviceable/repairable.

Always follow the battery manufacturer's instructions in determining the internal condition of a constant voltage level type battery. The following is a generalization of how the internal condition of a serviceable/repairable Nickel Cadmium battery might be checked.

First fully charge the serviceable/repairable Ni-Cad battery, and then discharge it at a specified rate measuring its ampere-hour capacity. If the battery's ampere-hour capacity is less than normal, some of the cells are unbalanced and/or one or more battery cells is possibly bad. To equalize the battery cells and check for any bad cells, the battery's cells must first be equalized by deep-cycling the battery. To deep-cycle a battery, discharge it at a rate somewhat lower than that used for the capacity test. When the cell voltage is down to around .2 volts per cell, short across each cell with a shorting strap (battery cover is off). Leave the strap across the cells for 4-8 hours to ensure that all the cells are completely discharged. Remove the shorting straps and charge the battery with a constant-current charger, charging it at the five-hour rate for six hours. This will give it 120 percent of its rated charge. If the battery has been properly serviced and is in good condition, each cell should have a voltage level range as specified by the battery manufacturer. If the voltage of any cell is not within that range, the cell is bad and needs replacing.

DETERMINING THE INTERNAL CONDITION OF VARYING VOLTAGE LEVEL TYPE BATTERIES Varying voltage type batteries are batteries whose voltage output decreases while internal resistance continuously increases during battery discharging. During charging, the battery's internal resistance decreases and the voltage level continues to rise till the battery is fully charged. Unfortunately, a very small portion of a battery's internal resistance can't be removed during charging from a moderately or highly discharged state, and therefore builds up cumulatively throughout a battery's life till eventually reaching a point where much of the battery's output voltage is dropped internally (hence a bad battery). Also, since this permanent increase in resistance mainly takes place when the battery is left in a partially or fully discharged state for a substantial period, varying voltage level type batteries last longest if kept in a near full state of charge.

• BATTERY LOAD TESTING

Accurately determining the condition (internal resistance) of a varying voltage level type battery is done by "load-testing" the battery while it is in a fully charged state. The steps in load-testing a varying voltage level type battery are as follows:

1. Make sure the battery electrolyte level is full (if serviceable), NOTE: Charging a battery with a low electrolyte level results in cell burn—so always maintain a serviceable battery's electrolyte level at the optimum level, which is usually just above the cell plates.
2. Make sure the battery is fully charged,
3. Measure the no load voltage of the battery,
4. Apply a load of fixed resistance to the battery that will draw

around 10 amps or more of battery current, and then after waiting a few seconds, measure the battery voltage (volt drop across the load),
5. Disconnect the load from the battery.

If the external load applied to the battery has a fixed resistance that didn't change substantially while loading the battery, the internal resistance of the fully charged battery can be figured using the following:
Vnl (no load battery voltage) = Vl (voltage drop across external load) + Vint.(voltage drop across internal battery resistance), therefore
Vint. = Vnl - Vl
I (circuit current) = Vl / Rl (fixed load resistance)
Rint (internal battery resistance) = Vint (voltage drop across internal battery resistance) / I (circuit current)

EXTRA: Cheap varying voltage level type batteries ("flooded" cell batteries) can have individual cells go bad from corroded cell plate material settling to the bottom of the cell that eventually builds up to the point of touching the base of the cell plates shorting out the cell(s).

DIGITAL VOLT/OHM/AMP MULTI-METER USE APPLICATIONS
A digital volt/ohm/amp multi-meter is used to measure electrical resistance (ohms), AC and DC voltage (volts), and electrical current (amps). Some multi-meters have the capability to measure other electrical parameters, such as hertz, capacitance, inductance, duty cycle, transistor beta, etc.
Owning and using a multi-meter will be useful to anyone living/working around electricity, such as when living/working in a privatized car. Having an inexpensive multi-meter and the knowledge of how DC electricity works will considerably enhance one's car living experience.

VOLT-METER APPLICATIONS In car living power applications, 90 percent of multi-meter use will probably be for measuring voltage levels. Possibly volt-meter applications include:
• Checking for correct polarity (positive/negative) before making an electrical connection.
• Measuring a battery's voltage level.
• Measuring voltage level during load testing a battery.
• Measuring voltage drop across electrical connections to check for electrical opens and shorts.

- Performing certain checks during car maintenance/repairs.
- Performing voltage checks when assembling and maintaining an auxiliary power source and solar charging system.
- Measuring a car's electrical system voltage level.

AMP-METER: CURRENT MEASURING APPLICATIONS Possible amp-meter applications include (1) measuring car battery current discharge to see if a car's starting battery is being drained excessively while the car ignition is off (generally should be less than 20mA), (2) measuring how much current a solar charging system is supplying, (3) measuring the current draw of 12-volt DC equipment, so as to better determine one's overall power needs, and (4) measuring "reverse current leakage" of solar panels and diodes.

OHM-METER: ELECTRICAL RESISTANCE MEASUREMENTS Checking for electrical shorts and opens, and measuring the resistance of certain electrical equipment are a few applications one might use an ohm-meter for. Checking the condition of fuses and light bulbs, and measuring the resistance of motor + alternator windings are applications that easily come to mind.

8.5 OPTIONS IN CHARGING 12-VOLT AUXILLIARY BATTERIES

CHARGING CONSTANT VOLTAGE LEVEL TYPE BATTERIES Constant voltage level type batteries, such as nickel cadmium, nickel metal hydride, lithium-ion, and lithium-polymer batteries are very expensive. Some of these batteries are susceptible to cell memory effect (cell imbalance) problems--all are susceptibility to damage from excessive temperature during charging and discharging. To ensure long battery life, constant voltage level type batteries should be charged, serviced and repaired strictly adhering to the battery manufacturer's guidelines, using the manufacturer's applicable equipment-- some battery manufacturers offer 12-volt car chariging and monitoring equipment for their batteries.

OPTIONS IN CHARGING VARYING VOLTAGE LEVEL TYPE 12-VOLT BATTERIES For general car living electrical power applications, I use totally sealed, varying voltage level type 12-volt batteries to meet my power needs (Note: much of the time I don't need an auxiliary power source). Varying voltage level type batteries, such as marine/RV/Aircraft lead acid batteries have a few advantages that make them well suited for use inside a car: (1) They are relatively inexpensive; (2) they're offered in totally sealed models; and (3) having no significant cell imbalance problems and having minimal charging restrictions allows them to be charged directly from a variety of charging sources without the need of an auxiliary regulator/filter. Some of the charging sources I've used for charging marine and lead acid gel cell batteries include (1) a car's 12-volt electrical system, (2) solar panels, (3) 120-volt AC battery charger, and (4) portable generator.

Extra: Absorbant Glass Mat lead acid batteries utilizing RG technology are pretty much maintenance free as a lead acid battery can be, mainly because they retain almost all electrolyte over their lifespan if not subjected to severe overcharging.

CHARGING A VARYING VOLTAGE TYPE 12-VOLT AUXILIARY BATTERY FROM A CAR'S ELECTRICAL SYSTEM A car's electrical system can easily charge many 12-volt auxiliary batteries, more than anyone would want to carry inside a car. An auxiliary 12-volt battery's positive lead can be connected at many locations throughout a car's electrical system, such as at the fuse box, car starting battery, and engine starter. If the auxiliary battery's positive lead is fuse protected, and if it's connected to a car's electrical system down circuit of the fuse box, both the auxiliary battery and car's electrical system will be electrically protected from a variety of electrical hazards. Since all interconnected car body metal acts as the car electrical system's negative terminal (ground), connecting an auxiliary 12-volt battery's negative lead to car body metal can be done at most any location.

CAR CHARGING DISADVANTAGES Since a lead acid car starting battery and deep-cycle auxiliary battery generally have slightly different fully charged voltage levels, auxiliary batteries of the appropriate type can only be connected to a car's electrical system while the engine is running; otherwise, the car starting battery lifespan could be drastically shortened. If connecting/disconnecting auxiliary batteries is inconvenient, a battery isolator can be installed to do so automatically whenever the engine is turned on or off.

Totally sealed batteries should not be subjected to extended periods of overcharging, as any loss of battery electrolyte generally can't be replenished. Therefore, it may be necessary to monitor an auxiliary battery's charge level and disconnect the battery from a car's electrical system to prevent it from being subjected to long periods of overcharging, such as when driving for long periods. Another option in preventing overcharging is to use an auxiliary charging regulator—many battery manufacturers offer 12-volt d.c. charging equipment when it is a better solution for car charging their batteries from a car's electrical system, as opposed to a direct hook-up.

CHARGING AUXILIARY 12-VOLT BATTERY(S) DIRECTLY FROM A CAR'S FUSE BOX A very accessible location in a car's electrical system to charge auxiliary 12-volt batteries from is the car fuse box. There is plenty of power at this location, and it is generally a very convenient and accessible location to connect an auxiliary battery's positive lead to. Also, connecting to the down-circuit side of a fuse provides protection for the car's electrical system. If a car's fuse box contains the old style round type fuses, simply clip the auxiliary battery's positive alligator lead to the down-circuit side of the fuse holder. If a car's fuse box contains thin-type fuses, one of the 20 to 30-amp thin fuses will have to be modified, such as in removing the side top corner portion of plastic and then soldering a small amount of stranded wire to the exposed fuse tang metal so that an auxiliary battery's positive lead can be clipped to it. An auxiliary battery's negative lead can be connected to almost any unpainted car body metal and hardware.

CHARGING AUXILIARY 12-VOLT BATTERY(S) USING SOLAR PANELS Solar panels have been a very useful type battery charger I've used in car living/working electrical power applications. When 12-volt auxiliary power has been needed, solar panels have allowed me to live and work comfortably inside privatized cars parked most anywhere. Solar panels can be used for many types of battery charging applications: (1) trickle charging a car's starting battery during periods of extended parking (especially beneficial during cold weather), (2) recharging a car's starting battery if ever inadvertently discharged, (3) charging auxiliary 12-volt batteries, and (4) charging a boat, recreational vehicle, or mobile phone battery whenever needed (excellent emergency backup).
 • SOLAR PANEL CHARGING ADVANTAGES

The main advantages of using solar panels pertains to their power production, construction, use applications, and lifespan.

POWER ADVANTAGES   Solar panels produce free power in a silent, clean, maintenance-free manner. The quality glass-covered solar panels I own have typically came with a 10-20 year power output warranty. Because of the broad spectral response of silicon, solar panels can supply power (less power) during cloudy days and even during thunderstorms.

CONSTRUCTION ADVANTAGES The lightweight, aluminum frame, low-iron tempered glass-covered panels I own are designed to withstand sustained 125 mph winds or impacts from 1" hail stones falling at 52 mph.

Solar panels that have a front clear plastic covering and a rear metal covering are highly unbreakable--some can take a bullet and keep right on producing power (less power).

SOLAR APPLICATION ADVANTAGES Solar panels are available in a variety of sizes to fit almost anywhere one would want to place them. Although 12 + 24-volt applications are what solar panels are typically designed for, there are many solar panels being manufactured that cover a broad range of operating voltages. Also, solar panels with like output voltages can be connected in series to create other operating voltages. Some solar panel manufacturers will build panels to the size and electrical configuration desired by their customers (large volume customers).

Plastic-covered panels with metal backing are highly unbreakable, thus are well suited for use in applications that would break glass-covered panels. Panel protective boxes are available for protecting aluminum frame, glass-covered panels that will be used in potentially damaging applications.

In the late 1990s an extremely flexible, thin solar panel came on the market. This panel can be comfortably carried to a remote site while rolled up, and then unrolled and used after reaching the destination.

Because of the emergency power a solar panel can supply anywhere there is sunlight (even when clouds are present), carrying at least a small solar panel (3.5 x 9") that can trickle charge a 12-volt battery (car/boat/RV/mobile phone/etc.) that will be used in remote areas is highly recommended.

SOLAR PANEL DISADVANTAGES: (1) Solar panels are fairly expensive to purchase; (2) Much of the sun's solar energy reaching a solar panel is absorbed by the panel and converted into heat--solar panels can become very hot (advantage during winter); (3) Although the glass covering of glass-covered solar panels is generally a strong low-iron impregnated glass, if cracked, the panel will eventually "expire" because of moisture entry. The rear plastic covering of applicable glass-covered solar panels can be scratched/torn; also, it will slowly deteriorate from UV rays reflecting onto the backside of the panel (if applicable); (4) The front plastic covering on applicable panels is easily scratched. Because the plastic covering of plastic-covered panels is susceptible to UV ray degradation, plastic-covered panels generally come with only a 2-5 year power output warranty.

I've found that manufacturers typically only warrant a panel's construction for 1 year; however, except for the front plastic trim on an amorphous type solar panel coming loose, and an electrical open occurring in an amorphous solar panel's power cord, I've never had any of my solar panels' construction fail.

Recently, an extremely flexible (stores rolled up), thin solar panel has come on the market; however, like most plastic-covered solar panels, their power output warranty is fairly short (2 years is what I've seen).

EXTRA: Chapter 3 discloses a solar panel heat dissipating option for panels being used/placed behind a car windshield.

• SOLAR CELL TYPES: STRUCTURE AND MATERIAL

Although there are materials that have a broader spectral response which can produce more power than solar cells made from silicon, because silicon has a fairly broad spectral response, can withstand high and low temperature extremes, is fairly easy to work with, and is cost effective in producing high quality solar cells, silicon is used extensively in the manufacture of solar cells.

The following information is a summary of the three type solar cells I've found most readily marketed (I've owned and used all three types). Since the manufacturing process of solar cells is highly guarded by solar panel manufacturers, and because certain manufacturing processes can enhance a solar cell's efficiency to some degree, the following information should only be considered as generalizations. One should consult the solar panel manufacturer for specific facts about their products.

SOLAR CELL STRUCTURE The two type solar cell structures I've widely seen manufactured and marketed to the general public are the (1) high efficiency crystalline structured solar cells, and (2) low efficiency amorphous structured cell (thin-film). Two structure variations of the crystalline solar cell is the mono-crystalline cell and the poly-crystalline cell. The amorphous solar cell has no crystalline structure.

MONO-CRYSTALLINE STRUCTURED CELLS Quality mono-crystalline structured cells intrinsically offer the highest efficiency. Mono-crystalline cells are the most difficult to manufacturer (grow), thus they are generally a bit more expensive than poly-crystalline cell structured solar panels, and they are much more expensive than amorphous cell solar panels. In converting the sun's solar energy into electricity, my quality mono-crystalline cell solar panels are probably around 10-15 percent more efficient than my quality poly-crystalline cell solar panels and 50 percent more efficient than my amorphous cell solar panels.

POLY-CRYSTALLINE STRUCTURED CELLS Poly-crystalline cells are generally a bit less expensive to manufacture and a little less efficient than mono-crystalline cells. However, since manufacturers may be able to more fully fill up a solar panel with poly-crystalline cells as compared to mono-crystalline cells, the power output of a poly-crystalline cell solar panel might be as high as that of a mono-crystalline cell panel of the same surface area.

AMORPHOUS CELLS Amorphous silicon cells have no crystal structure, thus they are easy and inexpensive to manufacture. Because there is no crystal structure in amorphous cells, size limitation is minimal. Since amorphous solar cells can be manufactured laid out on a metal plate, they are generally thinner and stronger than most crystalline structured panels. I've found amorphous silicon cell efficiency to be less than half that of a crystalline structured cell of the same surface area. An advantage of amorphous panels is their stealthy appearance: amorphous panels are practically all one color.

SELF-REGULATING VS. NON-SELF-REGULATING CRYSTALLINE STRUCTURED SOLAR PANELS My crystalline structured self-regulating solar panels operate as if they have an internal voltage regulator that allows them to automatically reduce their power output when needing to prevent battery overcharging, thus a voltage regulator may not be required. In contrast, a non-self-regulating solar panel provides maximum available power at all times, thus use of a voltage regulator will be necessary.

SELF-REGULATING DISADVANTAGES Self-regulating panels don't always provide maximum power. Also, for a self-regulating panel's self-regulating feature to work properly, the total amp-hour capacity of batteries being charged must fall within a certain range specified by the panel manufacturer. Unfortunately, even when properly charging the amp-hour range of battery(s) specified by the panel manufacturer, I've found that when using self-regulating panels in hot climates, the heat build up tends to cause my self-regulating panels' output voltage (power output) to decrease a significant amount lower than what it normally provides during cool weather, and this can prevent battery(s) from becoming fully charged during hot weather.

WHEN SELF-REGULATING SOLAR PANELS ARE BEST USED Self-regulating panels are beneficial to use in small applications (one to two panels) where powering a voltage regulator might be an excessive drain. Also, self-regulating solar panels are convenient to use in applications where they will be connected and disconnected frequently, such as in car living applications where having to use, disconnect, and reconnect a voltage regulator often would be an added inconvenience.

WHEN NON-SELF-REGULATING SOLAR PANELS ARE BEST USED Non-self-regulating solar panels have the advantage of always providing their maximum power for the amount of sunlight available. Unlike self-regulating panels, I haven't found their power output to be significantly affected in high heat applications. Non-self-regulating panels used with a voltage regulator will probably be best in stationary applications in which many panels provide plenty of power, thus making any power draw from a voltage regulator insignificant.

GLASS COVERED, ALUMINUM FRAMED, MONO-CRYSTALLINE CELL STRUCTURE SOLAR PANELS. LivingInCars.com is hosted by www.CARTAMA.NET

SOLAR PANEL WARRANTY CONSIDERATIONS/RECOMMENDATIONS

My solar panels' warranties generally covered (1) solar panel power output, and (2) solar panel construction. Power output warranties of the solar panels I've owned generally guaranteed the solar panel to produce 80-90 percent of their rated power for X number of years. My glass-covered panels' power output warranties generally ranged from 10-20 years, and my plastic-covered panels warranty generally ranged for only 2-6 years (UV ray degradation of plastic being the reason).

Although the construction warranty of my solar panels has only been 1-2 years, they have never come a part during a decade of rough usage and handling (exception: plastic trim covering of metal backed amorphous solar panel, and an open in the power cord of an amorphous solar panel). Save your purchase receipt(s)!

IMPORTANT CONSIDERATIONS IN CHOOSING A SOLAR PANEL Depending on the application, one may wish to consider the following when choosing a solar panel: (1) physical size requirements/limitations of where panel will be placed, (2) application's power requirement: panel's efficiency (type solar cell), and number of panels needed, (3) stealthy appearance requirement, (4) panel covering: glass or plastic, (5) type frame: aluminum frame w/ rear plastic covering, or metal backing, (6) warranty length of coverage: panel power output warranty and panel construction warranty, (7) self-regulating vs. non-self-regulating (which is best for the application used in), (8) panel wiring, and (9) the physical hazards at the location used.

PANEL WIRING: CRYSTALLINE CELL TYPE PANELS SHOULD HAVE WEATHERPROOF WIRE JUNCTION BOXES (PREFERABLY NOT PRE-WIRED) The glass-covered, aluminum frame, crystalline structured solar panels that I own all have wire junction boxes, some junction boxes were pre-wired and others not. Some of my panels have had two separate junction boxes, one for the positive wire and one for the negative wire. Other panels have had only one junction box, generally pre-wired and sealed in which both a negative and positive wire extend from.

Being able to choose the quality, diameter and length of wire attached to a panel's junction box(s), as well as being able to replace the wire if ever necessary--may be very beneficial. In contrast, pre-wired junction boxes in which the positive and negative wires/leads can't be replaced will become a problem at some point when the wires need replacing.

SOLAR PANEL PURCHASING CONSIDERATIONS/RECOMMENDATIONS

To get the best price, I purchase solar panels at wholesale pricing from the manufacturer or manufacturer's authorized wholesale distributor (call the manufacturer to locate wholesale distributors or check the Internet). Although I've never had to do so, when dealing with a wholesaler it might be necessary to represent oneself as the type of business owner that would normally receive wholesale pricing, such as a home builder, home improvements specialist, RV repair business, etc. Also, one should verify the retail pricing of solar panels before purchasing from a wholesaler, to make sure the wholesaler is selling at wholesale pricing. Obviously, the Internet makes purchasing anything at the best pricing a much easier job to do.

• CHARGING AUXILIARY 12-VOLT BATTERY(S) USING A PORTABLE GENERATOR

I once used a portable generator while living in an isolated wilderness area only to find that it created many hassles while giving only minimal benefit. Also, the generator wore out rather quickly even though I maintained it extremely well. Thereafter, I never had the desire to use one again while living in a car. However, since a generator can easily charge auxiliary 12-volt batteries, and since it can be very useful in certain 12-volt DC and 120-volt AC high power applications at any location desired, I think it is appropriate to also include them as a possible auxiliary 12-volt battery charging source.

PORTABLE GENERATOR ADVANTAGES Portable generators can supply an abundance of 12-volt DC and 120-volt AC electricity. Except for slight frequency variations, generators closely duplicate the 120-volt AC electricity produced by power companies--and this can be very beneficial when powering certain types of electronic and inductive load equipment, as compared to using a modified sine wave inverter. Portable generators can provide maximum power for as long as one is willing to keep fuel and oil in them--that is, until they wear out or break.

Portable generators can be powered by gasoline or propane (propane carburetor conversion required if not already configured that way). Powering by gasoline has the advantage of gas being readily available most anywhere (siphoning gas out of a car's gas tank is easy). Powering by propane has the advantage of creating about only half the pollution of gasoline with no deadly carbon monoxide emission.

Using a portable generator may be very beneficial in severe cold weather, wilderness isolated car living situations. The hot exhaust of a portable generator can be directed onto containers of bathing water to warm them fairly quickly. Besides charging auxiliary batteries, a portable generator can be used to run power tools, microwave oven, electric heater, car engine block heater, etc.

*EXTRA: Using synthetic engine oil (-80°F pour point) and spraying "starting spray" into the carburetor will make starting the generator much easier during freezing weather.

PORTABLE GENERATOR DISADVANTAGES Portable generator disadvantages are too many for me to recommend their use in most car living situations. They're expensive to purchase, maintain, operate, repair, etc. They require fuel, oil, air + oil filters, repairs, adjustments, cleaning, electrical parameter measurements/adjustments, etc. The first major repair my portable generator needed cost 1/3 the price of the generator (alternator rotor went bad). Even when maintained extremely well, my portable generator's air-cooled engine wore out fairly quickly.

Portable generators are bulky, heavy, noisy, dirty/greasy; they emit toxic/flammable fumes when not operating and pollute when operating. The frequency of 120-volt AC electricity produced varies with engine speed variations -- and 120-volt AC electricity frequency variations have caused problems with my automatic 12-volt battery charger. Portable generators partially covered in plastic shrouding can be very difficult to work on because of inaccessibility caused by the shrouding; the shrouding also causes extra heating. Other than high power applications, and except for an extremely cold, isolated, wilderness car living situation, portable generators have too many deficits for me to recommend their use in charging auxiliary 12-volt batteries used in car living situations.

GENERATOR PURCHASING CONSIDERATIONS/ RECOMMENDATIONS
SMALLEST GENERATOR THAT WILL MEET ONE'S POWER NEEDS Having the smallest size generator that will adequately satisfy one's power needs has the benefits of less noise, less

pollution, less bulk, and less weight, along with having less fuel consumption. Also, using the smallest generator possible may allow for better electricity frequency stability when powering small loads.

MINIMAL SHROUDING IS DESIRABLE Portable generators that have no cosmetic shrouding operate cooler (last longer) and are much easier to work on and keep clean. Also, installing a larger gas tank and larger muffler on shrouded portable generators probably isn't an option.

EXTRA LARGE MUFFLER AND LARGE GAS TANK OPTION Less noise and fewer fuel refills will make using a portable generator much more enjoyable. Being able to install a larger gas tank and larger muffler is a desirable feature for a generator to have.

HIGH ENGINE OIL CAPACITY IS BEST Generator engines that have large oil capacities run cooler allowing the engine to lasts longer. Also, large engine oil capacity allows for a longer operating period between oil changes.

ENGINE OIL FILTER Unfortunately, there are many air-cooled generator engines on the market that aren't equipped with an oil filter. Having a portable generator that has a replaceable engine oil filter is extremely desirable, as having an oil filter that is replaced on schedule will substantially increase engine life.

BENEFICIAL GENERATOR OPERATING PRACTICES
MINIMIZING ENGINE WEAR DURING STARTING Running any 4-cycle engine at high rpm before engine oil has had time to fully circulate will produce significant engine wear. Unfortunately, portable generators start up and immediately rev to their high operating rpm.

   To prevent unnecessary engine wear, a generator engine can be started at idle rpm and allowed to operate for 10-15 seconds before being allowed to rev to its normal operating speed. This generally can be accomplished by holding the carburetor throttle valve lever partially closed during starting; another option is to close the engine choke to minimize engine rpm while starting.
*NOTE: Holding the carburetor throttle valve partially closed may cause the generator engine's constant speed controller to come out of calibration at some point.

ALWAYS START A GENERATOR WITHOUT ANY ELECTRICAL EQUIPMENT CONNECTED TO IT During starting, a generator has inadequate lubrication in its engine. Loading the generator down with an electrical load/equipment before the engine oil has had time to fully circulate will cause additional engine wear; therefore, a generator should be started and allowed to run for 30 seconds before any electrical load/equipment is connected to it.

REPLACE OIL, OIL FILTER, AND AIR FILTER ON OR BEFORE THE MANUFACTURER'S RECOMMENDED TIME INTERVAL Maintaining clean engine oil of the correct viscosity grade is the most important preventative maintenance that can be done to ensure maximum engine life. Therefore, one should always change the engine oil, oil filter, and air cleaner at or before the manufacturer's recommended time interval. I highly recommend replacing the engine oil filter during each oil change even if the generator manufacturer says that it can be changed at every other oil change. Also, whether or not the generator manufacturer's recommended time interval has been reached, if the engine oil has turned dark brown in color--I recommend changing it.

If the generator manufacturer approves of its use, I highly recommend using synthetic engine oil. Because of the -80 degrees Fahrenheit pour point temperature of synthetic oil, as compared to 0 degrees for conventional oil, using synthetic engine oil during freezing weather will be extremely beneficial in reducing engine wear during starting, and it will make starting a generator much easier during cold weather.

BEST VISCOSITY GRADE OIL TO USE IN A 4-CYCLE AIR-COOLED MOTOR DURING HOT WEATHER Many people own/use equipment, such as mowers, generators, edgers, etc., that are powered by air-cooled 4-cycle gasoline motors. High revving air-cooled motors can become extremely hot; high rpm and high heat can place extreme demands on motor oil. In my opinion, multi-grade oils (10w-30, 10w-40, etc.) become too thin when used in high-revving, air-cooled engines during warm weather. Therefore, to prevent motor oil from thinning out to a point of providing inadequate lubrication, I always use straight weight oil (40w or 50w) in air-cooled 4-cycle engines when operating in temperatures above 75°F.

GENERATOR LONG-TERM STORAGE CONSIDERATIONS

Whenever a single cylinder engine isn't being operated, it should be stored with the piston on the compression stroke so that the valves will be closed sealing off the cylinder. The compression stroke is easy to recognize when pulling on the starting recoil cord, as the cord gives the most resistance during the compression stroke.

When storing a generator for moderately long periods (1 month or more), the fuel shutoff valve (if equipped) should be closed and the engine should be run until the carburetor runs out of fuel (actually, this is good to do anytime the engine won't be operated for a week or more). Also, a carburetor's manual choke can be closed to help seal the carburetor during periods of non-use.

Generator engines that have metal gas tanks should be stored with the gas tank full of fuel to prevent the gas tank from rusting. Plastic fuel tanks can be stored full or empty: however, gas looses some of its good qualities if not stored in an all-metal container.

Before running a generator that has been stored for 5 months or more, a generator's fuel tank should be emptied and refilled with fresh gasoline. Otherwise, old fuel could cause varnish deposits to build up on engine valve stems causing stoppage of the engine and preventing its restart until the varnish is removed (difficult work).

• CHARGING AUXILIARY 12-VOLT BATTERIES USING A 120-VOLT AC-POWERED BATTERY CHARGER

In most of my car living/working situations: (1) There hasn't been a 120-volt AC outlet near my car; (2) I haven't needed any 120-volt AC power; or (3) I've had secret parking situations in which running an extension cord to my car from a nearby 120-volt AC outlet wasn't possible. Using a 120-volt AC-powered battery charger (voltage sensing type) for charging varying voltage level type 12-volt auxiliary batteries has primarily been performed at my external storage locations (rental storage room, friends' residence, etc.) in which I would drop off auxiliary 12-volt batteries for charging, but only when other means of charging weren't available or adequate.

120-VOLT AC-POWERED AUTOMATIC 12-VOLT BATTERY CHARGER ADVANTAGES

Twelve-volt battery chargers are relatively inexpensive, readily available, and simple to use. They don't directly pollute, and they operate almost maintenance-free with minimal noise. Being highly efficient using very little power makes battery chargers inexpensive to operate. If minimally taken care of, battery chargers can be expected to last an extremely long time. They're small and fairly light weight. They can be used/stored at one's external storage location (use light bulb plug adapter if a wall outlet isn't available). My automatic battery charger (voltage sensing type) can charge 12-volt lead acid starting batteries and deep-cycle Marine/RV batteries (one type at a time) automatically stopping when batteries are fully charged.

120-VOLT AC-POWERED BATTERY CHARGER DISADVANTAGES 120-volt AC-powered battery chargers are best powered only from a 120-volt AC wall outlet. 120-volt AC electricity produced by a portable generator generally isn't frequency stable, especially when powering a small load, thus using a portable generator to power a battery charger could cause problems with the battery charger, and it could cause problems with constant voltage output type batteries that are susceptible to cell memory effect problems. A modified sine wave inverter shouldn't be used to power a 120-volt AC-powered battery charger because the inverter's modified sine wave's extremely fast voltage rise/fall rate and voltage spikes would probably cause excessive heating and damage to a battery charger (especially automatic voltage sensing types).

CHAPTER 9

PROTECTING YOURSELF AND YOUR CAR WHILE LIVING IN CARS

Theft prevention, financial loss prevention, car protection, and personal safety/protection are the main topics covered in this chapter.

9.1 PERSONAL SAFETY

GLASS CONTAINERS AREN'T SUITABLE FOR USE INSIDE A CAR Glass containers shouldn't be used inside a car--they're just too dangerous. Splinters of broken glass could easily enter one's eye or get under one's skin. Knife/dagger shaped pieces of glass could easily become lethal and/or blinding during a car accident/crash. If using a glass container is absolutely necessary, it should be stored inside a protective container, such as a foam-lined plastic hunting storage box.

PREVENTING OXYGEN DEPLETION AND FIRE/SMOKE/CARBON MONOXIDE HAZARDS Never use any type of oxygen depleting device inside an enclosed car, such as a candle, fuel heater, propane refrigerator, etc., as oxygen depletion and smoke inhalation hazards could easily become lethal.

Using a smoke detector inside a car that is being lived in is a good idea, especially if using an auxiliary power supply. In certain parking situations, such as when parking in the bottom floor of a parking garage, it may be beneficial to use a carbon monoxide detector, too.

MINIMIZING RISK OF ELECTRICAL FIRE As described in chapter 8, splicing in an in-line wire type fuse assembly into an auxiliary 12-volt battery's positive lead as near to the positive terminal as possible will help prevent any type of electrical fire (use lowest amp fuse that will satisfy the application). When possible, electrical equipment should be disconnected from any auxiliary 12-volt power source while one is away from their car.

AUXILIARY BATTERY CHARGING HAZARDS It's best not to charge high capacity 12-volt totally sealed batteries from any type of powerful battery charger while inside an enclosed parked car. The reason being is that totally sealed 12-volt high capacity batteries can emit fumes/gases during periods of prolonged overcharging, possibly making a car's interior toxic or explosive. Fortunately, high capacity 12-volt auxiliary batteries can be removed and charged at an external storage location, they can be charged inside a well-ventilated car during driving, or they can be charged in a parked car while no one is inside. (See Chapter 8 for more details.)

PRIVATE ELECTRONIC COMMUNICATIONS DON'T EXIST
During the mid-1990s the government required phone companies to rewrite their phone system software to allow for easy wire-tapping. Shortly thereafter, the government used your tax money to install hubs throughout the entire phone system to make it easy for the government to physically tap into the phone system at any desired location (the phone companies rejected installing the hubs until tax payers were made to pay for this tremendous expense). The government is fantasizing about having all phone communications go through one central location, and the government fantasizes about making you thumb scan or retina scan each time you log onto the Internet, all of which someday may be a reality. Government computers and spy satellite systems have the capability to listen in on all phone communications worldwide at all times (a central hub would make doing so less expensive). Government computers listen for "trigger" words spoken, and they can identify a person by their voice.
Presently, the only way I know to prevent government computers and spy satellite systems from examining your phone conversation, e-mails, faxes, basically anything that travels across phone lines (some of which is wireless) is to encrypt everything--only sophisticated encryption programs that the government doesn't already have the key to will be successful in preventing government intrusion into your electronic communications.

MOBILE PHONE CONVERSATION IS EASILY LISTENED TO Conversations on mobile phones that use analog modulation (almost extinct) can easily be listened to by anyone using an analog scanner that picks up mobile phone frequencies. Newer scanners that have been programmed by their manufacturer not to scan mobile phone frequencies can usually be easily reprogrammed. Conversation transmitted from digital mobile phones is much more difficult for the general public to eavesdrop upon at present, but not impossible; obviously, the government monitors all electronic communications of every type.

Most anyone can purchase anyone's mobile phone records off the Internet.

The increasing speed/capability and decreasing cost of mobile phone systems (phones and phone company systems) is turning urban areas into a total surveillance grid. Phone company mobile phone systems are being installed everywhere to help accommodate rapidly increasing numbers of users and increasing bandwidth demand, along with building a surveillance state--public areas being video taped (regular, infrared, night vision, millimeter x-ray, etc.), with high resolution picture and sound being streamed into government control agencies via wireless phone systems...microphones located throughout cities being used to triangulate and locate gun fire are really mainly used to listen to anyone within range (gov. surveillance grid isn't something I want to live around).

LAND-LINE PHONE FAX/DATA TRANSFERS Land-line phone to land-line phone fax/data transfers are fairly secure from the general public, but not from the government (encrypt data for more privacy).

INTERNET COMMUNICATIONS AREN'T PRIVATE Transferring data over the Internet has the advantage of no long-distance charges, but has the disadvantage of government computers (and hackers to a large extent) monitoring all communications. Unfortunately, all your Internet activity can be monitored, and all the addresses you visit are recorded for a significant period.

Another problem of Internet use is that when a computer is connected to the Internet, it is susceptible to being invaded, read, and even altered by anyone else on the Internet who has the necessary knowledge, skills, software, and computer (British teenage boy invading U.S. military computer system during the mid-1990s--he had enough time). There is firewall software & hardware available to help prevent this, but it's not 100 percent effective--especially if the computer hacker has UNLIMITED TIME to work (actually, the software does much of the work). Therefore, I recommend physically disconnecting your computer from the Internet when not using the Internet.

BEST SOLUTION FOR INTERNET SECURITY--USE A SPARE "STRIPPED" COMPUTER THAT HAS NO PERSONAL INFORMATION IN IT, AND THAT IS RUNNING FIREWALL & ANTI-VIRUS PROGRAMS. HIGH-SPEED MODEMS SHOULD HAVE INTEGRAL FIREWALL HARDWARE.

COMPUTER VIRUSES Computer viruses can be brought into a computer when downloading any type of infected executable file off the Internet. The virus will then activate when the infected executable file is executed in the computer. Be extremely cautious about opening any file attached to a e-mail no matter what file extension the file has. Having the latest computer virus scan program to identify and delete viruses is the safest way to go.

 MAKING INTERNET BROWSING MORE SECURE
Use a firewall program that monitors traffic in and out of your computer while connected to the Internet. Among other things, a firewall program helps to make your computer invisible to computer hackers that are running a program that looks for vulnerable computers connected to the Internet. Read your firewall program's instruction manual to learn everything you can about its operation, optional settings, how to access all the settings, etc.
    Close your web browser while not in use, such as when listening to Internet radio. An opened web browser or e-mail program that has security flaws (they all do) is an easier avenue for hackers to break through, and this is true for any computer program that can communicate with computers over the Internet.
    Set your Internet browser security setting to the highest level at which you can still browse the Internet freely, and take a detailed look at and learn about all individual settings that can be accessed within the program, such as the advanced settings in the Internet Properties interface. After using the Internet and closing the Web browser, go to Internet Options in the Web browser program (right-clicking the web browser icon and then select Internet properties) and delete all temporary

downloaded data/files and "cookies." You should do this immediately after accessing very personal information over the Internet, such as your online bank and credit card accounts.

• Use an anonymous browsing service. (Unfortunately, the government is beginning to defeat certain benefits that these services once provided).

• Change the name of your passwords, usernames, and e-mail addresses often. Use upper and lowercase letters, numbers, and other symbols to make long passwords when allowable.

• Keep all personal information (anything you want kept private) off your Internet computer, such as by storing personal information on an external hard drive (turn off or disconnect external hard drive while online).

• Use a cyberspace e-mail provider service for more privacy, mainly pertaining to keeping your physical location private. Using your local Internet Service Provider's (ISP) e-mail service allows anyone you correspond with by e-mail to learn your ISP's physical address.

• Download lengthy information, disconnect from the Internet, and then read the information while offline. Your computer is vulnerable anytime it is connected to the Internet.

• Turn off power to high-speed external modem when not online. High-speed external modem should have internal firewall hardware. For utmost security, physically disconnecting your computer from the Internet is best when offline. If Microsoft and the U.S. military can't secure their personal information on their sophisticated computer systems connected to the Internet, you probably can't either (fortunately, you're probably not a target of most sophisticated computer hackers).

• Don't use wireless networks, as anyone nearby can connect to your network, or at least monitor what you are doing.

• Use a firewall software program----make sure you properly adjust the settings immediately after installing it! Read the firewall program's manual to learn about all its features, and how to adjust its settings properly. (Extra: it might be best to turn off your web browser's firewall while installing a firewall software program).

• Properly adjust the security settings for your web browser's firewall.

• If you're not absolutely sure that a downloaded program or e-mail attachment isn't infected with a virus, it would be best to delete it without opening it.

• Use an anti-virus program that checks data as it downloads onto your computer, not after.

• Create weekly system restore point dates, so that you can restore your computer to a previous date if it is ever taken over by a hacker on the Internet. Once my computer was taken over by a hacker who locked me out of my firewall program, so I simply restored my computer to a date previous of the attack.

CELL/MOBILE PHONE USE ALLOWS YOU TO BE PHYSICALLY TRACKED Before October 2001, mobile phone exact location could only be determined through triangulation anytime the phone was in use, but that wasn't automated in the phone companies' phone systems. However, anytime the mobile phone was powered on, the phone would initially contact the nearest cell tower, thus the general area of the phone was known immediately to the phone company. After October 2001, all U.S. cell phones are being equipped with GPS (Global Positioning System) electronics that provide the phone's location to the phone service company anytime the unit is on, and that information is probably being automatically provided to or is easily accessed by the government.

EXPOSURE TO MOBILE PHONE RADIATION Mobile phones transmit microwave energy, you know, the food heating energy in microwave ovens. Even though microwave energy transmitted by a .6-watt mobile phone is probably .00075 of that transmitted inside a medium size microwave oven, depending on the phone used, the antenna may be transmitting microwave energy dangerously close to one's brain (think of a mobile phone antenna being similar to a lit match -- up close it burns, several inches away it doesn't). In my opinion, one's brain being within an inch of a mobile phone antenna transmitting microwave energy is hazardous to one's health. I recommend using the speakerphone feature or a headset microphone and earpiece to keep the mobile phone antenna farther away.

MINIMIZING EXPOSURE TO PORTABLE COMPUTER RADIATION Computers are given designations as to how much electromagnetic energy (radiation) they emit: Class A and B is what I've seen. To minimize radiation exposure, I recommend not using a portable computer placed against your body. If it needs to be used on your lap, placing a spacer, such as a pillow, between the computer and your lap will be beneficial in limiting exposure to computer radiation. Better yet, use an external keyboard so that the portable computer can be placed several feet away.

EXTRA: For home computers, replacing cathode ray tube (CRT) electron-beam type monitors with a PLASMA/LCD/TFT monitor, which doesn't utilize an electron beam picture tube, will be helpful to your vision and will lessen your exposure to radiation. Fortunately, electron-beam type monitors are just about extinct.

MINIMIZING VISION DETERIORATION DURING COMPUTER USE

Many would agree that eyesight can be adversely affected by focusing on the same size object at the same distance over long periods, such as when reading or when using a computer. Fortunately, vision deterioration caused by using close-up eye focusing over long periods of time can probably be lessoned by using long-distance eye focusing as much as possible, to bring about balance.

OPTION #1: USE EXTERNAL KEYBOARD

Using an external keyboard to increase or vary the distance between my eyes and computer screen is my favorite way to balance close-up eye focusing with long-distance eye focusing usage. Since I use my eyes' close-up focusing very much each day in other activities, I choose to use my portable computer positioned about 6-7' from my eyes.

OTHER EXTERNAL KEYBOARD BENEFITS:

Using an external keyboard minimizes portable computer wear and tear (keyboard, screen hinges + ribbon, etc.). Positioning a computer away from one's body minimizes exposure to electromagnetic radiation. During cold weather car living, working off an external keyboard placed under one's covers allows one to stay much warmer.

OPTION #2: INCREASE THE RESOLUTION SETTING OF THE COMPUTER DISPLAY

Increasing the monitor resolution setting will generally cause everything to appear smaller. Increasing the computer monitor's resolution setting is generally done in the operating system software.

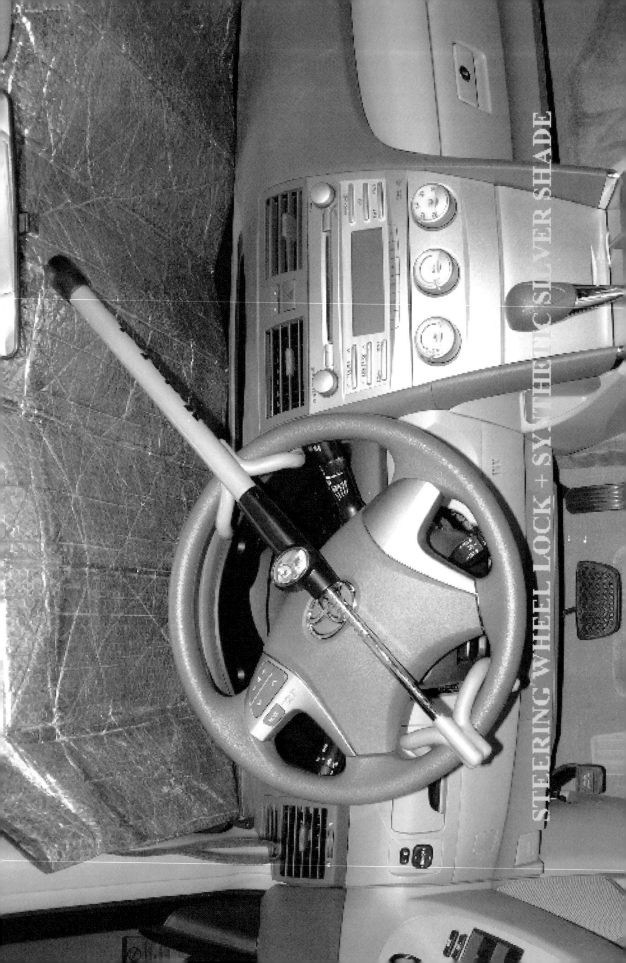

STEERING WHEEL LOCK + SYNTHETIC SILVER SHADE

DISCREET TRASH DISPOSAL RECOMMENDATIONS There are unlimited places to throw away garbage while living in a privatized car. However, it will appear strange to see someone throwing away substantial amounts of trash taken from their car in which normally would be disposed of privately at one's conventional residence. A couple ways I've dumped trash that has caused my living situation to be questioned include (1) dumping trash daily upon arriving at my place of employment, (2) dumping my yesterday's breakfast food containers at the place I purchase breakfast from each morning on the way to work, (3) dumping excessive amounts of trash during the day with lots of people around.

Being discreet when dumping trash, so as not to bring about any unwanted attention of one's secret living situation, will be beneficial while living/working in a privatized car. Some ways to limit exposure while disposing of trash include (1) using non-transparent trash bags to prevent anyone from knowing what is being dumped, (2) dumping trash at low-exposure times, such as during the night or early morning hours, (3) dumping trash at low exposure locations, such as at dumping bins located behind businesses, and (4) dumping trash at areas located far away from one's normal daily activities + nightly parking locations.

HIDING/STORING SPARE CAR KEY ON ACCESSIBLE CAR LOCATION TO PREVENT FROM EVER BEING LOCKED OUT

Being locked out of a car without having immediate access to a spare key can be extremely frustrating. Fortunately, a spare key can be stored hidden on the outside of a car that can be retrieved if ever locked out.

MAGNETIC KEY STORAGE BOX Storing a spare key inside a magnetic key storage box that adheres to car body/frame steel can work well. Fiber/plastic material type boxes help minimize key abrasion. If the key storage container is metal, the key can be coated with silicon sealant to prevent abrasion and corrosion.

SILICON ADHESIVE SEALANT KEY STORAGE Silicon adhesive sealant cures/dries to a flexible rubbery state; it adheres extremely well to a variety of materials. Sealing a spare car key to clean car metal (painted or non-painted), glass, or rubber surface using silicon adhesive sealant is generally a very secure way to store a spare car key. This key storage method minimizing possibility of corrosion, and practically eliminates possible abrasion.

A slight disadvantage of this storage option is that removing all the silicon adhesive sealant from the key is a bit difficult and time consuming. Also, the location the key is sealed to must stay below the sealant's maximum operating temperature.

PLACING KEY ON ACCESSIBLE CAR SURFACE Placing a spare key on an accessible car surface in which the key won't bounce off of may work out OK if the key can be accessed if you're ever locked out of your car.

CAR KEYS WITH IMBEDDED ELECTRONICS Car keys with imbedded electronics can be difficult to replace, sometimes taking a car dealership 2-3 weeks to obtain another. Therefore, it would be best to acquire a couple spare keys beforehand--and it's best to always drive with a spare key that you can access if you ever get locked out.

BREACH OF PRIVACY PREVENTION Several things can be done to help prevent breach of privacy in car living situations. To be able to live/work secretly and comfortably in a car, the car must be privatized (Ch. 1) so that anyone outside won't be able to see inside the car while it is parked with windshield shade installed. Using a small flashlight (1-2 AA batteries) to read by, closing the car's privacy/insulating partition (Ch. 1), and installing a windshield shade whenever parked will be helpful in preventing interior lighting from being noticed by anyone outside during nighttime. Listening to entertainment equipment using headphones will prevent sound from being heard by anyone outside. Body movement inside a car should be slow and smooth to prevent noticeable car body movement to anyone outside. Because of the lasting, fly-attracting, potent smell of urine---urine should be poured out far away from one's parking location.

During cool/cold weather, one can minimize or prevent condensation from forming on the inside of a car's windshield by (1) placing a windshield shade and custom cut 2-3 inch thick foam layer behind a car's windshield to seal it from the warm humid car living area air (minimally-moderately effective), (2) opening front-seat area air vents and sealing off the rear car living area from the front-seat driving area by using a well-insulated privacy/insulating partition (Ch.1), (3) coating the windshield's inner surface with scuba mask or motorcycle goggle anti-fogging solution, (4) smearing a dish washing soap and water solution on inner windshield surface, or (5) placing a custom-sized windshield shade behind the car windshield, including a pouch of drying agent between the windshield and shade, and then coating the edge of the shade with silicon sealant to seal the shade's outer edge to the plastic window trim or windshield's outer edge.

9.2 PHYSICAL RESIDENCE ADDRESS CONCERNS

- KEEPING YOUR CAR LIVING SITUATION SECRET IS BEST
While living and working in privatized cars, I generally never admit to doing so--even when it is obvious that I might be. I recommend not disclosing one's car living situation to anyone other than those who absolutely need to know, such as a friend whose address one uses when absolutely necessary (listing it on business forms, renewing a driver's license, opening a bank account, opening pager/cell phone service, etc.).

TO PREVENT POSSIBLE INVALIDATION OF CAR INSURANCE Many car insurance policies have exclusion of coverage clauses pertaining to cars that are being lived in. Therefore, it is very important to never admit to police that you live/camp/sleep in your car, as police records detailing one's admission could possibly materialize at some point, such as after having a car accident.

TO PREVENT PROBLEMS WITH POLICE FOR VIOLATING CITY ORDINANCES Many cities have local ordinances that ban any type of sleeping or camping on all city-owned property, including roads/streets (taxi cab drivers and park sunbathers break the law with no problems). During a police encounter occurring on city property, if one admits to living or sleeping in their car--they could be subject to arrest, time in jail, stiff fines, car impoundment, a talk with a judge, etc.
EXTRA: Having sexual relations inside a privatized cars while parked on city property is generally illegal (see Chapter 12).

TO PREVENT EMPLOYMENT AND PROFESSIONAL SERVICES DISCRIMINATION Keeping one's car living situation secret will prevent employment and business discrimination. While living in privatized cars, disclosing my inexpensive living situation to anyone who absolutely didn't need to know would have been counterproductive, possibly causing problems with my employer, fellow employees, clients (especially when working at image conscious type businesses). When self-employed running a business out of my car, my business wouldn't have benefited if clients new that I was living and working in a privatized car. Trying to open certain business services, such as mobile phone service, bank account, etc. would have been difficult had I disclosed living in my car.

TO PREVENT LIMITING AVAILABLE PARKING Having to avoid parking at some desirable location all because of someone in the area knowing about your secret living situation who might possibly cause you problems won't be necessary if your car living situation is kept secret.

TO PREVENT PROBLEMS WITH PEOPLE AND CONTROLLING ORGANIZATIONS It would be a waste of time and energy to try to get people's approval of your car living situation--keep it secret and you won't have to. Also, there are plenty of people who enjoy causing problems in other people's lives--keep your car living situation secret and there won't be any problems. People can cause problems for just about anything one exposes: religious beliefs, race, salary, personal possessions, bank account, etc. Believe it or not, paying no rent or taxes can make some people jealous if they find out about one's inexpensive, productive car living situation. Basically, keeping your car living situation secret will eliminate having to deal with negative feedback and negative constraints of all sorts.

EXAMPLE: AUTHORITARIAN GROUP CAUSING PROBLEMS WITH MY COLLEGE EDUCATION
    While attending a large university, I once unintentionally disclosed my secret living situation to the wrong person who then informed an authoritarian type organization of my living situation. Shortly thereafter, I was given the choice of renting a conventional residence on or off campus--or quit my education and move away! Fortunately, at that time I was able to satisfy the situation by disclosing that I had moved in with a friend at an off-campus residence; however, I just continued my education while living secretly in my privatized car parked on the university campus.

• MEETING RESIDENCE ADDRESS REQUIREMENT WHILE LIVING IN A PRIVATIZED CAR

Being successful living secretly in a privatized car requires that one always have a suitable physical residence address to give out whenever absolutely necessary. Some possible situations include (1) during a police encounter, (2) when applying for business services, (3) when opening a bank account, (4) when seeking employment, (5) filling out certain college forms, (6) when renewing a driver's license, (7) when applying for health insurance, (8) when purchasing car insurance, (9) when purchasing firearms, (10) when joining a health club, etc.

PHYSICAL RESIDENCE ADDRESS OPTIONS Using a family member, friend, or acquaintance's residence address to list or disclose as your own physical residence address may work out OK as long as the residence owner has given you his/her permission to do so.

In the past, a business rental mailbox address could be listed as a residence or business address, but as of April 26, 1999, that was ended by the government--at least pertaining to receiving mail from the United States Postal Service at the private business rental mailbox address.

Although a P.O. Box address isn't a physical residence address, one will be surprised how often a P.O. Box or business rental mailbox address will be accepted as a physical residence address when listing it on forms requiring a residence address.

POST OFFICE BOX Receiving mail at a post office box allows for privacy, and it prevents inconveniencing a residence owner/renter from having to receive your mail. Also advantageous is that renting a P.O. box may be relatively inexpensive, as compared to renting a business mailbox.

Post office box disadvantages include (1) the government can easily monitor and go through all mail received at a P.O. box whenever desired, (2) not being able to receive packages from any carrier other than the U.S. Postal Service, and (3) the records of who rented the P.O. box will probably never be destroyed. Although not so anymore, a local residence address once wasn't required to open a P.O. box--during this time period one postmaster went way beyond his/her job duties spending a significant amount of energy trying to verify whether I was living at the address I listed on my P.O. box application (the government can be very intrusive). Have you noticed the bar code on every piece of mail you receive . . . government computers track all mail.

MAILBOX RENTAL BUSINESS In the past, one could rent a business mailbox at a mailbox rental business and receive U.S. mail privately using an alias, but not anymore. In March of 1999, the U.S. Postal Service adopted rules that require the business rental mailbox address to be listed as "private mailbox #" or "PMB#"-- the U.S. Postal Service will no longer deliver mail to a business rental mailbox if "Private Mailbox #" or "PMB#" isn't listed on the mail. An alias can still be used in receiving mail at a business rental mailbox, but the U.S. Postal Service requires the business mailbox renter complete a U.S. Postal Service form listing all aliases that will be used in receiving U.S. mail. Also in effect, rental mailbox business owners must provide an alphabetical list of their present & former customers every three months to the local postmasters.

PREVENTING GOVERNMENT INTRUSION IN YOUR MAIL If you're being investigated by any agency of the U.S. government, examining your mail is extremely easy for the government to do if receiving mail at a government mail agency, such as at a P.O. box--and now even at Business Rental Mailboxes. To prevent government intrusions, one can have a friend open either a P.O. box or rental mailbox and have all correspondence sent in the name of their friend (box holder). Similarly, one's mail can be sent to a confidant's residence address using the confidant's name and address, which is something I had to do a long time ago to successfully receive my Florida employer W-2 forms.

BANK ACCOUNT CAUTION When traveling out of state, don't try to open a bank account without disclosing a verifiable physical residence address in your home state along with a legitimate reason as to why you need the account. Listing only a P.O. box or Business Rental Mailbox on the bank application and not disclosing a legitimate reason as to why you need the account may cause the banker to contact the government (FBI, Dept. of Homeland Security, etc.). Unfortunately, the government may then start looking through your mail, listening in on your phone conversations, listening in on all of your friends'/ acquaintances' phone conversations (roving wire-tapping), watching your bank accounts and financial transactions, review your IRS records, data-base your assets.... Once getting on the government's list--your name and file data will be there from then on (actually, the government already has many files about you, some of which you can obtain through the Freedom of Information Act).

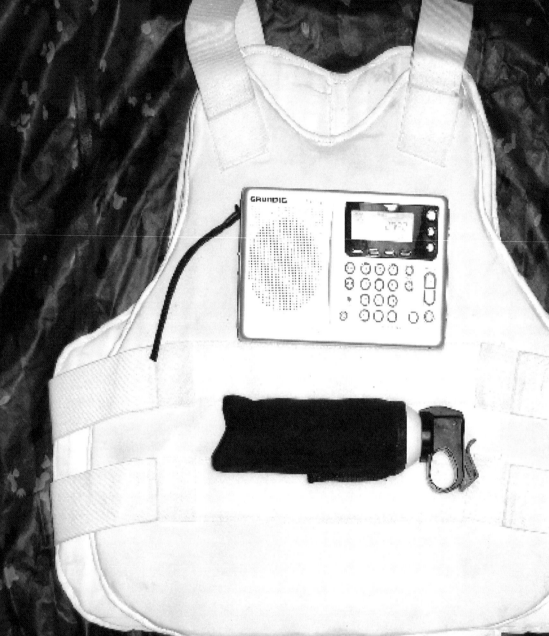

Deadly Wildlife, Remote Wilderness Tools:
BODY ARMOR VEST, PEPPER SPRAY,
SHORTWAVE RADIO, + RAIN PONCHO.

9.3 PREVENTING CAR VANDALISM / THEFT

• SIMPLE WAYS TO MINIMIZE THE RISK OF CAR THEFT/ VANDALISM
Living in a privatized car parked highly exposed almost anywhere, one will want to safeguard their car as much as possible against vandals and thieves. Besides the usual option of a car alarm, which can be used while away from one's car, there are inexpensive things that can be done to make a car less appealing to vandals and thieves.

CAR "PRIVATIZATION "Privatizing" a car as described in Chapter 1 will increase a car's theft/vandalism deterrence in a number of ways. If thieves can't see inside a parked privatized car (windshield shade installed), they won't know whether there are any valuables inside. Also, a privatized car may be more intimidating to thieves since they can't tell whether an armed person is inside or whether anti-theft devices are operating.

STORE POSSESSIONS IN NON-SEE-THROUGH CONTAINERS
What valuables thieves don't know exist aren't pursued. Storing possessions in non-see-through storage containers (Ch. 4) will prevent people outside from accidentally seeing them during certain situations: (1) when entering/exiting your car, (2) while at a business's drive-thru pickup window, (3) anytime the windshield shade isn't installed and the privacy/ insulating partition (Ch. 1) isn't drawn, (4) when car sunroof is open, front side windows are rolled down, etc.
EXTRA: Storing possessions in non-see-through storage containers will also be beneficial during a police encounter (see Ch. 12).

KEEP THE CAR'S APPEARANCE AS GENERIC LOOKING AS POSSIBLE Keeping a privatized car as generic looking as possible makes it less identifiable, thus allows it to blend in better. Anything that makes a car more identifiable, such as bumper stickers, white letter tires, custom license plates, expensive wheels and bumpers, physical dimension alterations, etc., makes a car more noticeable--and this includes being more noticeable to thieves and vandals. Also, keeping a car as generic looking as possible will make a car appear unbiased, making it less of a target to vandals.

While parked, it may be worthwhile to remove removable car antenna(s) that would otherwise signal thieves that expensive electronic equipment might be inside; also, an antenna that doesn't exist can't be vandalized.

HAVE YOUR CAR'S VIN# ACID-ETCHED INTO EVERY CAR WINDOW Having your car's VIN# (Vehicle Identification Number) acid-etched into every window of your car is another means of deterring car theft, as car thieves don't want to spend thousands of dollars to replace all car windows. At present, acid etching a car's VIN# into all car windows isn't much of a deterrent to car thieves who take the car out of the U.S., which is about one-fourth of all U.S. cars stolen.

PARKING TO PREVENT CAR THEFT/VANDALISM Whatever type of car alarm you have, always remember that if a thief has enough time--your car's alarm will be disabled and the car will be stolen. Therefore, when leaving your car, it will be best parked in an area that has lots of people nearby who will immediately report any attempted break-in upon hearing your car's alarm.

PREVENTING CAR THEFT/VANDALISM USING A FAKE CAR ALARM There are many types of car alarms that can be used to help prevent car theft/vandalism while one is away from their car, but generally not while one is inside their privatized car. Car alarms generally can't effectively be used while one is inside their privatized car because of two reasons: (1) Movement inside the car will generally sound the alarm; and (2) turning on the alarm manually when vandals or thieves make contact with one's car will cause most car alarms to give an "arming" signal (chirp, flashing light, etc.) that will allow thieves/vandals outside to know that the car owner is nearby or inside the car. Therefore, in car living and surveillance work applications, it may be useful to wire up a fake alarm that can be turned on manually from inside the car that will activate a siren/horn/ light//etc. without any "arming" indicator. Hopefully, this will scare away anyone outside making physical contact with the car (thief/vandal, security guard, police officer, children, pedestrians, nosy people, etc.).

9.4 INCREASING A CAR'S BULLET RESISTANCE

Car body steel MIGHT stop a .22 cal bullet, but it won't stop much else. Most all rifle bullets and many pistol bullets can penetrate car body steel easily--many like a hot knife cutting through room temperature butter.

Once during my U.S. travels, I stopped at a resort/vacation area for a week of entertainment where I had a fairly good time playing in the casinos, watching shows, hiking and biking on nearby mountains, visiting shopping malls and theaters, etc. One late night while sleeping in my privatized car parked on a casino parking lot, I was awakened by gunfire going off around my car -- some criminals were having a shootout. Almost as quickly as the gunfire erupted, it was over. Feeling that my car hadn't been hit, I quickly fell back asleep. This and other similar occurrences have convinced me of the need to increase the bullet-resistance of my cars.

OPTIONS IN INCREASING A CAR'S BULLET RESISTANCE

If desiring to own a bullet-resistant (B.R.) car, one basically has four options: (1) Pay a car manufacturer tons of money to custom manufacturer the desired model car in a B.R. version, (2) purchase a production armored vehicle, such as the armored vans that transport money and other valuables to/from businesses (may not sell to the general public), (3) pay a lot of money to have your car customized by a company that specializes in car bulletproofing, or (4) increase your car's bullet resistance doing the work yourself. Actually, at least one bullet and bomb-resistant car is now available to the general public as a standard model from one car manufacturer, thus one can expect many more models to follow (it's about time).

Options 1-3 above won't be possible for most car owners. Therefore, the following information is for those desiring to increase a car's bullet resistance doing the work themselves.

INCREASING YOUR CAR'S BULLET RESISTANCE DOING THE WORK YOURSELF

There are many types of bullet-resistant (B.R.) materials available that are suitable for use in car bulletproofing applications, some of which are much more suitable than others. Cost, weight, degree of B.R., B.R. material weaknesses, and installation difficulties are the main factors to consider when deciding which type B.R. material to use. Except for the difficulty in increasing the B.R. of a car's usable windows, increasing a car's B.R. is fairly easy to do.

INCREASING THE BULLET RESISTANCE OF USEABLE CAR WINDOWS

Increasing the bullet resistance (B.R.) of usable car windows, such as the windshield and front side windows, are the most difficult areas of a car to deal with. The reason being is that because these areas have to remain transparent, using a type of clear B.R. plastic, such as Lexan or Lexgard, is really the only suitable option.

Two options in increasing the bullet resistance of usable car windows using B.R. plastic is (1) mount clear bullet-resistant plastic sheeting behind useable car windows, or (2) if one can obtain them, replace usable car windows with custom made bullet-resistant windows (extensive window framing modifications may be required).

CAUTION: Businesses that sell B.R. car windows almost never sell their product to the general public--and they will give your name to federal agencies if you disclose it to them (Update: in recent years, some B.R. car window manufacturers have become a bit more open to selling product to the general public).

LEXAN AND LEXGARD BULLET RESISTANT PLASTIC

Lexan and Lexgard clear B.R. plastic are products developed by General Electric. Lexan is a high strength, bullet-resistant, polycarbonate plastic. Lexgard bullet-resistant plastic is made of Lexan laminates and bonding interlayer. Both are highly unbreakable and are available with a surface coating (MR5) that increases scratch and UV ray resistance. Both Lexan and Lexgard are heat resistant to 180 degrees Fahrenheit (continuous).

Although both Lexan and Lexgard are bullet-resistant, Lexgard is much more bullet-resistant than Lexan of equal thickness. Lexgard sheeting can handle repeat gunfire much better than Lexan sheeting, and it can do so without spalling. Bullet resistant thickness starts at around three-fourths-inch thick for Lexan and half-inch thick for Lexgard. (General Electric Company, 1994)

BULLET PROOFING NON-TRANSPARENT CAR AREAS IS EASY

Flexible B.R. materials stop bullets sort of like how fireman encircled around a "catching net" catch people who jump out of burning buildings. To be most effective, flexible B.R. materials must not be rigidly mounted. Basically, the more flexible it's mounted (up to a point), the more bullet stopping ability it has.

Covering a car's interior surfaces with blanketing material made out of flexible B.R. material, such as Kevlar, Spectra, nylon, etc., is easy to do. Bullet resistant blanketing can be loosely secured over car interior surfaces. However, an ultimate installation of B.R. blanketing is to cover the outer surface of "tube/shell" insulating foam (discussed in Ch. 1), loosely mounting the B.R. blanketing where necessary. The "tube/shell" insulating foam and minimal mounting holds the B.R. blanketing in place, but at the same time allows for extreme flexibility if ever hit by bullets. The front opening of the "tube/shell" can be made B.R. by simply hanging B.R. blanketing in front (i.e. making the "insulating/privacy partition" (Ch. 1) out of B.R. blanketing). Likewise, the rear opening can also be covered with B.R. blanketing. Obviously, covering a car's interior with B.R. blanketing can be customized in any number of ways.

A few of the many advantages of using B.R. blanketing material to line a car's interior include: (1) Car interior remains comfortable with negligible loss of interior space; (2) a car accident won't be anymore hazardous; (3) minimal mounting difficulties; (4) permanent damaging installation modifications generally aren't necessary; (5) minimal weight increase; and (6) negligible increase of interior condensation problems.

BULLET RESISTANT BLANKETING MATERIAL OPTIONS
Kevlar, Spectra, and nylon are just a few of the many types of B.R. threads available that can be woven into material for use in making B.R. blankets, clothing, vests, etc. One can obtain information from the B.R. fiber/thread manufacturer about the threads specifications/characteristics, such as degree of bullet resistance, tensile strength, effects from high humidity and UV rays, etc. After deciding which B.R. thread has the most desirable characteristics for your application, the thread manufacturer can be contacted for a list of companies that weave the thread into material.

9.5 SELF-PROTECTION WEAPONRY OPTIONS

Most people realize that they alone are individually responsible for their immediate safety and protection--the police aren't, the government isn't--only oneself (exception: paid personal bodyguard). Police help keep order and deter crime in society, and they are very helpful in solving crimes after they occur -- but they're not very effective in preventing random acts of violence in society.

Because of the type work I've been involved in, and in some instances, because of being in the wrong place at the wrong time, I've had many attacks from assailants, sometimes multiple assailants. Studying, stretching, and being proficient in martial arts is <u>highly worth the effort</u>; however, the fact is that during hand-to-hand combat--there is no guarantee of your safety. Another risk of hand-to-hand combat is the risk of catching AIDS, hepatitis, TB, etc. from an infected assailant (not likely, but possible). Therefore, using a weapon to deter the assailant(s) and, if needed, disable the assailant(s) without physically making bodily contact may be a healthier approach, especially when being attacked inside a car.

<u>NOTE: I highly recommend studying and training in martial arts—it's fun to learn, and its extremely effective (I can't recommend it enough). Carrying defensive spray is also highly recommended, as defensive spray is a weapon that can effectively be used in many adverse situations.</u>

This section of chapter 9 explores weaponry options that may or may not be suitable or legal for self-protection usage in car living situations.

• WHAT TO CONSIDER WHEN CHOOSING A WEAPON FOR SELF-PROTECTION

When choosing a weapon for self-protection, one should consider their physical and mental abilities, personality characteristics/deficits, personal preference, regulating laws, type encounters most likely to encounter, etc.

MENTAL AND PHYSICAL CAPABILITIES Coordination, eyesight, and strength are a few physical characteristics that may be important in operating certain types of weaponry. More importantly, being able to effectively operate a weapon includes having the mental ability and knowledge to effectively and legally deal with an adverse confrontation. The higher the degree of deadly force a weapon has, the more complicated the laws that regulate a weapon's usage, transportation, and concealment.

PERSONALITY CHARACTERISTICS Analyzing one's personality characteristics/traits is important when choosing a weapon for self-protection, especially one of deadly force. Characteristics such as one's degree of emotional or unemotional thinking (subjective/objective thinking), ease/difficulty to anger, degree of anger, history of stability/instability, poor/good judgment ability, degree of impulsiveness, etc. should all be considered.

POSSIBLE SITUATIONS MOST LIKELY TO ENCOUNTER The type confrontations most likely to encounter, such as number of assailants, assailant's armament, assailant's intent: theft, violence, vandalism; locations parking at, etc., should be considered.

LAWS REGULATING WEAPONRY USAGE, STORAGE, AND TRANSPORTATION* (if applicable) Knowing the laws that regulate a weapon's use, transport, and concealment will allow the user to escape legal problems by complying with the law or by temporarily "fixing" one's situation to be in compliance with the law whenever necessary.
EXTRA: Advice concerning highly regulated weaponry--keep its ownership secret! What people don't know about doesn't bother them--people can't cause problems with what they don't know exists.

PERSONAL PREFERENCE
   Most people understand their limits and capabilities better than anyone else, thus choosing a weapon yourself is probably best. However, it may be extremely beneficial to get other people's knowledge and opinions about various types of weaponry.
   Most important is choosing a weapon that one is comfortable with, as being comfortable with a weapon makes it more likely that one will practice with it enough to become proficient in its use. Being comfortable with a weapon also includes being at ease with the laws, if any, that regulate a weapon's usage, transport, and concealment. It also includes being comfortable with the amount of deadly force or injury a weapon is capable/incapable of inflicting.

The main concerns when considering a self-protection weapon for car living/working situations are:
• LEGALITY: is it legal to transport and conceal inside a car (must verify local, state, and federal laws).
• MAINTENANCE: a weapon's necessary maintenance/cleaning, etc. necessary to keep it in a ready to use condition.
• EFFECTIVE RANGE
• BODY ARMOR PENETRATION: whether the weapon is effective against assailant(s) wearing body armor.
• ASSAILANT DISABLEMENT: will use of the weapon result in partial or complete disablement of the assailant(s).
• CONCEALABITY: is the weapon easy to conceal inside a car.
• STORAGE: can the weapon be stored in a ready or near-ready to use condition.
• USAGE: how easy is the weapon to use against assailant(s) breaking into your car.
• ASSAILANT DETERRENT: how many assailants will stop their attack by simply showing the weapon.
• BODILY HARM TO ASSAILANT: will the weapon's use result in permanent or non-permanent physical damage of the assailant.
• USEFULNESS AGAINST GUN-CARRYING ASSAILANT: can use of the weapon completely disable the gun-carrying assailant instantly--if not, you'll probably be blown away.
• CONTROL & POSSESSION OF THE WEAPON: how well can you maintain control & possession of the weapon during an attack.

SELF-PROTECTION WEAPONRY
CULINARY/SPEARING TYPE WEAPONRY
BOW & ARROW
CROSS-BOW (Rifle/Pistol)
KNIFE/DAGGER
• LEGALITY: folding knife shorter than X inches may be legal to conceal inside car most anywhere (must verify local, state, and federal laws).
• USAGE SKILLS: If you prefer using a knife/dagger for self-defense, learning edged-weapon martial arts fighting skills will enhance your speed and lethalness--edged-weapon skills are vicious.
SPEAR GUN (Pistol/Rifle)
BLOW GUN
SWORD

- LEGALITY: probably illegal to transport and conceal inside a car under many/most circumstances (check local, state, + federal laws).

SLINGSHOT

STUN GUN

MISCELLANEOUS STRIKING TYPE WEAPONRY
   It's important that striking type weaponry be of a type that is legal to transport and conceal in a car (batons and clubs may not be legal items to carry inside a car).
WOODEN CLUB
- If you like this type weaponry, and if you would like to carry it legally at all times---simply have a wooden, metal, synthetic or combined material walking cane made to your desired specifications.
GOLF CLUB

FIREARM TYPE WEAPONRY
PAINTBALL RIFLE/PISTOL
PISTOL/RIFLE/SHOTGUN
- FIREARM LEGALITY: it once was legal to transport almost anywhere in the U.S. a rifle/shotgun in a car without a round chambered--not anymore: (1) School buffer zones, (2) businesses posting signs making it a felony to have a concealed weapon inside a car, (3) areas within states that have draconian gun laws. (4) some federal land and property, (5) some areas within city/state/national parks.
- FIREARM CONSIDERATIONS/RECOMMENDATIONS:
                        1. One needs to research all local, state, and federal laws pertaining to the transport and concealment of a pistol/rifle/shotgun stored inside a car--if the laws aren't researched, one would probably be better off transporting a weapon that is generally considered legal to transport inside a car under most circumstances.
                        2. In this age of command-and-control police state, draconian gun laws, circumventing the U.S. Constitution, loss of freedom, etc.--I RECOMMEND NEVER DISCLOSING YOUR FIREARM OWNERSHIP (covering gun serial numbers with CS3230 sealant is something I do—my firearm serial numbers are personal private information).
3. During a police encounter, if police ever ask if I'm transporting

any firearms--I always answer no, even if I'm "carrying" legally, as answering yes will cause the officer to run a serial number check on the firearm, data base that gun to you in a government computer--a corrupt cop might try to steal your firearm.

4. It is generally illegal to transport a pistol/rifle/shotgun with a round in the firing chamber—don't have a round in the chamber during a police encounter check that somehow finds the firearm!

5. If transporting a firearm inside a car, make sure it is being transported "legally" during a possible police encounter. Obtaining a concealed carry permit/license is an option in making transporting firearms legal under many circumstances; however, the government turning a right into a government-issued privilege is just more tyranny that allows more government data-basing of gun owners.

6. If a legal gun owner isn't a concealed carry permit holder, there are circumstances that may or may not (check the local/state/federal laws) make transporting a firearm legal. Transporting a firearm to a shooting range (must be in direct route) may be legal. Transporting a firearm <u>during overnight travel genrally offers the most protection;</u> however, minimum distance restrictions may apply, such as travel across two counties (carrying spare clothes and a toothbrush will help prove the travel is "overnight"). Transporting a firearm to a gunsmith for repair (must be a direct route) may be legal. Transporting a firearm to a pawnshop to possibly sell (must be a direct route) may be legal. Transporting a firearm to a friend's residence (must be a direct route) may be legal. Transporting a firearm to a gun dealer to pickup ammo and then to a rifle range may be legal.

EXTRA: Threadlocker (Loctite #414) can be used to seal bullets (bullet to case, and primer to case).

EXTRA: Oil penetration of ammo primers will ruin them.

EXTRA: Frangible bullets break into many pieces upon impact, thus are extremely hard to trace back to a firearm.

MIRAGE EFFECTS ON SHOOTING ACCURACY

Looking far down a highway on a bright sunny day, you'll probably see at a distance what looks like water (often referred to as a heat mirage). This mirage is caused by distortion of the light waves as they pass through different temperature air before reaching the viewer. Varying degrees of solar heating of the different colored ground surfaces is one cause of different temperature air.

To a shooter looking through a scope on a bright sunny day, the mirage effect can cause the actual aim of the barrel to be a significant distance off target from what the scope displays (the farther the shot and the more varying temperature air being shot through, the greater the potential of being farther off target). In my experience, the mirage effect can only affect accuracy when shooting at targets at distances greater than 180 yards. Every once in awhile, you'll hear about a police sniper who accidentally shot a hostage instead of the hostage taker--it was probably because of mirage effect.

Ways to counter the mirage effect include: (1) Get within 180 yards of the target, or (2) position yourself high above the target, such as in a tree or on top of a building, so that you will be shooting through air that has minimal temperature variations from you to the target (remember to properly compensate for less bullet drop), or (3) shoot late at night or during early morning hours before the sun has had time to create temperature variations between different colored surfaces.

CHEMICAL DEFENSIVE SPRAYS (D.S.): MACE, PEPPER SPRAY, COMBINATION MACE/PEPPER SPRAY
• LEGALITY: D.S. are generally legal to transport and conceal in car most anywhere, but not always (must check local, state, and federal laws)--probably not legal to carry in federal buildings or onto commercial aircraft.
• CONCEALABILITY: Small canisters of defensive sprays are easily concealed inside a car or on person.
• USAGE: easy to aim and use–I recommend practicing at least once with a practice bottle to gain proficiency in its use. Pepper spay must contact eyes, mouth, or nose membranes to be effective, thus is suitable for use inside a car. MACE fumes need to be breathed in to be effective, thus is not suitable for use in the close confines of a car; however, MACE is generally faster acting than pepper spray. Pepper spray is carried extensively by hikers who hike in areas containing dangerous wildlife--it seems to be very effective as long as it doesn't run out during an attack.
• STORAGE/MAINTENANCE: D.S. store ready to use; however, D.S. should be replaced at end of manufacturer's recommended shelf life.
• ASSAILANT DISABLEMENT: D.S. are highly disabling.
• ASSAILANT BODILY HARM: D.S. causes no permanent physical damage from normal exposure.

- EFFECTIVE RANGE: D.S. generally has a range of 10-15 feet.
- ASSAILANT DETERRENT: D.S. may not deter minimally armed assailants—but it will disable them!.
- USEFULNESS AGAINST GUN-TOTING ASSAILANT: Defensive sprays should never be used on an assailant who is capable of delivering immediate deadly force!

- THREE TYPES OF DEFENSIVE SPRAYS
  Three types of chemical agents are currently available in defensive sprays: Chloroacetophenone (CN), Orthochlorobe nzalmalonitrile (CS), and Oleoresin Capsicum (OC). Because special decontamination procedures may be required for a person sprayed with CS, Orthochlorobenzalmalonitrile (CS) defensive sprays generally aren't marketed to the general public.

CHLOROACETOPHENONE (CN) "MACE"
- ACTIVE INGREDIENT: Chloroacetophenone (CN)
- DEVELOPMENT/INTRODUCTION: CN was introduced to law enforcement in the 1960s. Commonly incorrectly referred to as "tear gas," but is actually a suspension of extremely fine particles, not a gas.
- EFFECT: CN is a fast acting irritant that causes copious tearing of the eyes, irritation of upper respiratory tract (including nose), and a very painful burning-like irritation of skin.
- HEALTH RISKS: No long-term health risks are known to exist from "normal exposure" to CN.
- USAGE: CN affects anyone breathing its fumes--it will affect the user if used in a small enclosed area.

ORTHOCHLOROBENZALMALONITRILE** (CS)
- ACTIVE INGREDIENT: Orthochlorobenzalmalonitrile (CS).
- DEVELOPMENT/INTRODUCTION: CS was developed in the 1950s for military use, and it has become the standard riot control agent in most western nations. Commonly referred to as "tear gas," but is actually a suspension of extremely fine particles.
- EFFECT: The effects of CS are similar to that of CN, only more severe and more irritating to the respiratory system. CS is approximately 10 times more potent than CN. Although relatively quick acting when used in an atomized or micro-pulverized format, CS is often much slower acting than CN, taking up to 30 seconds if not sprayed directly in the eyes.

- HEALTH RISKS: Special decontamination procedures may be required for CS.
- USAGE PROBLEMS: affects anyone who breathes its fumes--including the shooter using it in a small enclosed area.

OLEORESIN CAPSICUM** (OC) "PEPPER SPRAY"
- ACTIVE INGREDIENT: Oleoresin capsicum (OC). The active ingredient in OC is a powerful, colorless phenolic amide called capsaicin. It is capsaicin that gives hot peppers their "heat." Although it can be synthetically produced, OC is a naturally occurring substance found in the oily resin of chili peppers (capsicum frutescens).
- EFFECT AND USAGE: OC is an inflammatory agent that acts on the mucous membranes creating an intense burning sensation. Being non-volatile allows its use in a sealed off room without adversely affecting the user; however, OC must contact the mucous membranes (eyes, nose, and mouth) to be effective. (Nielsen, 1996).

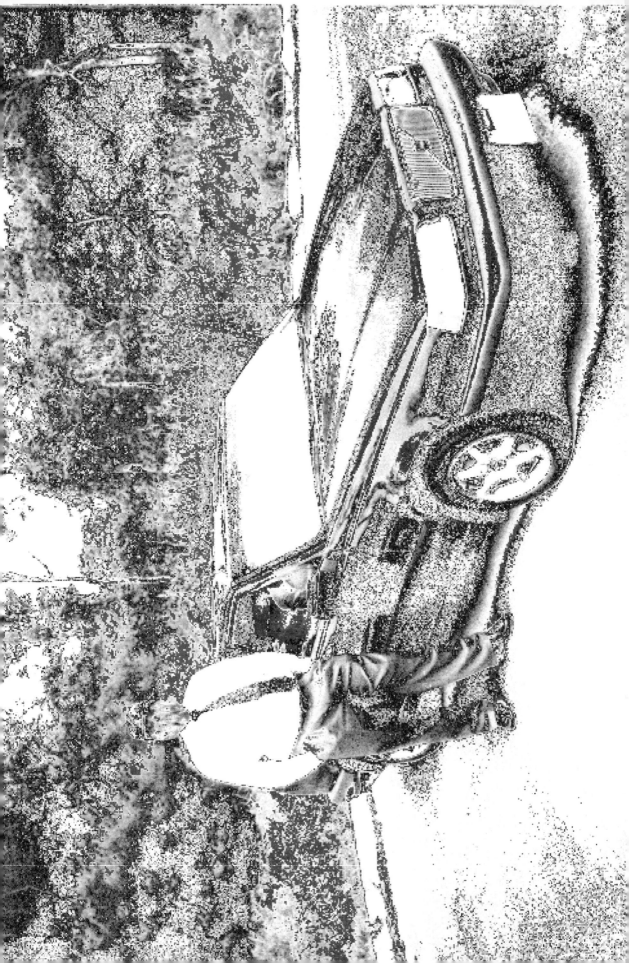

CHAPTER TEN

UNLIMITED PARKING OPTIONS FOR CAR LIVING AND SURVEILLANCE PARKING SITUATIONS

10.1 CHAPTER INTRODUCTION

There are almost unlimited free parking places to use while living/working inside a privatized car. Unlike with motor homes and RV campers, one can live undetectable inside a privatized car that blends in well parked almost anywhere--what people don't see (recognize) or know about doesn't bother them. There are locations where one can park without having to be concerned with the information in this chapter, such as on private property with the owner's permission. However, this chapter is about parking most anywhere desired while living/working secretly inside a privatized car. Also, since one can park most anywhere for one night without incurring any problems when traveling (use common sense), the information contained in this chapter is geared more toward helping one meet their semi-stationary and stationary nighttime parking needs. When reading this chapter, keep in mind that because of the low volume of people/traffic in sparsely populated areas, many parking locations that are easy to use in moderately to heavily populated areas can be very difficult to park at in minimally populated areas.

Picking excellent parking places requires knowledge of the many elements and conditions associated with suitable parking locations, and it requires developing the ability to "read" a parking location/area for visible and non-visible "conditions" that affect its suitability. This chapter describes the "conditions" that make up good parking places and then finishes with detailed examples of a variety of parking locations I've used while living/working secretly inside privatized cars. The information contained here and in Ch. 12: Making Police

<u>Encounters Successful/Productive</u> will be very useful for anyone beginning to live or work secretly in a privatized car--I just wish I had this information available to me when I began living in cars many years ago.

• THREE TYPES OF PARKING DURATION DEFINED

Parking durations are described in this chapter using the following three definitions.

<u>PARKING WHILE TRAVELING</u> <u>Parking while traveling</u> generally refers to parking at a location for one night (two nights maximum) before leaving the general area not returning for at least a few weeks. As long as a privatized car looks normal and not like it's being lived in, parking most anywhere overnight while traveling is generally very easy (use common sense).

<u>SEMI-STATIONARY PARKING</u> <u>Semi-stationary parking</u> refers to parking secretly at the same location for at least two nights per week, but generally not more than four nights per week on a continuous weekly basis. An enhancement to semi-stationary parking includes using two or more parking places rotating back and forth (1-4 nights here, 1-4 nights there), thus minimizing exposure at any one parking location keeping one's parking fresh, enjoyable, and somewhat exciting.

<u>STATIONARY PARKING</u> <u>Stationary parking</u> refers to parking at the same location at least 4 nights per week on a continual weekly basis. Limiting one's exposure through a variety of means is a very important aspect of successful stationary parking. I've been able to use the same parking location for more than a year when it has been necessary to do so; however, parking in the same location does become dull, thus using more than one parking location is probably how most will want to satisfy their nighttime parking needs.

10.2 GENERAL PARKING RECOMMENDATIONS (GPR)

The following General Parking Recommendations (GPR) generally applies to most any secret parking location/ situation.

GPR #1: DON'T TRY TO SECRETLY PARK IN A SINGLE-FAMILY HOMES RESIDENTIAL NEIGHBORHOOD

A single-family homes neighborhood is any neighborhood that consists only of houses without any apartment communities, businesses, etc. Attempting to park in this type of neighborhood is generally very difficult because there are no places to blend in. Because people are very protective of their residences, family/children, possessions -- a strange car parked in a houses only residential neighborhood is easily noticed. This type parking generally violates GPR #2 and #4 (soon to be disclosed). Therefore, unless one has a property owner's permission to park on or in front of their property, parking secretly in a single-family homes residential neighborhood isn't recommended.

ALL HOUSES RESIDENTIAL NEIGHBORHOOD SURVEILLANCE CONSIDERATIONS For those determined to do surveillance work out of a privatized car parked on an "all houses" residential neighborhood street for as long as one's supplies (food/water) and waste storage will last, the following guidelines may be helpful. Parking on the street midway between two houses will make neighbors unsure which house is possibly being visited by the owner of the privatized car. Houses separated by a privacy fence or hedge could signal that the owners might not be on good speaking terms, thus they may not discuss with each other the privatized car parked out in front of their property.

Arriving between 3:30-4:30 a.m. is generally a good time to arrive since most people are asleep at this time and because police patrols seem to be at a minimum during this period. However, this is a high exposure time to be seen arriving by police.

Cars used in neighborhood surveillance work should be nice enough to be pleasing to the neighbors, but not so nice as to draw excessive attention. One's privatized car should be as generic looking as possible, with no features that make the car easy to identify.

Movements inside the parked vehicle need to be very slow to prevent noticeable car body movement to anyone outside. Interior sound and lighting should be kept to a minimum to eliminate breach of privacy blowing one's cover.

During cool or cold weather, one may want to address the problem of condensation forming on useable windows (non-covered, non-insulated see through windows) possibly blowing one's cover. Possible ways to prevent condensation from forming include (1) covering the interior side of a window with scuba diving mask or dirt bike goggle anti-fog liquid, or a mixture of water and liquid soap, (2) installing a perfectly sized windshield shade against the windshield's interior surface and placing a pouch of drying agent between the windshield and shade, then sealing the outer edges of the windshield shade to the windshield's outer edge or plastic trim using a silicon adhesive sealant.

Having a "fake" alarm that can be activated manually to drive away anyone curious enough to touch one's parked privatized car can be very useful in driving away thieves/vandals, kids, walking pedestrians, curious cops, etc.

GPR #2:"DON'T PARK AT LOCATIONS WHERE THERE ARE SIGNIFICANT AMOUNTS OF CHILDREN

Most people are concerned about children's safety, thus parking around children can easily cause problems with parents, adults, and police. Therefore, parking where there are significant amounts of children, such as children's playgrounds, day-care centers, schools, skating rinks, movie theaters, etc., should be avoided. Another reason to avoid parking around children is that kids playing near one's parked privatized car might want to include it in their "fun + games." Fortunately, these locations are easy to identify and avoid.

GPR #3: "DON'T PARK IN DIRECT VIEW OF ANY POLICE STATION"

Police watch their surroundings very carefully, especially their residences and office/station areas. Although parking out of view but near to a police station can work out nicely because of the added security, parking within view of a police station will probably result in problems from officers eventually noticing and then investigating an unidentified privatized car parked often within view. Also, besides not parking within view of police stations, one will want to avoid parking on the main road(s) that police vehicles use when leaving/entering their station area, so as to minimize exposure to police.

GPR #3 EXAMPLE #1: PARKING UNSUCCESSFULLY IN DIRECT VIEW OF POLICE STATION/RESIDENCE AREA

Once while traveling in a mid-western state, I pulled over to take a nap in my privatized car not realizing that I had parked next to a police station cadet training/residence area. Within a few hours I was awakened by two cautious police officers.

The officers said they were a bit surprised to find me there because they didn't often find cars parked adjacent to their station/residences with someone napping inside. After running the "usual checks," I was told to move along.

GPR #3: EXAMPLE #2: COLLEGE PARKING At a large college I attended, I once tried parking on a dormitory parking lot that was in direct view of the campus police station. Even though I was over a block away from the police station, the police were able to see my car through a couple of the station's windows-- and they did sometimes notice that I entered my privatized car and spent unusually long periods inside before coming out or driving away. I could actually feel the police watching me, so I soon began parking in another location much farther away and out of view of the campus police station.

One day, when I went to the campus police station to try and talk my way out of a parking ticket, the officer listening to me yelled back to the captain, "Hey Captain, the guy living in his car over by the library wants you to dismiss his parking ticket...." As one can see, college campus police can be very supportive of students who work hard and don't cause problems; however, if I hadn't moved to another parking location out of view of the campus police station, or if I hadn't kept my car living situation completely secret from students/faculty who might otherwise have complained about my inexpensive living situation--- my being able to live in my privatized car parked on campus probably would have ended fairly quickly.

GPR #3 EXAMPLE #3: PARKING CLOSE TO BUT OUT OF DIRECT VIEW OF A CITY POLICE STATION Even though I don't recommend parking in direct view of police stations, I have had plenty of added security by parking out of sight but close to police stations. In a city where I once worked, during the night I would park on a city street a few blocks away from the city police station. I was off the main road(s) that police cars entered and exited the station from, so my exposure was minimal. It was a nice, safe, quiet area to park at during the night because of its proximity to the police station. The only drawback to this parking situation was having to wake up at 7 A.M. to feed the parking meter or leave the spot (parking was free from 5 p.m. - 7 a.m.).

GPR #4: DON'T PARK IN CLOSE, DIRECT VIEW OF ANY MAIN LIVING AREA WINDOWS OF ANY TYPE OF RESIDENCE

When parking near any type of residence, such as apartment communities, student dormitories, hotels/motels, hospitals, etc., one will want to implement GPR#4. Parking within close direct view of residence windows will result in too much exposure of one's vehicle. Even when a property owner has given permission to park at their residence, a vehicle parked close to any windows through which the resident looks often may become irritating to the resident owner. Therefore, positioning one's car much farther away or in a location not in direct view of main resident windows is a much better way to park around any type of "suitable" residence (don't violate GPR#1). Basically, if people don't see or hear you--you don't exist, so there is no problem.

GPR #4 PARKING EXAMPLE: HOTEL ROOM PARKING SITUATION Parking directly in front of a newlywed couple's hotel room window made the couple very nervous--they kept looking out at my car. I simply relieved the tension by moving out of view, parking on the adjacent city street.

GPR #5: DON'T DISCLOSE YOUR SECRET LIVING/PARKING SITUATION TO ANYONE UNLESS ABSOLUTELY NECESSARY

General Parking Recommendation #5 came about because of problems I've had after disclosing my car living situation to people who absolutely didn't need to know. The few times I've mentioned my inexpensive car living situation to people associated with my work (non-surveillance work) or education, it generally has been counterproductive. Disclosing one's secret car living situation can severely limit one's parking options. Chapters 1 and 12 thoroughly discuss reasons why one should never disclose their secret car living situation to anyone unless absolutely necessary (Ch. 1 Section: "Why 'privatize' one's car;" Ch. 12 Section: "What not to disclose during a police encounter").

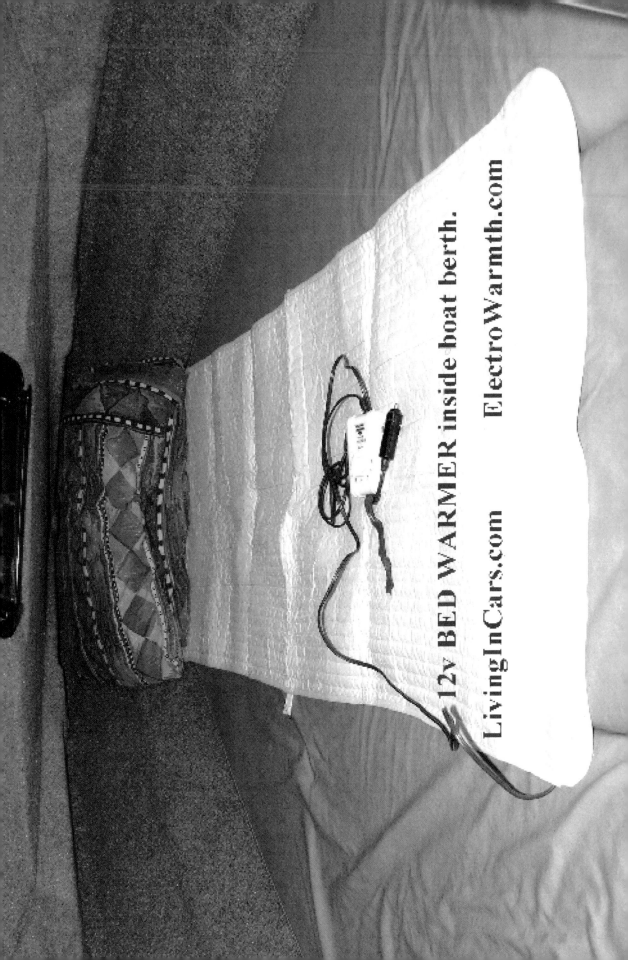

12v BED WARMER inside boat berth.

LivingInCars.com   ElectroWarmth.com

10.3 GOOD PARKING ELEMENTS (GPE)

Thinking about all the locations I've used over the years, I realize that most suitable parking locations have similar traits. For semi-stationary and stationary parking, choosing parking places with "good parking elements" may be very beneficial for a parking location to work out over the long-term. However, unlike General Parking Recommendations that should be followed when choosing most any secret parking location, the following Good Parking Elements (GPE) don't always have to be a part of a parking location to make it very suitable.

GOOD PARKING ELEMENT (GPE) #1: ELEMENT OF MANY POSSIBILITIES: COMBINATION AREA PARKING LOCATIONS

Some suitable parking locations have what I call the "Element of Many Possibilities." This element is present when people seeing a privatized car can easily think of more than one good reason as to why the vehicle is parked where it is during the entire parking stay. This can be found in combination area parking locations that have more than one activity taking place nearby at which the owner of a parked car could be involved. Generally, if people who see a parked privatized car can think of more than one reason why it is parked where it is, they will generally pay little or no attention to it, thus helping to ensure long-term, uninterrupted secret parking.

GPE#1 EXAMPLE#1: APARTMENT and GROCERY STORE COMBINATION AREA An example of a good combination area would be parking in between an apartment community located next to a 24-hour business, such as a 24-hour grocery store, or an 18/24-hour restaurant, or a 24-hour health club, etc. Anyone seeing a parked privatized car wouldn't know if the owner is living, working, or visiting at the apartment community, or whether the owner is working or shopping at the 24-hour grocery store--there are many possibilities.

GPE #1 EXAMPLE #2: UNIVERSITY/COLLEGE PARKING COMBINATION AREA

Attending college while living in a privatized car, one of the best places I found to park on campus during the night is between the college library and student dormitories. College libraries usually open early (6:00-7:00 A.M.) and close late (10:00-12:00 P.M.) and many times are located near student housing, thus making this type combination area parking easy to park at. The "element of many possibilities" comes from people seeing my privatized car not knowing whether I was a student or employee living/working/visiting at the dormitory, or whether I was a student or employee working or studying in the library.

GPE #2: DON'T PARK NEAR INVISIBLE PEDESTRIAN WALKING PATHS

Many people can sense the presence of another human nearby without actually seeing or hearing them; therefore, the less close-up exposure an occupied privatized car has to people, the better. For this reason, avoid parking near invisible pedestrian walkways, such as near to the shortest path across a parking lot between two buildings. If parked in an invisible pedestrian pathway, simply remedy the situation by moving a short distance away, move a few parking spaces to the right or left, or move to the next parking row.

GPE#3: YOUR CAR SHOULD BLEND IN WITH ITS SURROUNDINGS AS MUCH AS POSSIBLE

Having one's privatized car blend in with its immediate surroundings as much as possible is very important in semi-stationary and stationary parking situations in which one's car may be exposed to many of the same people on a nightly/daily basis. Being able to implement GPE#3 requires analysis of the events taking place around one's car during the entire time it will be parked. Depending on the type and difficulty of a parking situation, having one's car blend in with its surrounding requires consideration of several factors: (1) your car's arrival and departure times, (2) whether or not you enter/exit your car while parked; if so, the optimal time to leave/enter your car, (3) parking at the optimal, least exposed parking location in the parking area, (4) keeping one's privatized car looking as generic as possible so that it is difficult to identify/recognize from other like-model cars, and (4) considering the best direction in which to park one's car.

The following grocery store stationary parking example will help you better understand GPE#3.
• GPE#3: GROCERY STORE SEMI-STATIONARY/STATIONARY PARKING EXAMPLE
PARKING LOCATION The goal is to park at a location within the available parking area that is quiet, has minimal exposure to store entrances/windows and outside employee smoking areas, and looks natural to park there. Parking on the side of a grocery store out-of-the-view of store entrances and away

from heavily used parking lot entrances can be very suitable. Parking at locations in which people inside the store would have to strain to see through store windows may be suitable. Parking a good distance from the store where nighttime employees park can also be suitable, as one's car appears to be a nighttime employee's car and is parked far enough away from store entrance(s) and windows to be hardly noticed by anyone in the store.

OPTIMAL ARRIVAL AND DEPARTURE TIMES Depending on the parking situation and duration, using optimal arrival/departure times to minimize exposure may be very important. In my experience, grocery store daytime managers are the ones most likely to notice and investigate a car parked nightly on a store's parking lot. To avoid exposure to daytime store management, I've generally tried to arrive after 7:00 p.m. and depart just before 5:45 a.m. (optimal times vary). If one chooses to park far out in the parking lot near where the nighttime grocery store employees park, it would be best to arrive an hour before or an hour after the nighttime employees arrive.

SHOULD ONE ENTER/EXIT THEIR CAR WHILE PARKED AT A NIGHTTIME PARKING LOCATION?
    People generally only develop problems with people they are directly exposed to. To limit exposure and eliminate possible problems, I usually never leave my car at night while parking at a semi-stationary or stationary parking location (shop somewhere else--not where you park).

OPTIMAL DIRECTION IN WHICH TO PARK Another aspect to consider is the use of a front windshield shade when parking at night. Since a windshield shade in use to fully "privatize" a car during the night may look a bit odd, it's generally better to park the car in a direction and location in which the windshield shade has minimal exposure to passersby. Also, because all car windows can be tinted except for the windshield, during cold weather car living the windshield is the only window that readily shows condensation (if not eliminated by some means). Thus it is best to park in a location and direction in which store employees can't easily see the car's windshield.
    In certain parking situations, it's best if one can enter their car with minimal exposure. In these situations, park the car so that the driver's side door is away from what one is trying to limit exposure to.

GPE #4: PARKING AROUND FAST PACED, HIGHLY PRODUCTIVE, HIGH VOLUME, LOW CRIME, ECONOMICALLY SOUND AREAS CAN BE EXCELLENT LOCATIONS TO PARK AT

GPE#4 mainly applies when parking in densely populated areas where a car will be exposed to many people. In densely populated areas, I've found it beneficial to park around economically sound, highly productive, low crime areas that have a high volume of people/cars arriving and departing throughout the day. The reason being is that changing environments are fairly easy to blend into unnoticed. The productive people in these type environments generally don't have the time or interest to investigate whether someone may be living in a privatized car. Also, there are usually excellent "combination areas" located in these areas for parking.

GPE #4 EXAMPLE #1: PROFESSIONAL DISTRICT/AREA An example of a high volume, low crime, fast paced, economically sound, highly productive area that I once used for stationary nighttime parking was at a professional business area (lawyers, accountants, etc.) of a large city. The area was unique in that it also had some residential housing alongside some of the professional businesses. The city streets had parking meters that required payment during the day from 7am to 5pm, but parking was free during the evening and night.

In this parking situation, no one was concerned about my privatized car parked on the city street--the productive people in the area just didn't have the time or interest to notice my car. Also helping my car blend in was the combination area effect created by residential homes being located sporadically in the area, and by businessmen occasionally working late into the night.

GPE#4 EXAMPLE #2: UNIVERSITY CAMPUS PARKING In the GPR#1 "element of many possibilities" college campus-parking example previously discussed, GPE#4 was very much a part of the environment. Universities are the easiest to attend living in a privatized car because of their extremely productive, fast paced, high volume, low crime, ever changing environments that allow a privatized car to blend in well.

GPE #4 EXAMPLE #3: SEE HOTEL EXAMPLE AT END OF CHAPTER

10.4   PARKING LOCATIONS I'VE USED WHILE LIVING/ WORKING SECRETLY INSIDE PRIVATIZED CARS

Being familiar with my "general parking recommendations" (GPR) and "good parking elements" (GPE), you're ready to learn about some of the many possible parking locations I've used while living/working secretly in privatized cars. For each parking location disclosed, I've provided a brief summary that includes (1) personal/possible usage of the location in satisfying the three parking durations previously defined, (2) advantages and disadvantages generally associated with the parking location, and (3) considerations/recommendations for successful parking usage of the location. Keep in mind that parking conditions can vary considerably between similar type parking locations; therefore, the following parking location information should be considered as generalizations of what I've usually found during my parking experiences.

Before continuing, it may be helpful to review the previously disclosed parking duration definitions at the beginning of this chapter.

• HOTELS/MOTELS

PARKING CONDITIONS: Traveling (excellent-good), Semi-stationary (Very good-fair), Stationary (good-poor)

Hotels/motels may be suitable to use in satisfying all three types of parking: (1) parking while traveling, (2) semi-stationary parking, and (3) stationary parking. Stationary parking at hotels/motels usually isn't possible unless located in a combination area, has exceptional "minimal exposure" parking and building layout, or has adjacent city streets suitable for parking on. However, I've been able to use the same hotel/motel for stationary parking in excess of several months even when conditions weren't ideal.

HOTEL/MOTEL PARKING ADVANTAGES In heavily populated areas, hotels/motels are readily available for parking. With different people arriving each evening, hotel/motel parking can continuously be a fresh experience. Many hotels/motels are located in "combination areas," thus making them more suitable for stationary parking usage. Adjacent streets surrounding hotels/motels may be suitable for parking on.

Hotel/motel parking has minimal risk in that generally only two things will occur if caught (I've been caught once): (1)

You'll give a suitable excuse for being inside your privatized car, such as "it would look better to my employer if I don't check into a room until such-in-such time, and I accidentally fell asleep while waiting;" and (2) you'll apologize and proceed to check into a room or leave.

Parking at motels/hotels can offer other benefits outlined in Ch. 14 The Freebies, such as free ice, swimming, inexpensive quality subsidized meals, etc. Hotel parking garages can offer added comfort during severe weather.

HOTEL/MOTEL PARKING DISADVANTAGES Parking at hotels/motels can be a bit noisy, especially during early morning hours when many people leave. Air quality may be a bit poor depending on the location. Low volume hotels/motels located in sparsely populated areas or in high crime areas, and hotels/motels that have only one entrance/exit in direct view of the office generally aren't suitable for semi-stationary or stationary parking usage.

HOTEL/MOTEL PARKING CONSIDERATIONS/RECOMMENDATIONS Volume of people/traffic, condition of local economy, degree of crime in the area, hotel building and property layout, type businesses nearby (combination area), and other factors will affect how suitable a hotel/motel is for use in satisfying one's semi-stationary + stationary parking needs. Hotels/motels located in low crime, economically sound areas that do a high volume of business are generally easy to park at unnoticed. When considering a hotel's layout, the office generally should not be in view of one's parking location, and preferably not within good view of the parking lot entrance/exit one uses. When available, one may wish to take advantage of combination area parking. Adjacent city streets may be suitable for parking on.

To help make nightly parking successful, one will probably want to use low exposure arrival + departure times. Arriving during or slightly after peak check in periods is a low-exposure time to arrive. Depending on the hotel/motel, departure time is generally a bit more critical in that one should leave before housemaids are more than an hour into their work at cleaning used rooms, as housemaids may notice any "extra" cars and then contact the office to see what room the car owner is occupying.

To minimize exposure one generally shouldn't leave their car while using a hotel/motel for semi-stationary or stationary parking. For semi-stationary and stationary type parking, using more than one hotel/motel for parking will minimize exposure and help keep parking fresh and enjoyable.

• 24-HOUR CASINOS
PARKING CONDITIONS: Traveling (excellent), Semi-stationary (very good - fair), Stationary (good-poor) 24-hour casinos may be suitable for use in satisfying all three types of parking usage: (1) parking while traveling, (2) semi-stationary parking, and (3) stationary parking.

CASINO PARKING ADVANTAGES Parking at a 24-hr. casino looks normal anytime. Many casinos are built integral with a hotel, thus creating combination area parking that allows a privatized car to blend in even better. Casinos are often built with minimal view outside to prevent gamblers from recognizing the passage of time. If outside crime isn't a problem, parking area surveillance/monitoring may be minimal. Adjacent city streets may be very suitable for parking on.

   Like parking at a hotel, if one's parking situation were somehow discovered, casino personnel probably wouldn't cause any problems with a possible customer (exception: repeat offender). Casinos often have inexpensive quality meals that are subsidized by gambling profits. Unlike most parking locations being used for semi-stationary/stationary parking, leaving one's car to use a casino's facilities may workout satisfactorily--as long as one spends a little money while inside.

CASINO PARKING DISADVANTAGES Parking around casinos is generally what I would consider a very "worldly" experience (some people like it, some don't). Surveillance camera monitoring of casino parking areas may make stationary parking difficult. However, if parking lot crime isn't a problem, surveillance cameras could make parking easier, as all parking lot activity being recorded allows security personnel to spend most of their time monitoring the more important gambling areas inside the casino.

CASINO PARKING CONSIDERATIONS/RECOMMENDATIONS If available, using more than one casino for parking will minimize exposure at any one location and help keep the parking situation fresh and enjoyable. One may want to take advantage of combination area parking when available. Adjacent city streets may be suitable for parking on. Arriving during peak business hours, when casino security personnel are primarily focused on inside gambling and building entrances, will be helpful in limiting exposure of one's arrival. Parking with the driver's door and windshield out of direct view of surveillance cameras will also be beneficial. When available, use parking lot entrance/exit points located out of view of building entrances and windows.

- 24-HOUR GROCERY STORES   **ONE OF MY TOP 5 FAVORITE PARKING LOCATIONS**
PARKING CONDITIONS: Traveling (excellent), Semi-stationary (excellent - very good), Stationary (very good - poor). 24-hour grocery stores located in moderately to heavily populated areas may be suitable for all three types of parking usage: (1) parking while traveling, (2) semi-stationary parking, and (3) stationary parking.
24-HOUR GROCERY STORE PARKING ADVANTAGES There usually are 24-hour grocery stores readily located throughout moderately/heavily-populated areas. Parking at 24-hour grocery stores looks normal anytime. 24-hour grocery store parking lots generally have quiet parking places located out of view of store entrances and windows, and away from parking lot entrance/exit points. Different people arriving and leaving often allows a privatized car to blend in easily. Many 24-hour grocery stores are located in "combination areas," thus making them more suitable for semi-stationary/stationary parking usage.

Like casinos and hotels/motels, 24-hour grocery stores are fairly safe for parking, offering minimal risks if caught (I've never been caught). If caught, one could say that they were traveling and had just pulled over to rest awhile (never admit to sleeping/living/camping in your car).
24-HOUR GROCERY STORE PARKING DISADVANTAGES Daytime management may take notice of a car seen often, especially if they see a car's arrival or departure noticing that the driver isn't a store employee. Because of possible intrusive parking lot surveillance, parking at 24-hour grocery stores located in high crime or sparsely populated areas may be difficult.

Depending on the location, 24-hour grocery store parking areas may have substantial drug trafficking taking place. Any narcotics trafficking taking place at store parking areas will cause all car owners to be suspect.
24-HOUR GROCERY STORE PARKING CONSIDERATIONS/ RECOMMENDATIONS People can easily develop problems with anyone they're exposed to. Therefore, when using a 24-hour grocery store for semi-stationary/stationary parking, it's best

not to leave your car and expose yourself to store personnel (shop somewhere else).

The goal is to park in a quiet location that is out of view of and/or far away from store entrances + windows, but still looks normal to park at. Parking on the sides (if available) of a 24-hour grocery store or parking far out in a parking lot close to nighttime employee vehicles are locations I commonly use. If a 24-hour grocery store is located in a combination area, such as next to an apartment community or hotel/motel, parking in the fringe area where the two parking lots meet may be very suitable.

When using a 24-hour grocery store for semi-stationary or stationary parking, it will be necessary to minimize exposure to daytime management. In my experience, daytime management are the only store employees nosy enough to notice and investigate a privatized car they see often. Therefore, it is important for daytime management not to see your car's arrival/departure possibly noticing that the driver isn't a store employee. I generally avoid daytime management by leaving at around 5:30 a.m. and not returning until after 8 p.m.

Although I've used the same 24-hour grocery store to park at Monday - Thursday nights continuously for several months, I prefer using three or four different locations to alternately park at, so as to minimize exposure at any one location. Alternating between stores/locations will also help keep one's parking fresh, enjoyable, and somewhat exciting.

To totally "privatize" my car when parked during night, I always install a windshield shade. But since using a windshield shade at night may look unnatural and draw unwanted attention, I generally try to park in a location and direction in which my car's windshield isn't in view of store entrances and windows.

Pelican + SKS Airtight Plastic Storage Containers

- 24-HOUR DEPARTMENT STORES

**PARKING CONDITIONS: Traveling (very good), Semi-stationary (good - fair), Stationary (good - poor) 24-hour department stores may be suitable for all three types of parking: (1) parking while traveling, (2) semi-stationary parking, and (3) stationary parking applications. I've used them mainly when traveling and for semi-stationary parking applications.

24-HOUR DEPARTMENT STORE PARKING ADVANTAGES
Parking at 24-hour department stores looks normal anytime. They may be located in "combination areas," thus making them more suitable for semi-stationary/stationary parking usage. Depending on the location of the 24-hour department store, motor homes and truckers may park on vacated areas of store parking areas during the night, thus somewhat averting attention from regular parking areas.

24-HOUR DEPARTMENT STORE PARKING DISADVANTAGES
Because of minimal traffic and few low exposure parking places, one's car may be more noticeable parked at a 24-hour department store. Having to park near all the other cars parked near a single nighttime store entrance also makes a car stand out more (if applicable). Department stores sell some very expensive merchandise and are therefore quite security conscious, possibly having parking area surveillance cameras and frequent nighttime visits from patrolling police.

In the age of draconian gun laws, many department stores now have signs posted making it a felony to have a concealed weapon in one's car.

Any narcotics trafficking taking place at store parking areas will cause all cars to receive more attention.

24-HOUR DEPARTMENT STORE PARKING CONSIDERATIONS
In semi-stationary/stationary parking situations, to avoid exposure to store personnel and customers, it's best not to leave your car. Parking near other cars but as far away from store entrances as possible, while still staying within the general nighttime parking area, may be a very suitable parking location to use.

Concealed firearms inside a car may be a felony violation at 24-hour department stores posting the appropriate sign. In the age of draconian gun laws--I recommend not disclosing one's firearm ownership.

- SCENIC LOOKOUT/OVERLOOK POINTS

**PARKING CONDITIONS: Traveling (very good-poor), Semi-stationary (good-poor), Stationary (poor)

I've used scenic lookout points for nighttime parking mainly when traveling and for limited semi-stationary parking situations. A scenic lookout point would have to be located in an exceptional area and have exceptional parking characteristics for stationary parking to be successful (few do).

SCENIC LOOKOUT/OVERLOOK POINT PARKING ADVANTAGES Scenic lookout points can be located most anywhere there are beautiful scenic views. It's enjoyable and refreshing to park at an unfamiliar scenic overlook/lookout point during the night and then be surprised by the beautiful view/surroundings upon wakening the next morning.

SCENIC OVERLOOK/LOOKOUT POINT PARKING DISADVANTAGES If located on busy roads or in highly populated areas, scenic overlook/lookout points tend to be heavily visited by people, thus excessive noise, highly exposed parking, and less than desirable air quality may be present. I've found scenic overlook/lookout points to be frequented by police on routine patrol, especially when located around highly populated areas. Severe firearm restriction laws may apply at scenic overlook/lookout points. Scenic overlook/lookout points generally are not highway rest areas--sleeping in a car while parked at a scenic overlook/lookout point may be illegal.

SCENIC OVERLOOK/LOOKOUT POINT PARKING CONSIDERATIONS One should never admit to living/sleeping/ camping in their car during a police encounter occurring at a scenic overlook/lookout point. Severe firearm restrictions may apply--I never admit to transporting a firearm even when I'm doing so legally. Like at highway rest areas, one's safety and protection is only what one provides--make sure it is enough. In this age of draconian gun laws, one would be better off not disclosing their gun ownership to anyone.

• **HIGHWAY REST AREAS**
PARKING CONDITIONS: Traveling (excellent - poor), Semi-stationary (excellent - poor), Stationary (very good - poor)

Depending on the parking duration allowed, highway rest areas may be suitable for all three types of parking usage: (1) parking when traveling, (2) semi-stationary parking, and (3) stationary parking. Although I've used highway rest areas for semi-stationary parking, I mainly use them when traveling.

HIGHWAY REST AREA PARKING ADVANTAGES Highway rest areas are always available to legally park at, but with possible time restrictions. They make an excellent backup parking place if ever needed. Some may be located in quiet minimally-traveled areas making them pleasant to park at (quiet with good air quality). They're easily located on road maps.

HIGHWAY REST AREA PARKING DISADVANTAGES If located in highly populated areas or adjacent to busy highways, highway rest areas can be extremely noisy, somewhat polluted, highly exposed, and even dangerous to park at. Many states have time restrictions limiting use of highway rest areas.

HIGHWAY REST AREA PARKING CONSIDERATIONS/ RECOMMENDATIONS I've experienced car vandalism and an attempted break-in while parking at highway rest areas. Safety/ protection is only what you provide--make sure it is enough for any situation that might arise.

- TRUCK STOPS

PARKING CONDITIONS: Traveling (excellent - very good), semi-stationary (very good - fair), stationary (good - poor).

Truck stops may be used to satisfy all three types of parking: (1) parking when traveling, (2) semi-stationary parking, and (3) stationary parking. Because of moderate pollution and noise, I only use them minimally when traveling and for limited semi-stationary parking usage.

TRUCK STOP PARKING ADVANTAGES Truck stops are 24-hour businesses where truck drivers can gas up, park and sleep, eat, and possibly shower; they are intrinsically combination area parking locations. Showering at a truck stop may be free or cost little. They generally are located adjacent highways on the outskirts of cities/towns and at points along isolated stretches of highway.

Parking among the big rigs is fairly safe, as truckers are generally well armed. Truck stop employees are generally a bit overworked, excessively exposed, and could care less about what is going on outside as long as crime isn't being committed.

TRUCK STOP PARKING DISADVANTAGES Many of the big rigs' motors are left running all night to provide climate controlled comfort for the driver sleeping inside, and this can result in quite a bit of noise and pollution for anyone parked nearby. Truck air brakes make loud noises when the trucks leave and arrive.

TRUCK STOP PARKING CONSIDERATIONS/ RECOMMENDATIONS It's best to park in a location that is out of sight of truck stop business's windows and entrances. Avoiding exposure to daytime management is recommended, thus using optimal arrival/departure times will be beneficial.

Not exposing oneself by not doing any business at the truck stop will be beneficial during semi-stationary/stationary parking usage.

• STORAGE RENTAL UNITS

PARKING USAGE -- POSSIBLE ONLY FOR THOSE RENTING STORAGE SPACE Use of a rental storage business to park or live at is generally only possible for those renting storage space, as a non-renter seen at a rental storage business would be presumed criminal trespass/intent. As a renter renting rental storage space, living in a storage rental room (motorcycle/bicycle easily fits inside) or living inside a privatized car parked at a rental parking space may be suitable for use in all three types of parking or similar usage.

RENTAL STORAGE BUSINESS PARKING/LIVING ADVANTAGES AND CONSIDERATIONS Living secretly in a rental storage room or parking at a rented parking space is generally very quiet at night with no neighbors to bother one's sleep. It is also a place that one can use to "disappear" or use to support operations that one would rather keep private.

As disclosed in chapter 6, a storage rental room is an excellent place to store and use a three-way or household freezer to help satisfy food storage and ice making needs. Simply dropping by my storage room for a 3-5 days supply of ice and frozen food, whenever necessary, has allowed me to eat extremely well while living/working in privatized cars. Using a refrigerator/freezer inside a rental storage room helps keep the room dry. Recharging batteries at a rental storage room may also be convenient.

To power electrical equipment in a storage room that has lighting, a light bulb can be replaced with a "light bulb plug adapter" in which electrical equipment can be plugged into. If the electrical equipment uses more power than what the light bulb plug adapter can supply (600 watts typical), temporarily removing the light bulb fixture and wiring in a 110-volt AC outlet in its place may be possible.

Using a sleeping cot in a rental storage room allows for enhanced comfort during any temperature weather. Covering a portion of each of the sleeping cot's legs with petroleum jelly or automotive grease will prevent most any crawling type bug from reaching the cot's surface. If flying bugs are a problem, a military mosquito netting tint-like covering can be hung over and around a sleeping cot.

Storage room doors whose doorknobs only lock from the

outside can be held closed by several means. If a storage room door opens inward, it can be held shut by jamming the bottom of a door with a door wedge(s). Better yet, it can be held closed by placing a 2x4" wood piece of appropriate length between the door and opposite wall. A storage room door that opens outward can be held closed by chaining the inner doorknob to a piece of wood/pipe placed across the door's frame (using spacers at each end of the pipe/wood will aid in keeping the door held tightly shut).

DISADVANTAGE OF PARKING/LIVING AT STORAGE RENTAL ROOM OR RENTAL PARKING SPACE

One can possibly secretly live at a rental storage business only if renting storage or parking space--a non-renter seen at a rental storage business would be viewed as criminal trespass/intent. If theft or vandalism were committed at a rental business, anyone found to be living at the rental storage business would automatically be investigated. Rental storage businesses that are monitored by security cameras, electric gates that record arrival/departure times, and/or rental storage businesses where the owner lives on-site are probably difficult to secretly live at.

Living in a rental storage room using a three-way refrigerator/freezer powered by propane fuel has the risk of being exposed to minute propane fuel leaks that can adversely effect one's health. Propane fire/explosion is another possible hazard. Be sure to use smoke, carbon monoxide, and LP gas detector alarms when living in a rental storage room, as what is being stored in the rest of the building could pose additional hazards.

Surprisingly, quite a bit of illegal narcotics are stored at rental storage businesses.

Obviously, rental storage rooms that are locked with a pad lock on the outside of the room/door aren't suitable for living in.

• 24-HOUR LAUNDROMATS

PARKING CONDITIONS: Traveling (very good-poor), semi-stationary (good-poor), stationary (fair-poor).

Twenty-four-hour Laundromats may be suitable for all three types of parking usage: (1) parking while traveling, (2) semi-stationary parking, and (3) stationary parking. However, because Laundromats generally have dull atmospheres/surroundings (exception: resort areas), I've used them minimally when traveling and minimally for semi-stationary parking situations.

TWENTY-FOUR-HOUR LAUNDROMAT PARKING ADVANTAGES
Laundromats located in resort areas can be quite nice to
park near and/or use. Twenty-four-hour Laundromats may
be located in combination areas. There may be adjacent city
streets suitable for parking on.

Hot water can easily be obtained from a Laundromat for
use in the two jugs of water or car privacy bathing options
(Ch. 5) if ever desired, such as when traveling. Laundromat
bathrooms generally have drainage provisions installed in the
floor, making them suitable for use in an emergency "two jugs
of water" showering application.

24-HOUR LAUNDROMAT PARKING DISADVANTAGES
Laundromats generally have dull atmospheres. Laundromat
owners/personnel may pay close attention to their business
and business parking areas during their routine visits.

24-HOUR LAUNDROMAT PARKING CONSIDERATIONS
Although most 24-hour Laundromats are easy to park at
overnight while traveling, a Laundromat generally needs to be
located in a combination area or have an adjacent street to
park on if semi-stationary parking is to be successful. When
parking at Laundromat parking areas, avoid parking during
times when the Laundromat owner and/or maintenance
personnel routinely visit.

• 18/24-HOUR RESTAURANTS
PARKING CONDITIONS: Traveling (excellent-fair), semi-
stationary (very good-poor), stationary (good-poor)

Eighteen to twenty-four-hour restaurants can possibly be
used for all three types of parking, especially if located in an
exceptional combination area. One of the best 18-hr. restaurant
combination area parking locations I've used for stationary
parking usage was being parked on an adjacent city street
mid-way between an 18-hr. restaurant and apartment building
(included in end-of-chapter parking examples).

18/24-HOUR RESTAURANT PARKING ADVANTAGES Many
restaurants are located in combination areas, such as around
apartments, hotel/motels, truck stops, and other 24-hour
businesses that make them more suitable for semi-stationary
and stationary parking usage. Many restaurants are built for
interior privacy, having limited view of the outside. Restaurant
personnel generally aren't concerned with what is taking place
outside (exception: if crime is a problem). Many restaurants
have adjacent streets suitable for parking.

18/24-HOUR RESTAURANT PARKING DISADVANTAGES

Isolated 18/24-hour restaurants that do little business and/or restaurants located in high crime areas may be unsuitable for parking at because of the excessive exposure/attention all cars receive. Certain restaurants seem to attract a large patronage of police officers.

18/24-HOUR RESTAURANT PARKING CONSIDERATIONS/ RECOMMENDATIONS Restaurants generally need to be located in a suitable combination area or have adjacent streets suitable for parking on if semi-stationary/stationary parking usage is to be successful over the long-term--fortunately, many are.

People aren't bothered by anyone they're not exposed to, thus parking away from points of high exposure (i.e. windows, entrance/exit, parking lot entrance/exit points, etc.) is desirable. Like during most semi-stationary and stationary parking situations, one shouldn't leave their car and risk exposure to restaurant personnel. Arriving during peak nighttime business periods is a low exposure time to arrive.

Restaurants attracting a large patronage of police should be avoided.

Pelican + SKS Cases Opened

- BUS STATION

PARKING CONDITIONS: Traveling (very good-fair), semi-stationary (good-poor), stationary (fair-poor)

Bus stations may be suitable for all three types of parking usage: parking when traveling, semi-stationary parking, and stationary parking. Because of dull atmosphere/surroundings, I seldom use bus stations to park at.

24-HOUR BUS STATION PARKING ADVANTAGES Depending on a bus station's size, location, and traffic flow, blending in unnoticed may be very easy. Adjacent city streets may be suitable for parking.

24-HOUR BUS STATION PARKING DISADVANTAGES Bus stations generally have somewhat dull atmospheres/surroundings. Depending on the size, location, and traffic flow, excessive noise and poor air quality may be present.

24-HOUR BUS STATION PARKING CONSIDERATIONS People aren't bothered by anyone they're not exposed to; therefore, it's best not to leave your car during semi-stationary and stationary parking situations. Surrounding adjacent roads may be suitable for parking on.

- 24-HOUR PUBLIC BOAT LAUNCH PARKING AREAS

PARKING CONDITIONS: Traveling (excellent–very good), semi-stationary (excellent-good), stationary (good-poor)

Public boat launch parking areas may be suitable for use in all three types of parking usage: (1) when traveling, (2) semi-stationary parking, and (3) stationary parking. I've mainly used them when traveling and for semi-stationary parking usage.

24-HOUR PUBLIC BOAT LAUNCH PARKING ADVANTAGES Twenty-four-hour public boat launch parking areas may be located in beautiful, quiet areas anywhere there is a useable body of water. They're often located in scenic areas that have restrooms, trash bins, drinking water, etc. Parking near a 24-hour boat ramp looks normal anytime. They're easily located on road maps. Depending on the location of a public boat ramp, it may be legal to carry a firearm while boating, thus firearm restrictions may be minimal while parking at public boat launch parking areas.

24-HOUR PUBLIC BOAT LAUNCH PARKING AREA PARKING DISADVANTAGES If located within a city's limits, city "no camping/living/sleeping on city property" ordinances may apply. Boat launches located underneath heavily traveled bridges may be noisy and have poor air quality. Boat launch areas are few in number and may be located far away from one's daily activities. Many public boat launches have parking duration limits and may charge a fee for parking.

24-HOUR PUBLIC BOAT LAUNCH PARKING AREA PARKING CONSIDERATIONS A public boat ramp located within a city's limits may have "no sleeping/camping bans," thus one should never admit to sleeping or living in a privatized car. Installing a trailer hitch will allow a car to blend in better during stationary parking situations. Protection of yourself and car while parked at public boat launch parking areas is only what you provide-- make sure it is enough.

- 24-HOUR HEALTH CLUBS

PARKING CONDITIONS: Traveling (excellent-poor), Semi-stationary (very good-poor), Stationary (good-poor).

All three types of parking usage may be possible: (1) parking when traveling, (2) semi-stationary parking, and (3) stationary parking. However, for successful long-term stationary parking, a 24-hour health club really needs to be located in a combination area or have adjacent city streets suitable for parking on.

24-HOUR HEALTH CLUB PARKING ADVANTAGES Health club buildings are usually built for interior privacy, quite often having minimal view of outside parking areas. Unless local area crime is a problem, there probably will be minimal surveillance/ monitoring of parking areas, especially if the health club is located in a combination area. City streets adjacent to 24-hour health clubs may be suitable for parking on.

24-HOUR HEALTH CLUB PARKING CONSIDERATIONS

A 24-hour health club needs to do lots of business, needs to be located in a suitable combination area, or needs to have an adjacent city street suitable to park on if stationary parking is to be successful over the long term. Like in any secret parking situation, try to park where your car will receive the least exposure and still blend in well. Unlike most secret parking situations in which I recommend not leaving one's parked car, joining a health club to exercise and shower at may work out OK if there are suitable parking locations to park at in which no one inside the club can easily see you enter/exit your car.

- 24-HOUR MANUFACTURING COMPANIES

PARKING CONDITIONS: Traveling (excellent-good), Semi-stationary (excellent-good), Stationary (very good-fair).

I've used manufacturing facility parking areas and their adjacent streets for all three types of parking: (1) parking when traveling, (2) semi-stationary parking, and (3) stationary parking.

24-HOUR MANUFACTURING COMPANY PARKING ADVANTAGES Twenty-four-hour manufacturing facility parking areas can be very quiet throughout an 8-hour shift. Many manufacturing facilities have minimal parking lot security/surveillance monitoring. There may be adjacent city streets suitable for parking on. Manufacturing facilities can generally be located on street maps or in phone books. Some manufacturing facilities I've parked at have been located in the most beautiful areas in or around cities.

Twenty-four-hour manufacturing companies may be one of the few parking locations in which stationary parking works out better than semi-stationary parking. The reason being is that anyone directly or indirectly monitoring the parking area(s) may notice a strange car that sporadically shows up for only one or two nights, whereas a car used in stationary parking applications would appear to be an employee's car.

24-HOUR MANUFACTURING COMPANY PARKING DISADVANTAGES Depending on the manufacturing facility's location along with what is being manufactured/produced, poor air quality and excessive noise may be present. Some manufacturing companies have surveillance/security monitoring of parking areas, making parking difficult (try adjacent streets). Parking around manufacturing companies that have secret/sensitive government contracts could easily cause an FBI file to be created on anyone whose secret parking situation is discovered.

24-HOUR MANUFACTURING COMPANY PARKING RECOMMENDATIONS Avoid parking at manufacturing facilities involved in secret government contracts, have high crime in the local area, have designated parking spaces or require parking stickers, have small parking areas, have excessively monitored parking areas, or that have fenced-in parking areas that display "no trespassing" signs. Parking on adjacent city streets may be very suitable.

For stationary parking situations, it probably will be beneficial to use optimal arrival/departure times. Parking in a location in which the car windshield and driver's side window has minimal exposure to the manufacturing facility windows, entrances, and security cameras will be beneficial.

High technology firms have been some of nicest manufacturing facilities I've parked at or near to, as many are located in beautiful, clean, prosperous areas.

- HOSPITALS

PARKING CONDITIONS: Traveling (excellent), Semi-stationary (excellent-fair), Stationary (good-fair)

I've used hospitals for all three types of parking usage: (1) parking while traveling, (2) semi-stationary parking, and (3) stationary parking.

HOSPITAL PARKING ADVANTAGES Hospitals are generally easy to park at and blend in unnoticed. Much of the area inside hospitals has little or no view of outside parking areas. Hospital parking areas are generally relatively large. Activity taking place outside hospitals is generally concentrated at specific areas (drop off points, emergency entrance, etc.) a good distance away from patient parking areas. Except when located in extremely congested areas or in areas high in crime, I've found hospital parking to be minimally monitored. Patient parking areas are generally used by different people who won't be back anytime soon after their business at the hospital is completed--having one's car not being exposed to the same people for very long periods allows it to blend in better. A large percentage of hospital workers are highly educated and are extremely productive--they're generally focused on their work inside the hospital and aren't concerned with what is going on outside in patient parking areas.

Being in business to heal the sick and injured, hospitals are usually fairly quiet, calm, tranquil, relaxing, restful locations to park at, as compared to the local area.

Some hospitals have adjacent city streets that are very suitable to park on during the night.

HOSPITAL PARKING DISADVANTAGES Hospitals generally aren't located in combination areas. Hospitals located in high-crime areas may be difficult to park at because of excessive parking area monitoring/surveillance. If located in extremely congested areas, hospital parking may cost money (possibly free to senior citizens).

HOSPITAL PARKING CONSIDERATIONS/RECOMMENDATIONS Parking in patient parking areas at locations least exposed to hospital personnel are generally good places to park. Locations out from a hospital building's corners, where anyone looking out hospital windows would have to look to a window's extreme side (right or left) to see one's parked car, can be excellent locations to park at because people generally look straight out windows, not looking to the side extremes. To limit close-up exposure of one's car, avoid parking near invisible pedestrian walking paths (GPE #2), employee parking areas, parking lot entrances/exits, building entrances/exits, and any other high exposure location. Using optimal arrival/departure times may be beneficial in semi-stationary/stationary parking situations. Adjacent city streets may be suitable for parking.

- CITY PARKS

PERSONAL/POSSIBLE USAGE: WHILE OPEN Most city parks are generally closed during the night; however, people who work at night may find city parks very suitable to park at during the day. Some city parks are located in "combination areas" that have adjacent city streets suitable for parking at night.

CITY PARK PARKING ADVANTAGES A city park may be a relaxing, conveniently located, somewhat quiet place to park in a congested city. Police patrols may help make them relatively safe places to park. Bathing and swimming facilities may be available. Some city parks located in residential neighborhoods have adjacent city streets somewhat suitable for parking on at night because of the combination area effect that the neighborhood houses and park provide. City parks are easily located on street maps.

CITY PARK PARKING DISADVANTAGES AND PARKING CONSIDERATIONS Many, if not most, city parks have laws banning camping or sleeping in the park, thus one should never admit to sleeping/living in one's privatized car--especially during a possible police encounter.

City parks generally have severe firearm restrictions/penalties; not disclosing one's firearm ownership to anyone will be beneficial (what doesn't exist isn't a problem).

Park police may investigate a car that appears to be unoccupied with no one nearby, and this is especially true during a park's opening and closing times or when parking in certain "suspect" areas of a park, such as stolen car drop/ditch points.

Parks that are visited mostly by young children generally aren't suitable for parking at/near.

- STATE AND NATIONAL PARKS

PARKING CONDITIONS: Traveling (excellent), Semi-stationary (excellent-good), Stationary (good-poor)

I've used state and national parks for all three types of parking

STATE AND NATIONAL PARK PARKING ADVANTAGES State and national parks can be beautiful, relaxing, non-polluted, sparsely populated locations to park at. Park rangers generally won't bother people who obey the park rules, aren't noisy, and don't litter. Visiting a state/national park can make for a fun and relaxing weekend or non-workday excursion. Drinking water, restroom facilities, and showering facilities may be available. State and National parks are easily located on road maps. Privately owned, vacant land around (and within) state and national parks may be suitable for parking, too. If the state/national park is large, there are probably non-designated campground areas that can be parked at for free during the night.

STATE AND NATIONAL PARKS PARKING DISADVANTAGES State and national parks may be located too far away from one's daily activities to be conveniently used during the night. Overnight parking may cost money; many parks require payment just to enter. There probably are time restrictions limiting how many days one can park.

STATE AND NATIONAL PARKS PARKING CONSIDERATIONS/ RECOMMENDATIONS Park rangers tend to think of their working location (park) as their own land; therefore, taking good care of the land/environment when visiting a state/ national park will be beneficial.

If planning to stay awhile, it will be best to acquire a park map and park rules, as knowing the park land boundaries and the park rules/regulations may allow one to figure out ways to circumvent any parking duration time restrictions. Unoccupied, privately-owned land that is adjacent to or within state/national park land may be suitable for parking.

Protection in a national/state park is mainly what you provide. Pepper spray is a somewhat effective weapon to use against dangerous wildlife (park rangers possibly sell it).

Some states offer annual park passes that can save one much money depending on how often used.

• PARKING GARAGES
PARKING CONDITIONS: Traveling (very good-fair), Semi-stationary (very good-poor), Stationary (fair-poor)

Parking garages may be suitable for use in satisfying all three types of parking usage: (1) parking while traveling, (2) semi-stationary parking, and (3) stationary parking. My usage has mainly been parking when traveling and for semi-stationary parking.

PARKING GARAGE PARKING ADVANTAGES Hotel, high-technology manufacturing facility, and hospital parking garages have been some of the most satisfying parking garages I've used. During hot/sunny weather, parking garages may offer plenty of shade and a cool breeze (upper levels). During cold weather, they can offer warmer temperatures by minimizing a car's exposure to cold wind, sleet, ice, snow, etc. Privately-owned parking garages probably aren't patrolled by police unless asked to do so by the owner. Parking in a parking garage can add privacy and comfort to a car living situation by making one feel less exposed.

PARKING GARAGE PARKING DISADVANTAGES Sporadic car noise and less than desirable air quality may be present at certain times. Some parking garages charge a fee. Many parking garages have intrusive surveillance/monitoring, making them more difficult to park at unnoticed. Any crime committed at a parking garage may draw unwanted attention to any unidentified privatized car, possibly causing one's living situation to be discovered.

PARKING GARAGE PARKING CONSIDERATIONS Parking garages located in low-crime, economically sound areas are generally some of the most suitable to use. In contrast, parking garages located in high-crime areas should be avoided because of excessive surveillance/monitoring. Many parking garages that have excessive parking area monitoring/surveillance often have non-monitored adjacent city streets suitable for parking. If parking at a parking garage that has surveillance cameras, arriving/departing during high activity times along with parking far away from cameras, and with the driver's door and windshield facing opposite surveillance cameras will be beneficial.

• COLLEGE/UNIVERSITY CAMPUSES **Not Attending College** (If Attending College, see Ch. 11.)
PARKING CONDITIONS: Traveling (excellent-good), Semi-stationary (good-poor), Stationary (poor)

Parking at a college one isn't attending, in my experience, has only been possible when traveling and for limited semi-stationary parking usage. Fortunately, there are many off-campus locations around colleges that are suitable to use for any parking duration.

COLLEGE CAMPUS PARKING ADVANTAGES The highly productive, low-crime, continuously changing environments (GPE #4) at most colleges (especially universities) make them easy to blend in unnoticed. The majority of people at colleges being in their early-mid twenties is beneficial, as students generally pay minimal attention to parking areas (exception:

close-up and easy-to-view parking areas). College campuses usually have many parking locations suitable for parking, some being in combination areas. College campuses are generally very safe, as compared to off-campus areas.

College libraries have a lot to offer and are comfortable to hang out in. Private study rooms are nice places to sleep at and/or charge rechargeable equipment, especially during extreme temperature weather.

COLLEGE CAMPUS PARKING DISADVANTAGES Small colleges that don't have campus student housing probably aren't suitable for parking at during night. Overnight parking on a college campus may require a campus parking sticker--any car not having one may be investigated and/or towed away. College campuses generally have severe firearm/weaponry restrictions (leave your weapons at your external storage location). Colleges tend to have parking areas that have minimal shade and are highly exposed.

COLLEGE CAMPUS PARKING CONSIDERATIONS/ RECOMMENDATIONS The larger a college is and the more on-campus student housing available, the easier it will be to park at.

If a campus parking sticker is required, one would be better off finding an off-campus parking location to use during the night. However, I've been successful parking without a parking sticker at large colleges during the night, usually in the middle of huge crowded student dormitory parking lots (car owner appears to be visiting someone at the dorm, or a student is borrowing someone's car).

Adjacent city streets may be suitable for parking.

College campuses generally have severe firearm restrictions, thus one should never admit to owning/transporting any type of firearm. Better yet, leaving firearms at an external storage location will be best when parking secretly at a college campus.

Read Chapter 11: "Attending College Living in a Privatized Car" for other helpful information pertaining to college campus parking.

• 24-HOUR SKI RESORTS
PARKING CONDITIONS: Traveling (excellent), Semi-stationary (excellent-very good), Stationary (very good-fair). I've used large ski resorts for all three types of parking usage.
24-HOUR SKI RESORT PARKING ADVANTAGES Many large ski resorts have free 24-hour parking very close to ski slopes in

which most any type of vehicle is welcome to park. There are usually plenty of swimming pools and whirlpools to enjoy. At small ski resorts there may be hotels/motels and condominiums nearby where one can secretly park. Ski equipment rental shops located at the ski slopes may have shower facilities.

24-HOUR SKI RESORT PARKING DISADVANTAGES Parking around motor homes that run gasoline generators during the night can be a bit noisy with poor air quality. Twenty-four-hour free parking is generally only available during winter months of ski slope operation.

SKI RESORT PARKING CONSIDERATIONS/ RECOMMENDATIONS To thoroughly enjoy living in a privatized car during freezing weather, a car will need to be insulated as described in Chapter 1. Some of the information discussed in Chapters 2 and 3 will also need to be implemented.

Because snow and ice increase the risk of car crashes/ accidents, choose parking locations and car positioning very carefully. Also, it is best to sleep with one's head in the least vulnerable car interior location in the event a car crashes into one's parked car.

• CHURCHES

PERSONAL/POSSIBLE USAGE: DAYTIME USE ONLY (exception: adjacent city streets or combination area parking).

Although generally not suitable for overnight parking, church parking areas may be convenient to use during daytime. While traveling, parking my privatized car at a church when desiring to nap or go on some excursion away from my car are a couple of my church parking area uses.

CHURCH PARKING ADVANTAGES Churches are located almost anywhere and are generally safe, relaxing places to park at during the day, but only if the church is occupied/open. Churches are private property, thus police won't be a problem unless called by church members/clergy. Some churches are located in combination areas, and some have adjacent streets suitable for parking.

CHURCH PARKING DISADVANTAGES AND PARKING CONSIDERATIONS/RECOMMENDATIONS

Small churches that aren't open during the day generally aren't suitable for parking at, as parking there may look like the car owner is involved in possible criminal activity. Churches that care for children during the day should be avoided.

In the event of a police encounter, having a Bible in one's car while parking at a church may allow one to say that they are parking there waiting to ask church clergy questions about Bible scriptures.

Churches located in combination areas or that have adjacent streets suitable for parking may possibly be suitable for nighttime parking.

- CITY STREETS

PARKING CONDITIONS: Traveling (excellent-fair), Semi-stationary (excellent-fair), Stationary (excellent-poor)

If parking conditions are optimal, city streets may be suitable for all three types of parking usage: (1) parking while traveling, (2) semi-stationary parking, and (3) stationary parking. I've included one of my best city street stationary parking examples at the end of this chapter.

CITY STREET PARKING ADVANTAGES If at an optimal location, city street parking can be quiet, fairly safe, and relaxing. One need not worry about any trespassing violation while parked on a city street. City streets offer unlimited parking locations to use anytime. City street parking locations are often located in excellent combination areas. Metered parking may be free during evening and night.

CITY STREET PARKING DISADVANTAGES It probably is illegal to sleep/camp/live in a privatized car parked on city property/ streets (taxi drivers and park sunbathers do so). Parking on a street increases the risk of a car crashing into one's privatized car. It also increases a parked car's exposure to moving cars and walking pedestrians, both of which increase the possibility of attempted car vandalism/theft.

CITY STREET PARKING CONSIDERATIONS/ RECOMMENDATIONS

While parked on a city street, sleep in a position and location inside your privatized car that is least likely to cause head and neck injury in the event that you're struck by another car.

Having a fake alarm that can be activated while inside your car may be useful in driving away anyone outside making physical contact with your car.

Because of "no sleeping/camping on city property laws that many cities have, it is important that your car be thoroughly privatized (Ch. 1) to prevent anyone from possibly seeing that your car is being lived in. Also, never admit to living/sleeping/ camping in your privatized car--especially to police.

City streets near police stations may be suitable for parking, as these locations have the advantage of extra security. However, the parking location should be out of sight of any police station, so as to prevent police from continuously noticing your privatized car.

SYNTHETIC WINDSHIELD SHADE

- APARTMENT COMMUNITIES

PARKING CONDITIONS: Traveling (excellent-good), Semi-stationary (very good-fair), Stationary (good-poor).

I've used apartment and condominium community parking areas and their adjacent streets for all three types of parking usage: (1) parking while traveling, (2) semi-stationary parking, and (3) stationary parking. Apartment communities that have excellent parking conditions are one of my top five favorite parking locations.

APARTMENT COMMUNITY PARKING ADVANTAGES

Apartment communities are readily available throughout most populated areas. They can be very pleasant, relaxing, quiet, and enjoyable places to park during the night. Large "privately laid out" communities can be extremely easy to park at. City streets adjacent to apartment communities may be extremely suitable for parking. Some apartment communities are located in combination areas, thus making them more suitable for stationary parking usage.

Apartment swimming pools and clothes-laundering facilities can be enjoyable to use while charging rechargeable equipment at an apartment community one doesn't use for nighttime parking (exception: when traveling).

APARTMENT COMMUNITY PARKING DISADVANTAGES AND PARKING CONSIDERATIONS

Some apartment communities are built with highly exposed parking areas. Completely fenced apartment communities and communities that have excessive parking area surveillance may not be suitable for parking.

One should avoid leaving a privatized car while secretly parking at any apartment community used for semi-stationary/stationary nighttime parking usage (OK when traveling). Also, one should swim, wash clothes, charge rechargeable equipment, etc. somewhere other than the apartment community where one secretly parks.

One should avoid parking at apartment communities that (1) have significant amounts of children playing (2) are located in high-crime areas, (3) are completely fenced and gated, (4) have only designated parking spaces, (5) have only highly exposed parking locations (GPR #4), and/or (6) have significant amounts of police as tenants.

There are several conditions that help make apartment communities easy to park at: (1) large parking areas with non-designated parking spaces, (2) large, privately laid out communities that have lots of trees and foliage, and that have many parking locations out of sight of main living area windows, (3) communities with adjacent city streets suitable for parking, (4) communities located in suitable combination areas, such as adjacent to a 24-hour businesses.

- AIRPORT TERMINAL PARKING AREAS

PARKING CONDITIONS: Traveling (excellent-good), Semi-stationary (very good-fair), Stationary (good-poor).

Depending on the airport's size, location, security, layout, etc., airport terminal area parking may be suitable for all three types of parking usage: (1) parking when traveling, (2) semi-stationary parking, and (3) stationary parking. I've minimally used airport terminals for parking, but I've used other more suitable airport parking locations for all three types of parking usage.

AIRPORT TERMINAL PARKING ADVANTAGES Airport terminal parking areas can be excellent emergency backup parking locations to use if ever needed. Parking at an airport terminal looks normal anytime. Airports are generally safe/secure places for parking. Many airports are fairly quiet at night. Large airports that cost money to park at generally have aircraft storage and maintenance businesses that may have free parking.

AIRPORT TERMINAL PARKING DISADVANTAGES Busy airports may have less than desirable air quality--possibly to the point of adversely affecting car body paint. Obviously, noise can be excessive, and this is especially true around large aircraft maintenance facilities that "run up and trim" jet aircraft engine. Airports are few in number and are likely to be located far away from one's daily activities. Terminal parking areas at large airports generally cost money--lots of money. Except for parking garages, airport parking areas are generally highly exposed.

Passengers can legally ship unloaded firearms (no ammo) on commercial aircraft if proper disclosure and shipping is arranged beforehand. Ammo can also be shipped in a separate lockable container.

AIRPORT TERMINAL PARKING (and AIRCRAFT STORAGE & MAINTENANCE FACILITY PARKING) CONSIDERATIONS/ RECOMMENDATIONS During a police encounter, a loaded firearm found I one's car while parked on federal airport property would probably result in felony arrest. An unloaded gun locked inside a suitable shipping container, and ammo locked in a separate suitable shipping container would possibly be OK if one discloses to police that he/she will be flying to such-in-such place tomorrow and will be shipping the gun and ammo on the plane (separate shipping containers required: locking metal boxes). Therefore, make sure a gun and ammo is locked in separate containers before responding to police knocking on your car door. Also, if police ask about a plane ticket, I would say that I purchase heavily discounted last-minute plane tickets 30 minutes before the flight leaves.

For successful parking, non-commercial aircraft storage areas need to be separated from the customer parking areas with a security fence--do not park around aircraft that are easily accessible.

Large 24-hour commercial aircraft maintenance facility businesses that have large employee parking areas and minimal parking area surveillance are probably the easiest aircraft maintenance facilities to park at and blend in unnoticed. If the parking area has surveillance cameras, park at a location that is far away from the camera but still around other cars, and park in a location and direction in which the surveillance camera has minimal view of the driver's door and car windshield.

To minimize noise when parking at noisy airports, one might want to use soft spongy earplugs, a thin sheet covering one's ears to prevent skin irritation, and earmuffs.

• AIRCRAFT STORAGE CUSTOMER PARKING AREAS
PARKING CONDITIONS: Traveling (very good-poor), Semi-stationary (good-poor), Stationary (fair-poor)

Aircraft storage businesses generally have customer parking areas that may be suitable to use for all three types of parking usage: (1) parking while traveling, (2) semi-stationary parking, and (3) stationary parking. I've mainly used aircraft storage business' customer parking areas when traveling and for limited semi-stationary parking.

AIRCRAFT STORAGE CUSTOMER PARKING AREA PARKING ADVANTAGES Airports are generally safe/secure places for parking--the reason being is that penalties for crimes committed on federal property are much more severe. Parking near personal/business aircraft storage areas during nighttime may be quiet and relaxing. Parking may be free.

AIRCRAFT STORAGE CUSTOMER PARKING AREA PARKING DISADVANTAGES Airports aren't readily available and are probably located farther away from where most people would want to park. Depending on the airport, nighttime parking can be sporadically irritatingly loud. Air quality may be less than desirable, possibly to the point of adversely affecting car body paint. Most airport parking areas are highly exposed, having minimal shade or protection from adverse weather (exception: parking garage).

Vehicle parking areas at aircraft storage businesses may be monitored by security personnel and/or surveillance equipment. A security guard could easily notice a privatized car's arrival/departure, car window condensation, any car body movement while parked, and any light or sound minimally emitted while parked.

Federal laws generally apply to all areas of an airport no matter if the business is privately-owned or government owned.

AIRCRAFT STORAGE CUSTOMER PARKING AREAS PARKING CONSIDERATIONS
See above: AIRPORT TERMINAL PARKING CONSIDERATIONS/ RECOMMENDATIONS

• AIRPORT 24-HOUR AIRCRAFT MAINTENANCE FACILITY EMPLOYEE PARKING AREAS
PARKING CONDITIONS: Traveling (excellent-good), Semi-stationary (very good-fair), Stationary (very good-poor). I've used aircraft maintenance facility employee parking areas for all three types of parking usage: (1) parking while traveling, (2) semi-stationary parking, and (3) stationary parking usage.
AIRCRAFT MAINTENANCE FACILITY PARKING ADVANTAGES:
See above: AIRPORT TERMINAL PARKING (and AIRCRAFT STORAGE & MAINTENANCE FACILITY PARKING CONSIDERATIONS/RECOMMENDATIONS)
AIRCRAFT MAINTENANCE FACILITY PARKING DISADVANTAGES
See above: AIRPORT TERMINAL PARKING DISADVANTAGES
AIRCRAFT MAINTENANCE FACILITY PARKING CONSIDERATIONS/RECOMMENDATIONS
See above: AIRPORT TERMINAL PARKING PARKING CONSIDERATIONS/RECOMMENDATIONS

• PRIVATELY OWNED PAY CAMPGROUNDS
PARKING CONDITIONS: EXCELLENT FOR AS LONG AS ONE WANTS TO PAY While living in cars, I've never had the need to pay to park anywhere. However, I have desired to visit privately-owned campgrounds located in extremely beautiful areas.
PRIVATELY OWNED PAY CAMPGROUND PARKING ADVANTAGES   Privately owned

campgrounds can be excellent emergency backup parking locations to use if ever needed. Police generally don't patrol privately-owned campgrounds unless the campground owner request it. Shower, restroom, swimming facilities, and drinking water may be available. Privately owned campgrounds are generally well taken care of. Privately owned campgrounds may be located in extremely beautiful locations with access to fishing, skiing, swimming, hiking, scuba diving, etc. Unless "firearm restriction" signs are posted, firearms inside one's car may be legal.

PRIVATELY OWNED CAMPGROUND PARKING DISADVANTAGES Who wants to pay to park anywhere? Some campground owners lock the campground car entrance/exit points at night to prevent any vehicle from leaving or checking in during the nightly lockdown. Some campgrounds have time limits on how many days a camper can stay. Privately owned campgrounds may not be included on street/road maps.

PRIVATELY OWNED CAMPGROUND PARKING CONSIDERATIONS While traveling, one may wish to purchase a campground directory for ease in locating privately-owned campgrounds.

• PRIVATELY OWNED VACANT LAND *WITHOUT LAND OWNER'S PERMISSION*

PARKING CONDITIONS: Traveling (excellent-poor), Semi-stationary (excellent-poor), Stationary (very good-poor). I've used vacant, privately-owned land for all three types of parking usage: (1) parking while traveling, (2) semi-stationary parking, and (3) stationary parking. For semi-stationary/stationary parking usage, the privately-owned, vacant land I've parked on usually has been fairly large in acreage, had no "no trespassing" signs, wasn't fenced (not always), had no owners checking on it, and had the type landscape/foliage that hid my car fairly well.

ADVANTAGES OF PARKING ON PRIVATELY OWNED, VACANT LAND Depending on the location, there may be much privately-owned, non-fenced, conveniently located vacant land on which to park. An unexposed, private, neighbor-less place to park at can be very peaceful and relaxing. Beautiful wildlife and vegetation can make this type parking extremely satisfying. Trees, foliage, and landscape may hide one's car extremely well.

Parking on privately-owned, vacant land that is adjacent to government/state/county land or other tracts of privately-owned vacant land may create a sort of combination area parking effect, in that anyone coming across your car won't know whose land you're parking on. Parking on privately-owned, vacant, fence-less land that is adjacent to national/state parks will probably allow one to escape any restrictions pertaining to the nearby park land, such as nighttime parking fees, maximum days one can park, etc.

City/local laws banning camping/sleeping on city property may not apply when parked on privately-owned vacant land located within a city's limits. Depending on the U.S. State, it's unlikely and maybe impossibly for one to be charged with trespassing on vacant, fence-less, non-improved, privately-owned land that has no "No Trespassing" signs posted.

DISADVANTAGES OF PARKING ON PRIVATELY OWNED, VACANT LAND   Many conditions make privately-owned, vacant land unsuitable for parking on: (1) land posted with "no trespassing" signs, (2) land is completely fenced, (3) land that has crops growing or livestock grazing on it, (4) land that doesn't hide one's car from nearby roads (may not be necessary), and (5) land that has had costly improvements done to it.

Vacant land in the city may have homeless people living on it, some of which may be violent.

In some U.S. States, landowners living in the countryside whose land is fenced and posted with "No Trespassing" signs may have the right to shoot trespassers without question during the night, and without question during the day if the trespasser is armed.

PRIVATELY   OWNED,   VACANT   LAND   PARKING CONSIDERATIONS To prevent possibly being ticketed (or shot) for trespassing, one will want to avoid parking on privately-owned, vacant land that is (1) posted with "no trespassing" signs, (2) has expensive property improvements, (3) is partially/fully fenced in, and/or (4) has crops growing or livestock grazing on it. For stationary parking situations, it's best if one's parking location is out of sight of people and adjacent roads.

Generally, the more traveled a road or highway is the more developed and inhabited the area will be.

When traveling on minimally-traveled highways, I love to exit onto a county road and park on isolated privately-owned or government owned vacant land.

• COUNTY ROADS
PARKING CONDITIONS: Traveling (excellent-good), semi-

stationary (excellent-good), stationary (very good-poor). I've used county roads and adjacent land for all three types of parking usage: (1) parking while traveling, (2) semi-stationary parking, and (3) stationary parking.

COUNTY ROAD PARKING ADVANTAGES Depending on the location, county roads can be extremely private places to park at. Vacant, government-owned land and/or vacant, privately-owned land adjacent to county roads might be extremely suitable for parking. Beautiful wildlife and vegetation, and pollution-free living may abound.

COUNTY ROAD PARKING DISADVANTAGES   Parking near county roads that have lots of livestock grazing or crops growing in adjacent pastures may be viewed as criminal intent by anyone seeing your car. Depending on the location, game wardens may frequently patrol county roads, mainly during the evening and night.

County roads that intersect minimally-traveled highways are generally the least developed and least populated. Parking off the road in a location where one's car can't easily be seen will be beneficial (what people don't know about doesn't bother them); however, 10 feet off the road may be considered trespassing, depending on the local law. Purchasing a county road map may be very beneficial in allowing one to know what county roads exist in the local area.

• UNDEVELOPED CITY-OWNED LAND

PARKING CONDITIONS: Traveling (good-poor), Semi-stationary (good-poor), Stationary (fair-poor)

UNDEVELOPED CITY-OWNED LAND PARKING ADVANTAGES: There may be plenty of it available for parking.

One would be surprised by the beauty of some secluded inner city undeveloped land.

Some of the undeveloped city-owned land I've parked on was never visited by police.

UNDEVELOPED   CITY-OWNED   LAND   PARKING DISADVANTAGES:

Possible laws that severely infringe on a person's second amendment gun rights.

Vacant inner-city land may be full of homeless people, some possibly being violent.

Bans against camping/sleeping on city property may apply.

Undeveloped city-owned land may be difficult to access by car.

UNDEVELOPED   CITY-OWNED   LAND   PARKING

CONSIDERATIONS/RECOMMENDATIONS:
There is usually quite a bit of vacant city land near train tracks.
I recommend never disclosing one's firearm/weaponry ownership to anyone.

• STATE/FEDERAL LAND
PARKING CONDITIONS: Traveling (excellent-good), Semi-stationary (excellent-fair), Stationary (good-poor)
STATE/FEDERAL LAND PARKING ADVANTAGES:
Depending on the location, there may be tons of it available for parking on.
It may be a very peaceful, beautiful, and relaxing location in which to park.
Hunting may be allowed.
STATE/FEDERAL LAND PARKING DISADVANTAGES:
It may be located much farther away from where one would like to park.

10.5 PARKING EXAMPLES DESCRIBED IN DETAIL

HOTEL PARKING EXAMPLE

While living/working at a popular resort/vacationing area, I was able to park Monday through Thursday nights for a period of several months at a nice hotel. The hotel was located on a main thoroughfare with other businesses, condos, and apartments; residential neighborhoods were nearby. The local economy was exceptionally good, area crime was low, people were well educated and highly productive, and the area had much activity taking place--all of which helped my car blend in unnoticed.

The two-story, 60-room hotel was square-shaped, and it had an open middle portion containing foliage and a pool. Parking areas were adjacent the sides and rear of the hotel building. A privacy fence surrounded all but the front of the hotel property. The hotel office/lobby was located in the front center section of the building, thus entering and exiting the parking areas through either of the two (and only) front side entrances allowed for minimal exposure to office personnel. The hotel parking areas weren't electronically monitored but only minimally monitored by hotel employees.

During my nightly stay, I would park next to the perimeter privacy fence, avoiding close-up exposure to hotel room doors and windows (GPR #4). To prevent housemaids from contacting the hotel office to see which room the owner of my car was supposedly staying at during any late morning, I usually left before 8:00 a.m. To minimize exposure to office personnel, I generally arrived during busy evening check-in periods or after sunset. To farther minimize exposure, I never exited my car to use the hotel's facilities (ice machine, swimming pool, restroom, etc.).

18-HOUR RESTAURANT AND APARTMENT BUILDING "COMBINATION AREA" CITY STREET PARKING EXAMPLE

While living in a crowded, fast-paced, highly productive area in the northwestern U.S., I found an apartment building located next to an 18-hour restaurant in which an adjacent road was extremely suitable for parking. On the north side of the apartment building and restaurant was a two-way, six-lane thoroughfare; a center median with foliage growing on it blocked the view of opposite traffic lanes. Adjacent the restaurant's and apartment building's south side was a minimally-traveled road that I used for parking during the night and sometimes during the day. Across this south-side, wide, minimally-traveled road was the beginning of a huge single-family homes residential neighborhood.

I parked on the minimally-traveled, south side road adjacent the property line that separated the 18-hour restaurant and apartment building. My car was positioned about the same distance from the restaurant building as it was to the apartment building (slightly closer to the restaurant), so as to maximize the element of many possibilities effect. This combination area parking allowed people seeing my car to not know whether I was a tenant/visitor/worker at the apartment building or whether I was a worker/customer at the restaurant. The people in the restaurant had minimal view of my car because of a fenced-in garbage dumping area that was located between my car and the restaurant.

The neighborhood houses across the street from my parking location were built facing roads that ran perpendicular to and intersected the minimally-traveled road I was parking on, thus the houses' main living area windows weren't facing in my direction. Also helping to minimize my car's exposure to the neighborhood houses was that the minimally-traveled road I parked on was quite wide, so I was a good distance from the nearest home.

The apartment building was built like a three-story box with an open atrium area in the middle in which all apartment doors and main windows faced. The only windows on the outer walls were small non-transparent bathroom windows. This type of building layout maximized the tenant's privacy and peacefulness. More importantly, it allowed me to park very close by and still be out of view of the apartment residences. Also beneficial was that the only time tenants ever saw my car was when they used the rear apartment building entrance/exit that was in view of my car, and this was seldom done since the apartment's main car-parking area was located alongside the well-traveled road on the opposite side (north side) of the building.

Because of the exceptional parking characteristics of this parking location, it could easily be used for stationary parking applications during both day and night for as long as desired. (MORE PARKING EXAMPLES ARE INCLUDED AT THE END OF CHAPTER 12)

10.6 EXAMPLES OF PARKING LOT CAR ABUSE

HOW OFTEN DO PEOPLE BUMP/SLAM THEIR CAR DOORS INTO ADJACENT CARS? During an extended period living in a privatized car traveling around the U.S., I spent many daylight hours parked at the parking lots of shopping malls, grocery stores, parks, college campuses, hospitals, etc. Hanging out inside my privatized car, no one knew that I was inside. During these times, I was surprised to find out how often people will carelessly let their car doors bump or slam into an adjacently parked car when entering/exiting their cars. Depending on the location in the parking lot along with the size of the parking spaces, I found that owners of adjacently parked cars would carelessly let their car doors bump into my car about 50 percent of the time. This also has held true during my surveillance work while working out of many different models of privatized cars. Fortunately, car alarms may activate if the car is hit hard enough by an adjacent car door, and this has reduced the previously mentioned 50 percent car abuse in half, depending on the area parked at.

FUNNY HAIR COMBING INCIDENT PARKED AT A GROCERY STORE Working surveillance while parked on a grocery store's parking lot during the day, I heard a soft tapping sound coming from the right side of my car. After carefully climbing to where I could get a better view of my car's right side mirror, I found that a mother outside was frenetically brushing her daughter's hair, banging the side of my car with each stroke of the brush.

ELDERLY COUPLE AT HOTEL On one occasion I had parked at a nice hotel for the evening and was deeply asleep when I was jolted awake. Waking up, I wasn't sure what had awakened me--that is until a car outside crashed into my car's rear bumper a second time. After quickly climbing to the front of my car and looking out at the driver's side mirror, I was able to see the third and final impact of the car outside as it backed into my car's rear bumper. When I saw that it was an elderly couple trying to maneuver their car into the adjacent vacant space, I fell down on the car floor laughing uncontrollably (like children, elderly people can brighten an otherwise dull environment). Fortunately, after the third impact, the elderly couple was able to successfully maneuver into the adjacent parking space without incident, so soon I was asleep again.

CHAPTER 11

ATTENDING COLLEGE LIVING SECRETLY INSIDE A PRIVATIZED CAR

11.1 CHAPTER INTRODUCTION

If there's one place best suited for living secretly in a privatized car, it's medium/large size college campuses, but only for those attending classes or working at the college. College environments, especially at universities, are generally fast-paced, highly-productive, low-crime, continuously changing environments--all of which make them easy to blend in with unnoticed.

Although I've had no trouble living secretly in a privatized car parking at any small college I've attended, generally, the larger and more productive the college is, the more satisfying one's secret living situation will be. Some reasons for this are: (1) It's usually easier to blend in unnoticed; (2) there are usually more on and off campus nighttime parking places available; (3) there are usually more options and available times to satisfy one's bathing and exercise needs; (4) there are usually more clothes laundering facilities available; (5) there are usually more options in satisfying nutritional needs; and (6) campus library operating hours are generally longer.

Depending on the college, a student living secretly inside a privatized car generally enjoys minimal expenses, extreme privacy, helpful campus police, highly productive people/ environment, safe on-campus living, fine athletic and swimming facilities, nice showering facilities, inexpensive quality health care, inexpensive medications (if applicable), inexpensive student health insurance, etc. Basically, one's needs can easily be met while attending college while living secretly in a privatized car.

Extreme organization and efficiency, minimal financial

burdens, and extreme privacy + inaccessibility make attending college living secretly in a privatized car a most productive way to live while furthering one's education.

DISTRACTIONS ARE MINIMIZED It's nice being able to be a part of everything and then be a part of nothing by simply disappearing into one's privatized car whenever desired. Because of extreme privacy and inaccessibility, distractions are kept to a minimum. Interpersonal relations problems with non-existent neighbors aren't possible. Loud noises at apartment communities, school dormitories, etc. won't be a part of one's car living situation either.

EXTREME ORGANIZATION AND EFFICIENCY PREVENTS WASTING ENERGY/RESOURCES One doesn't have to drive back and forth to a conventional type residence to satisfy any of his/her needs, as one's needs can be satisfied inside his/her privatized car or on the way to the next appointment. One is always organized, with everything important contained inside the privatized car, thus losing or forgetting things is very difficult.
EXTRA: Clear plastic, stick-on shelf covering makes an excellent book cover. Resealable freezer storage bags are excellent book storage containers.

LIVING/PARKING ENHANCEMENTS Getting the best parking place is easy, as one can arrive early and sleep or study inside his/her privatized car until class begins. If a parking location isn't working out for any reason, simply move to another location. Parking on campus, living secretly in a privatized car is generally much safer than living off campus; also, one's possessions are generally safer inside a privatized car that is always nearby on campus. Being able to immediately leave for a night or weekend excursion, without having to do much preparation or planning, is convenient to do anytime.
MINIMAL FINANCIAL BURDENS It's extremely beneficial not having to sign a 6-month apartment lease, possibly having to live at a community that is too loud or uncomfortable in some way. Paying rent and utilities for an apartment or dormitory would have been an unnecessary burden during my college years.

11.2 MEETING BATHING NEEDS: SUITABLE LOCATIONS FOR SHOWERING

During my college years, there were probably less than 20 days total in which unusual circumstances prevented me from using college campus showering facilities. Fortunately, using the two jugs of water or car privacy bathing options (Ch. 5) is possible if campus showering facilities are ever unavailable.

COLLEGE ATHLETIC FACILITY SHOWERS   College athletic showering facilities are one of the most hassle-free places to shower, that is, when they are open and available for student use. Waking up to a workout or swim session and then taking a hot shower at a college athletic facility can be an excellent way to start the day. College athletic showering facilities usually contain lockers that allow one the convenience of storing bathing supplies securely at the facility.

DORMITORY COMMUNAL SHOWERS   College dormitory communal showers can be excellent places to shower at. Paying a building use/lab fee as part of my tuition, I always considered my showering at dormitory communal showers as being fully paid for. However, one must remember that they are showering at someone else's residence somewhat invading the resident's privacy. Therefore, it is very important to be considerate of dormitory residents by being quiet and clean, and by using dormitory showering facilities during non-peak use periods.

DORMITORY SHOWERING SUITABILITY Things to consider in whether a dormitory is suitable for showering at are (1) how security conscious are the dormitory tenants, (2) how much traffic flows in and out of the dorm (how much of the flow is non-resident), (3) if there is more than one dormitory entrance/exit suitable to use (use the less exposed entrance/exit), (4) how much exposure one receives when arriving/leaving the dormitory (carry bathing items in a private bag/backpack), (5) the dormitory location not being in close view of one's nightly parking location, as this would cause too much exposure of one's secret living situation, (6) showering facilities that are large enough to meet the needs of the residents and oneself without being crowded (showering before/after peak showering use times is best), and (7) is the dormitory is monitored by staff?--if so, does the staff pay much attention to or disapprove of non-resident students possibly using dormitory communal showers.

POSSIBLE RESPONSES IF SOMEONE QUESTIONS WHY YOU'RE SHOWERING IN A DORMITORY If a dormitory resident questions why I'm showering at his/her dormitory, I might say that I'm getting my money's worth out of my tuition's "building use/lab fee." A more considerate response might be to say that it is more convenient to shower at the dormitory instead of driving all the way home (off campus). Saying that your off-campus residence's water heater is broken may be an even better response.

Surprisingly, I've only had three to four incidents of vocal objection from dormitory residents and one custodian during my years of using communal dormitory showers while attending college. Dormitory showering situations are similar to parking situations--if one place isn't working out satisfactorily, simply find another location (or change showering times).

COLLEGE BUILDING RESTROOM SHOWER FACILITIES College buildings sometimes have restrooms that contain showering facilities. For maximum privacy, use them during class time, not between classes.

PRIVATE HEALTH CLUB SHOWERING FACILITIES If the cost is reasonable, and if one's bathing and exercise needs can be better satisfied, belonging to a private health club may be worthwhile. Also, a private health club that is open 24-hours/day may be a suitable location to occasionally use for nighttime parking.

BATHING INSIDE A PRIVATIZED CAR USING THE "CAR PRIVACY" BATHING OPTION (SEE CH. 5) I've had to use the "car privacy" bathing option inside my privatized car less than a dozen times during the years I attended college. It is an excellent backup bathing option that one will want to be familiar with.

TWO JUGS OF WATER BATHING OPTION (CH. 5) The two jugs of water bathing option can be used just about anywhere one can drive to and then step just outside one's car and not be seen for about 45-90 seconds, such as behind a grocery store or on a vacant isolated road. However, unless it can be done at a location where one won't be seen, the two jugs of water bathing option shouldn't be used at or near the college one attends, as doing so would possibly bring too much exposure to one's secret living situation if ever seen by college students/faculty/employees.

11.3 MEETING NUTRITIONAL NEEDS_

As discussed in Chapter 6, I use a double cooler ice chest inside my car to store block ice and a 3-5 days supply of perishable/frozen food in. At an external storage location, I store and use a portable three-way freezer to store quantities of frozen food and to make block ice in. Block ice and a 3-5 day supply of pre-cooked frozen food can be retrieved whenever needing to replenish my double cooler ice chest.

Instead of using an expensive three-way freezer, an inexpensive household freezer could be used if a 120-volt AC wall outlet is available at one's external storage location, or if a light fixture is available in which a "light bulb plug adapter" could be screwed into, or if a 120-volt AC outlet can be temporarily wired to a light fixture's wiring. However, I've generally used a three-way freezer powered by propane because of its silent operation, portable LP power source, and its ability to operate in extreme cold or hot temperatures.
(SEE Ch. 6 for more information about meeting food storage, cooking, and eating needs.)

DRINKING WATER I generally purchase purified drinking water from water dispensing machines located around grocery stores and other businesses, or I purchase bottled water directly from a grocery store. Water can be additionally filtered through a small hiking water filter inside one's car, or through a larger gravity type filter at one's external storage location.
(See Ch. 6 for more information about drinking water sources, retrieval, and storage options.)

11.4 MEETING EXERCISE NEEDS

CAMPUS EXERCISE/ATHLETIC FACILITIES Depending on the college, a variety of options may be available to use in meeting one's exercise needs, such as weightlifting equipment, jogging track, exercise machines, swimming pool, aerobics classes, etc.

PRIVATE HEALTH CLUBS Joining an off-campus private health club may be a good solution in meeting one's exercise needs. Unlike college athletic facilities, off-campus private health clubs have the added benefit of no time usage constraints during normal business hours. Also, health clubs may be used for satisfying one's bathing needs, and they may be suitable to use for occasional nighttime parking if open 24-hours/day.

CITY PARKS/PLAYGROUNDS
EXERCISING AT AN EXTERNAL STORAGE LOCATION

• EXERCISING INSIDE A PRIVATIZED CAR
 Because of more suitable exercise options being available, I've never had to exercise inside my car while attending college. However, I have done so when traveling and when working for days at a time in a stationary car (all it takes is a bit of creativity).
 To create resistance in each of the following exercises, I've mainly substituted ankle weights for metal bars and weights, as ankle weights are comfortable to use and store inside a car. When living on my boat, I use water-filled barbells and ankle weights as a source of resistance when exercising.
PUSHUPS Lay ankle weights across your back to increase resistance. Place books under your hands to allow for greater chest muscle usage.
SIT-UPS Strap on ankle weights to help keep legs stationary when doing sit-ups.
DIPS (exercises triceps) Open car door and place one hand on roof and other hand on top of door while performing "dips." Placing a folded towel over the top of the opened car door will be more comfortable to your hand.
CURLS Hold ankle weights' securing straps in palm while doing curls one arm at a time.
FRONT LEG EXTENSIONS With ankle weights strapped around the ankle + lower calf muscle, extend leg straight out while sitting on a chair or like surface.
REAR LEG CONTRACTIONS (one leg at a time) While standing with ankle weights secured around the ankle and calf muscle of one leg, contract the leg, bringing ankle weights up toward one's buttocks while using the other leg for standing.
SQUATS (one leg at a time) While standing on one leg, raise and lower your body repeatedly.
CALF RAISES (one leg at a time) Standing on a slightly elevated surface, such as a step, using only one leg with the front of the foot contacting the edge of the elevated surface--raise and lower your body up and down, pivoting at the ankle.
PULL-UPS: (front-of-head/behind-the-head pull-ups) Find a

structure that has a horizontal bar suitable to use for doing pull-ups; strap on ankle weights to increase resistance. City parks/playgrounds usually have horizontal bar type structures; however, many buildings are abundant with suitable horizontal bar type structures, too. Finding a structure from which a chain and bar can be temporarily hung will also work.

BACK PULLS Leaning over and grasping a chair's seat with one hand and resting the forearm on the chair seat to support one's torso/chest in a parallel position to the ground, grasp ankle weights (straps) with other hand raising the weights up to one's side torso and then lower, repeatedly – keep elbow in toward one's torso while lifting.

SHOULDER SHRUGS Standing while holding suitable weight in both hands with arms positioned at one's side, raise and lower shoulders repeatedly.

NECK EXERCISES Lying on a suitable horizontal surface with neck and head positioned off the end of the surface, raise and lower head. Do so while lying on your back, sides, and stomach.

FOREARM CURLS While sitting on a chair or other suitable surface, rest the portion of your arm from wrist to elbow on your upper leg (right arm on right leg; left arm on left leg), with hands positioned forward of knees holding ankle weights' straps. Raise and lower ankle weights, flexing at the wrist. Do a "set" with palms facing up, and then do a "set" with palms facing down.

MILITARY PRESS Same movement as behind-the-head pull-ups, but doing so while standing and holding weight in each hand.

11.5 CAMPUS POLICE/SECURITY

College campus police are generally commissioned police officers that have the authority to enforce the law on and off campus. However, they generally are concerned with what takes place on campus and leave most off-campus work to the local police, and this can be an asset if one is ever required to move one's secret car living situation off campus (I never have). Campus police are generally very productive to deal with, as their job duties are mainly to enforce the law and campus policy, and to be helpful to students and campus faculty/employees (low stress type work).

ATTITUDE ABOUT A STUDENT POSSIBLY LIVING SECRETLY IN A PRIVATIZED CAR

If attending a medium to large size college, campus police probably won't recognize that a student may be sleeping in his/her privatized car at night parked on campus. However, if attending a small college, which is more easily monitored, campus police might suspect that a student may be sleeping in a privatized car at night parked on campus.

Although campus security has sometimes suspected that I was living in my privatized car, they have never bothered me. Even though it is against campus policy for a student to live in a privatized car parked on campus, campus police probably won't bother to investigate whether campus policy is being violated as long as one's secret car living situation isn't brought to their attention. Basically, if no one knows about one's secret living situation, there won't be any complaints made to campus police, thus there should be no problem.

To ensure success in living secretly in a privatized car parked on campus, three things must be maintained: (1) One's car must be thoroughly privatized so that anyone outside can't tell whether the car is occupied (see Ch. 1 Section: Car "Privatization"); (2) one shouldn't use any nighttime parking locations that are within view of the campus police station, as campus police thoroughly notice their immediate surroundings; and (3) one's car living situation must be kept secret from everyone except for those who absolutely need to know, such as the person whose local off campus residence address you give out as your own when absolutely necessary. Also, it is best to limit exposure to and dealings with campus police as much as is naturally possible.

11.6 SUCCESSFUL NIGHTTIME CAMPUS PARKING

CAR NEEDS TO BE THOROUGHLY PRIVATIZED As disclosed in Chapter 1, a car must be thoroughly privatized if it is going to be lived in secretly and comfortably. During nighttime parking with windshield shade in place, anyone outside shouldn't be able to see inside one's privatized car. Also, a privatized car should not emit any discernible interior light or sound that could possibly be noticed by anyone outside during nighttime.

During daytime parking with windshield shade in place, the window tint on front side windows should be dark enough to prevent anyone from seeing your silhouette just after entering the car. Placing static window tint over legally tinted side windows is an excellent way to temporarily gain extra window darkness while parked.

• SUITABLE NIGHTTIME CAMPUS PARKING LOCATIONS
Read Chapter 10 to gain a thorough understanding of the "conditions" that make up good parking places, as doing so will make the following information clearer.
"COMBINATION AREA" PARKING LOCATIONS Combination areas are parking locations in which anyone seeing your car can think of more than one good reason as to why it is parked there. Basically, there needs to be two or more activities taking place nearby in which the car owner could be involved in during the entire stay.

COMBINATION AREA PARKING EX. #1: LIBRARY LOCATED NEAR STUDENT DORMITORY If a campus library and student dormitory are located near to or adjacent one another, parking in between the library and dormitory can be an excellent nighttime parking location. In this situation, people seeing a privatized car won't know whether the car owner is working or studying in the library, or whether the car owner is living, visiting, or working at the dormitory. During the 6 hours the library is closed from 12:00 a.m.-6:00 a.m. (if applicable), students in the dormitory are probably asleep; a patrolling campus police officer would probably think that the car owner is a dormitory resident, or is a student visiting someone at the student dormitory, or that a student left his/her car parked there overnight for some valid reason.

COMBINATION AREA PARKING EX. #2: CAFETERIA LOCATED NEAR STUDENT DORMITORY Although not an excellent combination area parking location, I've successfully parked between a student dormitory and student cafeteria. The cafeteria's limited hours of operation made my parking a bit noticeable during the night, as it was a combination area location only during the day. Fortunately, dormitory-parking car stickers weren't required in this parking situation, as not having a dormitory parking sticker would have made my car in violation of campus policy had stickers been required. In this type parking situation it's important that one's car not be parked in the invisible pathway students use to travel back and forth between their dormitory and the student cafeteria (invisible pathway being the shortest distance between the two building entrances).

COLLEGE CAMPUS COMBINATION AREA PARKING EXAMPLE #3: ADJACENT DORMITORIES Parking between adjacent dormitories can be a suitable combination area to park at as long as dormitory resident car-parking stickers aren't required. It's best to park away from dormitory windows (Ch. 10: GPR #4) and main entrances so as to minimize exposure.

CAMPUS PARKING EXAMPLE #4: ADJACENT STREET TO CAMPUS HOUSING (DORMITORY, APARTMENTS, ETC.) Campus streets adjacent to student housing may be suitable for parking. The adjacent streets may have the benefit of not requiring a campus housing parking sticker (if applicable).

At a huge college I attended out west, there was a dormitory that had a minimally-traveled adjacent street in back that was very suitable for parking on during the night. The dormitory and road were built on a steep hill (sloping toward the road). The part of the road I parked on was cut into the hill, thus my parking location was physically much lower than the first floor of the dormitory and not in good view of dorm widows/entrances. There was a fence that ran along the dormitory property at this location to prevent anyone from falling onto the street below, thus my parking location was minimally visited by walking pedestrians.

At this college, dormitory area parking permit stickers were required on all cars parking in designated dormitory parking areas, but being parked on the adjacent street made my car exempt. This parking location also had the benefit of minimal car traffic at night. During sunrise and morning hours, the adjacent dormitory blocked the sun, leaving my car in the shade, which allowed me to sleep comfortably till late morning whenever desired. It was an exceptional parking location.

CAMPUS PARKING EXAMPLE #5: LARGE COLLEGE DORMITORY PARKING AREAS At large colleges that have huge crowded dormitory parking areas, it's easy to blend in well by parking far out in the parking lot away from dormitory's/apartment's/residences' main windows and parking area entrance/exits. However, one's car generally should not appear extremely isolated from other cars.

Depending on the parking lot, it probably will be best to park in locations where one's car isn't positioned in a straight out view of student dormitory main windows (exception: far out in huge dormitory parking lot is OK). The reason being is that when people look out windows, they tend to look straight out in front and not to the side extremes. Therefore, one will be better off parking at "off-center" locations, and this is true when parking around most any type of building.

SUITABLE OFF-CAMPUS PARKING LOCATIONS ARE DISCLOSED IN CHAPTER 10

WHAT TO SAY IF EVER ASKED WHERE YOU LIVE OR WHY YOUR CAR IS PARKED NIGHTLY ON CAMPUS

Having attended a number of colleges while living in privatized cars, there have been a few times when I've been asked where I live or why my car is always parked on campus at night. When someone wants to know where I live, I might respond by saying that I live off-campus in such and such direction, and then ignore any farther questioning. If someone wants to know why my car is parked on campus all night, I might say that I get a ride home with a friend and leave my car on campus to save money, or because it is safer left on campus.

UNSUITABLE CAMPUS PARKING LOCATIONS

Close up directly in front of dormitory/residence main living area windows. Very close to invisible pedestrian walking paths (example: shortest path between two buildings).
Child care areas. Where other cars aren't parked 24 hours per day (there are exceptions).

OFF-CAMPUS BACKUP PARKING LOCATIONS

I've never been prevented from parking on campus at any of the colleges I've attended (I came close once); however, since there is that possibility, having a few alternate off-campus places to park will make any campus parking situation much more carefree, productive, and enjoyable. Suitable backup parking locations might include a friend's residence, nearby rest area with no nighttime parking restrictions, 24-hour grocery store, 24-hour health club, city street adjacent to a 24-hour business, apartment community, hospital, etc. (See Ch. 10 for more off campus parking options).

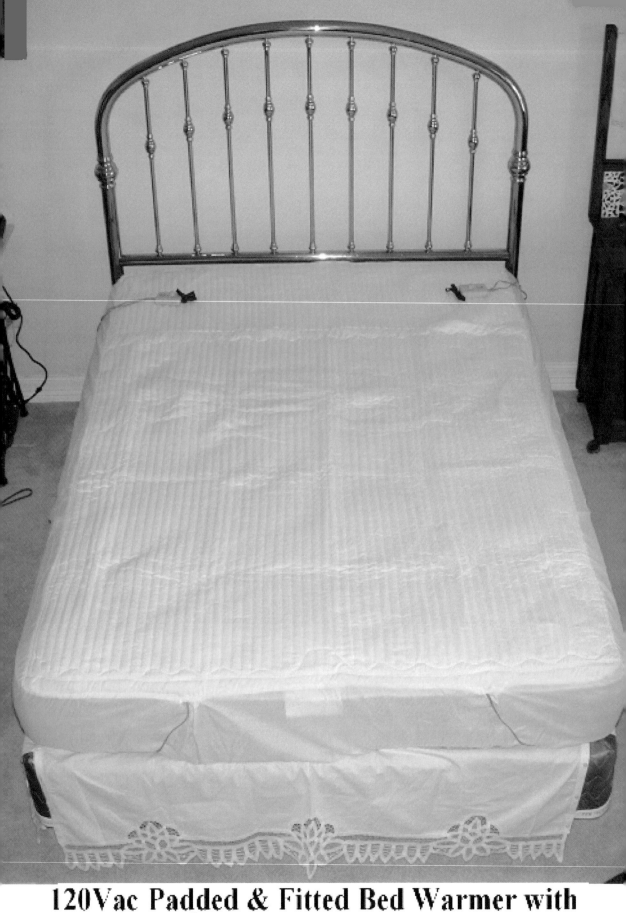

120Vac Padded & Fitted Bed Warmer with dual controls. www.LivingInCars.com

11.7 MEETING PHYSICAL RESIDENCE ADDRESS REQUIREMENT

WHAT TO USE AS YOUR LOCAL PHYSICAL RESIDENCE ADDRESS

I've always been able to park on campus living secretly in a privatized car while attending college; however, I've usually needed an off-campus address to list on college forms and for when opening business services (bank account, cell phone service, etc.). Fortunately, one has a number of options in having an off-campus residence address to list or give out when absolutely necessary.

Listing/disclosing a friend's local residence address only when absolutely necessary may work out well if the friend gives his/her permission for you to do so--but only if the friend can keep your secret living situation secret. A business rental mailbox address at one time could be listed to appear as a residence address, but as of April 26, 1999, this is no longer true (at least as far as being able to receive mail from the U.S.P.S).

My favorite option in having an off-campus address is to open a post office box, as a P.O. Box is relatively inexpensive and allows one to receive their mail somewhat privately without inconveniencing anyone. The disadvantages of a P.O. Box is that a P.O. Box address won't always be accepted as a valid residence address by those who absolutely need a physical residence address, such as when opening a bank account or renewing a driver's license, purchasing firearms, etc. However, when filling out college application/forms, disclosing a P.O. Box address was usually accepted during my years of college.

One now has to provide a physical residence address when applying for a P.O. Box, but it generally doesn't have to be a local physical address. (See Ch. 9 for more information about meeting one's physical residence address needs).

11.8 MEETING ELECTRICAL POWER NEEDS

MEETING AUXILIARY 12-VOLT POWER NEEDS WHILE ATTENDING COLLEGE

While attending college living secretly in a privatized car, depending upon one's electrical power needs, it may or may not be necessary to have an auxiliary 12-volt power source to use inside one's car. For instance, if using battery powered equipment and rechargeable equipment, one can charge batteries and rechargeable equipment at a campus library and possibly even in class (external storage location is another option). However, if one's electrical power needs require the use of a 12-volt auxiliary power supply inside one's car, using one or two totally sealed, deep-cycle, high-capacity 12-volt marine/RV batteries may be the best solution.

AUXILIARY BATTERY TYPE While attending college, I've mainly used totally sealed 12-volt marine/RV deep-cycle batteries when having an auxiliary 12-volt power source was necessary, such as when using cooling fans during September and May. I've chosen to use marine batteries because: (1) They're relatively inexpensive and readily available; (2) being available with totally sealed construction allows them to be safely used inside a car without having to store them in a sealable vented battery box; (3) they have negligible "cell memory" problems, thus they can be charged/discharged intermittently without adverse effects; and (4) they generally can be charged directly from a car's electrical system without the use of an auxiliary regulator/filter.

CHARGING TOTALLY SEALED, HIGH CAPACITY, 12-VOLT BATTERIES Three ways I've used to charge totally sealed marine 12-volt batteries while attending college are (1) using solar panels placed behind my car's windshield or below the opened sunroof, (2) using a 120-volt AC-powered battery charger at a friends' residence or at my external storage location, and (3) by charging them directly from my cars' electrical system while driving.

AUXILIARY 12-VOLT BATTERIES CONNECTED IN "PARALLEL" ALL NEED TO BE OF THE SAME TYPE, SAME CAPACITY, AND HAVE GOOD SIMILAR INTERNAL CONDITION

SEE CHAPTER 8 FOR DETAILED INFORMATION ABOUT MEETING ELECTRICAL POWER NEEDS

11.9 OTHER BENEFICIAL INFORMATION

COLLEGE LIBRARY USES & BENEFITS
College libraries can be excellent places to study, nap, and hang out at, especially during hot/cold weather extremes. Most have a vast selection of magazines, newspapers, periodicals, reference materials, books, etc. that can be used in completing school work and in keeping up with one's special interests. Many college libraries have a plethora of high technology equipment for students to use: computers; printing, copying, scanning, video, graphics, music equipment; Internet/e-mail and fax services, etc.

If located near college dormitories, parking in between a college library and student dormitory may be a suitable nighttime parking location.

College libraries are excellent places in which to charge rechargeable equipment/batteries. Placing all rechargeable equipment/batteries inside a carry bag, and plugging all equipment into a multiple plug adapter inside the bag, and then running a short extension cord out of the bag to a nearby wall outlet allows for charging in a less noticeable way.

COLLEGE STUDENT HEALTH CARE BENEFITS
Student health insurance plans are usually inexpensive and well worth the coverage provided.

The student health care facilities (clinic) at many colleges, especially at well-funded universities, are very impressive, possibly being staffed with nurses, a pharmacist, and doctor (on call). The health services provided for students are generally very inexpensive. If a college healthcare facility has its own pharmacy, prescription medications can probably be purchased very inexpensively.

SECURE COMMUNICATIONS (See Ch. 9)

CHAPTER 12

MAKING POLICE ENCOUNTERS SUCCESSFUL/PRODUCTIVE

12.1 CHAPTER INTRODUCTION

Living ten consecutive years in privatized cars, I've had less than a few dozen police encounters while parked. Most of these encounters occurred during the night while parking at high-risk locations. Some occurred when officers on routine patrol came upon my somewhat suspiciously parked car; a few have occurred because of concerned citizens reporting my suspiciously parked car to the police. Most of my police encounters could easily have been avoided had I chosen a less risky parking location, possibly being just a bit farther away. However, I have had several unexpected police encounters while parking at low risk parking locations where I thought an encounter wouldn't have occurred.

During a police encounter it is most important to know how to effectively deal with police, so as to prevent being ticketed and even arrested. Therefore, I've created this chapter to share information about how to successfully deal with an unexpected police encounter that occurs while living secretly in a privatized car.

POLICE OFFICERS: WHAT THEY'RE ALL ABOUT

Police officers are people just like you and I; most are good--a few are corrupt. The majority of police officers are professionals who uphold the law by protecting citizens and serving society; a very small percentage is corrupt, possibly being destructive and even dangerous to citizens/society.

My experience with police officers during police encounters that have occurred while living/working in privatized cars has been from very good to very poor. Stressed inner-city police officers have been some of the most degrading and abusive to deal with (not always), while dealing with officers in sparsely populated areas has generally been fairly productive (not always).

RECOMMEND LIMITING EXPOSURE TO POLICE AS MUCH AS POSSIBLE Depending on the type work an officer performs, the area/environment the officer works in, and the people/criminals an officer has to deal with, police work can be very abusive and stressful (obviously, police work is dangerous)--abuse, danger, and stress don't bring out the best in people. A police officer's mindset is to seek out criminals, thus almost anyone an officer comes in contact with is a possible suspect for some type of criminal activity. Power, having the tendency to corrupt along with the "temptations" that are a part of police work, most officers have to battle a variety of temptations daily. Because of the nature of police work and because of the almost unlimited power a corrupt police officer has in destroying people's lives--I recommend minimizing exposure to police as much as possible while living/working in a privatized car.

On a darker note, police today are called to enforce unconstitutional laws, whether created through illegal executive order, activist federal judges (charlatans), International banker puppet politicians (prostitutes), or otherwise, that make a joke out of the U.S. Constitution by decimating the individual freedoms outlined within, and that are quite destructive to society (the U.S.A. is a Constitutional Republic, not a command-and-control police state—www.freedomtofascism.com). Many police officers willingly enforce these unconstitutional laws, mainly out of ignorance, or for self-interest reasons.

12.2 WHAT EXACTLY TAKES PLACE DURING A TYPICAL NIGHTTIME POLICE ENCOUNTER

The purpose of a police encounter is to verify that a suspiciously parked car isn't stolen, that the possible occupant(s) inside isn't a wanted criminal, and that no criminal activity is taking place. Once police verify that everything is legal and that the car owner/occupant isn't breaking any laws or causing any problems, the officers (usually two) will either leave quickly to perform their duties elsewhere, or if parked where one shouldn't be parked, the officers will wait till one has left the area before leaving, too.

THE FOLLOWING IS WHAT TYPICALLY HAS TAKEN PLACE DURING MY NIGHTTIME POLICE ENCOUNTERS:

When police, usually two officers, stop to investigate my suspiciously parked car, they park directly behind my car, leaving their patrol car lights flashing. Before exiting their patrol car(s), the officer(s) runs a radio/computer check on my vehicle's license plate to make sure it's valid (not stolen), that they're installed on the correct make/model car, and to find out who the license plate is registered to and if that person has a criminal record.

As police Officer #1 approaches my car, he/she checks for current license plate sticker and current vehicle inspection sticker (if applicable), and also notices anything about my car that would make it illegal to drive (not a problem if car is parked). Officer #2 positions him/herself aft of my car acting as backup to Officer#1, possibly with gun drawn.

Since my car is completely privatized with windshield shade in place, Officer #1 knocks on the driver's side door to see if anyone possibly inside will answer. Upon waking I make sure that I'm suitably dressed before climbing to the front of my car, as I know I'll be required to get out of my car and provide my driver's license to the police outside (if it is the police). Climbing to the front of my privatized car I see flashes from the patrol car lights, thus I know that it is the police who are interrupting my sleep. After I slightly roll down the driver's door window, Officer #1 outside shines his/her flashlight into my eyes and asks me to exit my car and provide my driver's license. Because my car is parked, Officer #1 doesn't ask to see proof of car liability insurance.

Upon exiting my car and handing Officer #1 my driver's license, Officer #1 asks whether the physical residence address shown on my license is correct. The officer radios in information off my driver's license to farther check for possible arrest warrants, criminal record, and whether I'm presently under any type of investigation. Strangely, Officer #1 or #2 may ask whether I'm transporting any drugs or guns--obviously, my answer is "No."

If not already asked, Officer #1 will ask whether anyone else is inside my car. Without physically entering my car, the officer then will shine his/her flashlight into my car to verify that no one else is inside, and to see if there is any evidence of anything that would warrant a farther search of my car. If my privacy/

insulating partition (Ch. 1) is drawn, Officer #1 may ask me to slide it open so he/she can get a better view into my car. The officer may want me to verify ownership of any expensive equipment/possessions seen inside my car; fortunately, an owner's manual, sales receipt, or computer record is usually enough to satisfy the officer (recommend storing possessions in non-transparent storage boxes).

If Officer #1 sees anything suspicious when looking into my car, the officer may feel that he/she has the legal right to inspect my car by physically entering it and going through my stuff. Storing possessions in non-transparent storage boxes will help prevent this type of intrusion. While outside my car looking in, if Officer #1 doesn't see any type of possibly incriminating evidence, but still desires to search my car, the officer will ask for my permission to do so. When asked, I tell the officer that I honor the U.S. Constitution and would prefer not having my car searched. At this point the officer would have to get a search warrant to legally search my car; unfortunately, obtaining a search warrant is very easy to do in this age of circumventing the U.S. Constitution.

Two ways I've had police illegally search my car: (1) Once an officer just started doing so without my permission, without probably cause, and without a search warrant; and (2) Officer #1 has me go back to Officer #2 positioned aft of my car to answer questions. While answering Officer #2's questions with my back to my car, Officer #1 minimally enters my car to do an illegal search.

If everything has checked out OK up to this point, and if not already asked, the officers may ask what I'm doing parked there (see next section "Best Ways to Respond to Police Questioning").

After the officers have verified that nothing illegal is taking place and that I'm not causing any trouble, depending on the location where I'm parked, the officers will either quickly leave to continue their police work elsewhere, or they may ask me to "move along" and then wait till I have left the area before leaving, too.

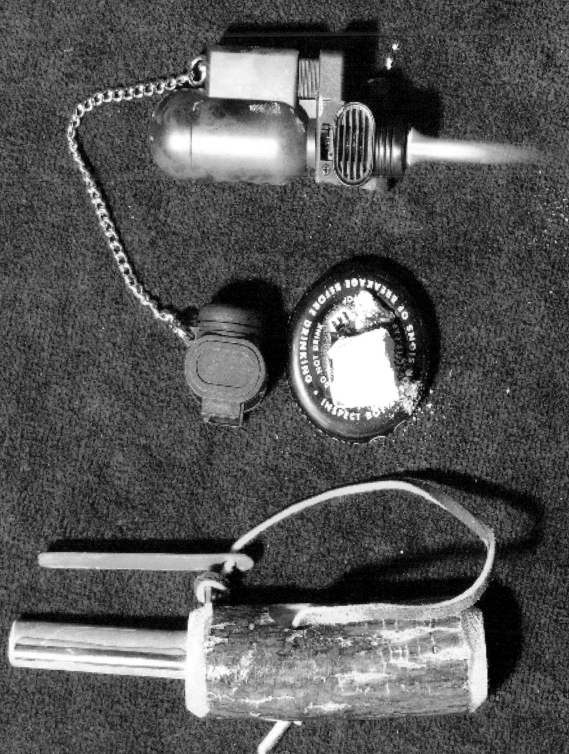

TORCH LIGHTER W/ 2500° F FLAME,
TRIOXANE FUEL ON CAP, FLINT ROD
AND STRIKER.

12.3 BEST WAYS OF RESPONDING TO POLICE QUESTIONS

GIVE MINIMAL INFORMATION Always remember that a police encounter is about investigating possible criminal activity. A police officer's job and mindset are about seeking out criminals, gaining evidence against them, and then ticketing or arresting them. Since an officer's mindset is geared toward analyzing all information for possible violations of the law, it's best to respond to an officer's questioning by disclosing only the minimal amount of information necessary to satisfy the situation. Providing more information than what is absolutely necessary will only conjure up negative, law-breaking type fantasies in some police officers' minds. Any additional, unnecessary information given might be recorded in writing or electronically by the officer, which, in a worst-case scenario, could cause problems at some time (example: insurance coverage voided because of one's recorded admission that a car is being lived in). One doesn't want to make an officer feel that his/her questions are intentionally being evaded; however, one doesn't want to provide an officer with more information than what is absolutely minimally necessary.

GIVE VAGUE RESPONSES WHEN POSSIBLE Most responses to an officer's questioning should be somewhat vague. For example, if an officer asks where I'm headed, instead of giving the exact location, I say that I'm traveling north or that I'm headed to the north side of town, etc.

ANSWER INCRIMINATING QUESTIONS WITH NON-INCRIMINATING RESPONSES--STAY CALM An officer asking incriminating questions generally wants you to respond with an incriminating answer, so as to gain evidence for any charge the officer brings against you. For instance, if an officer asks you why you think he/she pulled you over--never respond with an incriminating answer, such as "You probably pulled me over because I was speeding." Saying that you have no idea why you were pulled over because you're an "excellent driver who always obeys traffic law" would be an appropriate non-incriminating response. Answering incriminating questions with non-incriminating responses while not losing your composure will help prevent disclosing any type of possibly incriminating information.

KEEP THE OFFICER FEELING GOOD ABOUT THE ENCOUNTER When responding to an officer's questioning, do so amicably with decency and respect. Keeping the officer comfortable in his/her dealings with you will be extremely beneficial. EXTRA: Always have your hands where the officer can see them, especially at the beginning of a police encounter.

TWO THINGS TO NEVER ADMIT DURING A POLICE ENCOUNTER: (1) LIVING/CAMPING IN A CAR, (2) SLEEPING IN A CAR

Because there may be laws that make it illegal to sleep, camp, or live (even have sex) inside a privatized car while parked on city/government property and possibly anywhere within a city's limits, during a police encounter--NEVER ADMIT TO SLEEPING/LIVING/CAMPING IN YOUR CAR, even if it is obvious that you probably are. Another reason for this non-disclosure is that many car insurance policies have "exclusion of coverage clauses" pertaining to cars that are being lived in. Therefore, it would be best to not have any police documentation on record in which one admitted to living/camping/sleeping in a car.

Surprisingly, during nighttime encounters, police have seldom asked me if I was sleeping in my car, as it was obvious that I was most likely "resting" (NEVER ADMIT TO SLEEPING). If an officer questions why I'm parked "here," I view this as a possible incriminating question and therefore answer with a non-incriminating answer, such as: (1) "My car quit running, so I was waiting till morning arrived before looking for help," (2) "I was waiting for the sun to rise before traveling on," (3) "I had a dizzy spell, so I stopped to rest" (not sleep) (4) "I was traveling and had just pulled over momentarily to work on my computer, get a bite to eat, rest my eyes, listen to music, watch TV, read a book, write a letter, meditate, exercise, etc." Also, if police ask why the inside of my car is outfitted like it is being lived in, I might say that I enjoy camping at campgrounds and/or state/national parks during the weekend, or that I do wildlife photography out of my car.

USING IMAGE IN YOUR FAVOR During a police encounter, it may or may not be worth the energy and time required to correct an incorrect perception an officer has of you. Basically, if a somewhat distorted perception an officer has of you will allow the officer to finish his/her duties and quickly leave--not correcting the officer's incorrect perception may be beneficial. For instance, if an officer wants to feel sorry for me because he/she thinks I might be living in my car (don't admit to living/sleeping in a car) because of poor financial circumstances, and therefore desires to quickly finish the encounter without causing me any problems--I generally won't try to correct the officer's misperception. In fact, depending on the type car I'm driving, I might embellish the situation by initially placing a box of powdered milk in the front seat of my car for the officer to see when I open my car door at the beginning of the police encounter. In contrast, an unproductive false perception, such as an officer thinking that I'm a troublemaker who is hanging out and possibly involved in criminal activity, will certainly need to be corrected by convincing the officer(s) otherwise.

WHERE TO GO AFTER POLICE TELL YOU TO MOVE ALONG At the end of a police encounter, depending on where I'm parked, the officer(s) may or may not ask me to move along. If asked to move along, I'll drive to a risk-free parking location within the officer's patrol area, such as 24-hour boat launch parking, airport terminal parking (no longer recommended), highway rest area parking that has no overnight parking restrictions, private property where the owner has given me permission to park, etc. If risk-free parking isn't available within the officer's patrol area, I'll find a parking location outside the officer's patrol area to use for a couple weeks before parking within the officer's patrol area again. Fortunately, designated patrol areas generally aren't very large and tend to be economically mapped, both of which make an officer's patrol area fairly easy to determine.

12.4 HAVING SEX INSIDE A PRIVATIZED CAR--WHAT YOU NEED TO KNOW

The following material is not meant to promote behavior that would go against one's values, religious beliefs, good judgment, etc. (sex outside of marriage is lethal to millions every year). However, since humans are sexual beings, I feel that it is important to include the following material.

Car air conditioning and heating systems can make a privatized car's living area a very comfortable place to enjoy an intimate relationship. Having sex in a privatized car is fun, most pleasurable, possibly exciting, and can be done parked almost anywhere. However, there are some possible hazards to take precautions against before having sexual relations inside a privatized car.

PARKING LOCATIONS WITH ADVERSE SEX LAWS If parked on government property, such as federal, state, and city property, it probably is illegal to have sex in the privacy of a privatized car. Arrest, heavy fines, criminal record, and jail time are some of the possible penalties. Therefore, it is very important to be prepared for a possible police encounter while having sex inside a privatized car parked on any type of government property.

IMPLEMENTING PRECAUTIONARY MEASURES BEFOREHAND WILL BE VERY HELPFUL IF A POLICE ENCOUNTER OCCURS One's car should be completely privatized as outlined in Chapter 1. With windshield shade installed and privacy/insulating partition drawn (if applicable), no one outside should be able to see into the car, especially the car living area. During undressing, it's best to place and organize clothes so that one can re-dress quickly if needed. Keep lovemaking accessories, such as condoms, contraception, etc., organized and out of view from an officer looking through an opened car door during a possible police encounter. Realize that movement during lovemaking will cause car body movement that will be noticeable to anyone nearby outside. Make sure your mate understands these considerations/recommendations so that you'll both be prepared if a police encounter does occur.

EFFECTIVELY DEALING WITH POLICE WHO INTERRUPT YOUR LOVEMAKING If an officer knocks on your car door during your lovemaking, redress quickly and hide away all lovemaking evidence before answering the door. When talking to police--

NEVER ADMIT THAT YOU WERE HAVING SEX INSIDE YOUR CAR, as the possible penalties previously disclosed can be severe. If the police ask about any noticeable car body movement observed before knocking on the car door, give a plausible reason for the car body movement, such as you were exercising doing push-ups, sit-ups (redressing into workout type clothes may be a helpful guise), or that you were playing a joke on anyone outside, etc.

PREVENTING POSSIBLE CAR ENGINE PROBLEMS DURING IDLE OPERATION Since car engines aren't designed to run at idle rpm over long periods, there are a couple precautionary measures one may want to implement while having sex inside a parked privatized car with engine idling.

POSSIBLE EXCESSIVE ENGINE TEMPERATURES Depending on ambient temperatures, cooling system design/capacity, whether a car's air conditioner is operating, along with other factors, a parked car's idling engine may overheat (not likely, but possible). Therefore, it may be important to monitor the engine temperature gauge periodically.

If engine temperature becomes excessive, there are a few options in reducing engine temperature: (1) Opening the car hood will allow for extra cooling (may not be suitable depending where one is parked); (2) turning off the car engine will cool the engine, and (3) turning off a car's air conditioning and turning on the heater will also bring down engine temperature.

POSSIBLE INSUFFICIENT ENGINE OIL LUBRICATION DURING IDLE OPERATION Car engine cylinders are generally lubricated by a crankshaft's journals/throws splashing and slinging oil into the cylinders from beneath as the journals/throws rotate in and out of the oil pain oil. Slow engine rpm during idle operation may not be fast enough to create sufficient splashing/slinging of oil onto the cylinder walls, thus it may be providing insufficient cylinder wall lubrication. Fortunately, this condition can be easily remedied by slightly increasing the engine rpm (speed). Increasing an engine's idle speed by 200-300 rpm should provide thorough cylinder wall lubrication in most car engines. However, increasing engine idle speed causes more engine heat to be generated, thus engine temperature may need to be monitored more closely/often.

A car must be parked on level ground to have the engine crankshaft's journal/throws evenly rotate in and out of the oil pan oil. Being parked off-level on a hill/slope may prevent adequate cylinder wall lubrication of some of an engine's cylinders. Therefore, a car really needs to be parked on level ground while the engine is idling for substantial periods.

12.5 NIGHTTIME POLICE ENCOUNTERS DESCRIBED IN DETAIL

PRODUCTIVE POLICE ENCOUNTER: PARKING AT A SINGLE-FAMILY HOMES RESIDENTIAL NEIGHBORHOOD

I first really began living in cars when I took off and traveled around the U.S. for an extended vacation. It was during the first week of travel in which I learned that nighttime parking as a stranger in a single-family homes residential neighborhood would be very difficult.

Traveling down an interstate late at night feeling very tired, I exited the interstate to look for a place to park and sleep. Having less than a week of car living experience, I didn't know what type locations were suitable to use for overnight parking. Being extremely tired, I stopped and parked at the first place I thought might be suitable, which was a vacant lot located in a lower middle-class neighborhood consisting of single-family homes.

After about an hour of sleep, I was awakened by someone knocking on the driver's side door. Climbing to the front of my car I quickly realized it was the police, as the flashing colored patrol car lights were embarrassingly flashing throughout and waking up the neighborhood. One of the two officers (Officer #1) was at my driver's side car door; the other officer (Officer #2) was positioned about 20 feet behind my car acting as backup.

Upon rolling down the driver's door window, Officer #1 outside shined his flashlight into my face and asked me to exit my car and provide my driver's license. As I stepped out of my car, Officer #1 could see from looking in the opened car door that I was probably living in my car, and this seemed to have a sorrowful effect on him. After Officer #1 verified that nobody else was in my car, and seeing that I wasn't a threat, Officer #2 moved over by Officer #1 and helped him run the usual checks: valid driver's license, valid car registration, valid license plates, arrest warrant, criminal background check, etc.

From the officers' behavior, I could sense that they seemed to feel sorry for me, as they probably thought I was a homeless young man. Actually, I was a young man having fun traveling, skiing, scuba diving, meeting people, etc. However, since the officers' incorrect perception of my situation was beneficial to me during the encounter, I didn't try to correct it.

After finishing the regular police checks, the two officers were almost apologetic about waking me up; they asked me if I would like for them to contact the landowner to see if it would be OK for me to park there the rest of the night. Since I was a bit shaken, this being my first police encounter while living in a car, I chose instead to leave and find a more suitable place to park.

APARTMENT COMMUNITY UNPRODUCTIVE POLICE ENCOUNTER

COMMUNITY LAYOUT After starting a new job in a large city, I soon began looking for a quiet, comfortable place to park at that was within minimal driving distance from my work. The quietest place I found nearby (w/in 2 miles) was a very nice, fenced apartment community consisting of eight two-story apartment buildings, each building housing around eight to twelve apartments each. The apartment buildings were spaced about 250 feet apart. In front of the apartment community was a well-traveled four-lane road to which the community's single entrance/exit drive connected. Fortunately, the community was set back a good distance from the road and was surrounded by a wooden privacy fence, both of which helped to block out noise. To the left side of the community was the beginning of a large shopping strip/center. The rear of the community was adjacent to environmentally restricted, undeveloped land. Immediately to the right of the community was a patch of undeveloped land and then individual businesses.

The apartment community was very much designed with security in mind. Apartment main windows faced the parking areas, leaving no parking location unexposed. All tall trees having their branches cut off to 10 feet up and minimal foliage throughout the community allowed for all areas to be highly exposed. It was unlike any other medium size apartment community in the area because of its being almost entirely surrounded by a tall wooden privacy fence (exception: single car entrance/exit point) and because it only had one car entrance/exit point. "Residents and guests only" signs were posted on the privacy/security fence every 75 feet, leaving no doubt as to who was welcome. Paying a preliminary visit to the pool and mailbox area allowed me to find out that the tenants seemed to be a bit paranoid and that the tension in the community was fairly high (invisible condition).

Besides the security type design of the apartment community and the somewhat paranoid tenants, there was another problem that brought more risk into my possibly parking there. Because it was during warm summer weather and because the parking area was made of black top (high heat absorption and thermal radiation), I had to arrive at around 8:00-9:00 p.m. to avoid summertime sun and excessive black top heat, instead of a low-exposure 5:30 p.m. arrival time. This late arrival time made it very easy for many tenants to see my arrival through their apartments' main windows, very possibly noticing that no one ever exited my privatized car.

I knew that parking at the community during nighttime would be risky, but because of its quietness and close proximity to my work (w/in 2 miles), I decided to go ahead and do so Monday through Thursday nights. Sleeping in my privatized car at the apartment community was fairly quiet; however, because of all parking areas being highly exposed to apartment main windows, I felt that my car was always being watched--I could actually feel the tension in the community. Therefore, it was a blessing to be awakened by police a couple weeks into my parking there, which then forced me to find a much more private, cooler, and somewhat quieter apartment community located about twice as far away from my work.

THE ENCOUNTER During my second week of parking, at around 1:00 a.m. I was awakened by someone knocking on my car's driver's side door. Being suitably dressed, I went to the front of my car and rolled down the driver's side window to find an out-of-uniform officer (#1) with a gun in one hand and police badge and flashlight in the other.

Shining the flashlight in my face, Officer #1 told me to exit my car and provide him/her my driver's license. Another out-of-uniform officer (#2), with gun drawn, was positioned aft of my car acting as backup. Because there was no patrol car nearby, I quickly realized that the two relatively young out-of-uniform officers were residents at the apartment community. This was my first police encounter in a highly populated, economically sound area in which police officers initially had their guns drawn, and this seemed a bit extreme when considering the secure surroundings of where I was parked.

Officer #1 told me to move over to the fence in front of my car and then shined his flashlight into my privatized car verifying that no one else was inside. Officer #1 disclosed that word of my parking there nightly for over a week had come from a concerned tenant. About this time, two city police cars containing one officer each (#3 and #4) arrived and parked behind my car, leaving their flashing lights on, waking up the entire apartment community. Upon the arrival of officers #3 and #4, a third resident officer (#5) came from around the corner of the nearest apartment building where he had been acting as secondary backup watching the entire situation unfold. The older city officers #3 and #4 stayed back by their patrol cars letting the younger resident officers #1, #2, and #5 conduct their investigation of me.

One of the resident officers asked me what I was doing

there and where I worked, so I told him that I had been resting (NEVER ADMIT TO SLEEPING OR LIVING IN A CAR) and that I was employed about two miles away. Although all the officers were professional in their conduct, the three resident officers (#1, #2, #5) were very abusive in their communications with me---especially Officer #5, who acted like a first time hunter with "buck fever" in his attempts to find something criminal about me. From the incriminating type questions being asked, it was clear that the resident officers were looking for someone who had been stealing parts off apartment tenants' cars, or at least that's what they led me to believe.

Since I had employment nearby, had a "physical residence" within driving distance, and had no evidence of criminal activity inside my car, the officers' criminal law-breaking type fantasies about me began to disappointingly fade from their minds. Since I was parked on private property, I wasn't breaking any of the city's "no living/camping/sleeping on city property" bans (NEVER ADMIT TO SLEEPING/CAMPING/LIVING IN A CAR, EVEN WHEN IT'S OBVIOUS THAT YOU PROBABLY ARE). The officers didn't seem to be concerned with whether I might have been trespassing (I wasn't, as the community wasn't gated----although I obviously wasn't a welcome guest).

All three resident officers (#1, #2, #5) apparently had never been camping before, as they couldn't understand why I wasn't paying rent to live somewhere when I had a decent job. They just couldn't seem to grasp the idea of living in a privatized car increasing one's savings. It blew my mind when officer "Cranka" (#5) climbed into my car and very thoroughly started going through my stuff, performing an illegal search (no search warrant, no probable cause/evidence), as this was during a period in which the U.S. Constitution's Amendment #4, preventing unlawful search and seizure, wasn't being circumvented as it is today. To satisfy officer "Cranka's" curiosity, I had to produce receipts or equipment manuals for some of the expensive equipment stored in my car. When officer "Cranka" (#5) found my bank bag containing money, he feverishly yelled out to the other officers that I had money--again, grasping that I had a decent job with few bills didn't seem to register. It was a bit miraculous when officer "Cranka" (#5) didn't find the pistol I was somewhat illegally transporting, as it wasn't well hidden.

After officer "CRANKA" (#5) finished his illegal search, finding nothing illegal or suspicious inside my privatized car, and after the other usual checks about me and my car turned up nothing illegal--I could tell that the officer's criminal fantasies about me had painfully faded from their minds. Next, resident Officers#1 and #2 began making verbal threats as to how they would arrest me for vagrancy if I ever showed up there again. Although a vagrancy charge probably wouldn't have stuck because of my nearby employment and having a "physical residence" within daily driving distance--I would hate to have had to spend the time and money having to fight a false charge in court; therefore, I remained amicable and respectful in my dealing with the officers.

After finishing their verbal threats, the resident officer(s) told me to move along, so soon I was on my way, driving to what turned out to be a much more suitable location located outside of the city Officers' (#3 and #4) patrol area. This backup parking location was an apartment community located about twice as far from my employment. It turned out to be a much quieter, private, relaxing location in which to park because the apartment parking areas and a minimally-traveled adjacent city street could both be used for minimal-risk nighttime parking.

REMOTE WILDERNESS ROAD CLEARING TOOLS.

www.INFOWARS.com

NEGATIVE POLICE ENCOUNTER AT AN INNER-CITY PARK

I was living in a city working mainly at night. Because of convenience, I chose to park at one of the city's many parks during the day and sleep out of sight inside my privatized car. The park would open at 7:00 a.m., but no entrance fee would be charged until after the fee collector arrived at his/her park entrance position at around 8:00 a.m. Because it was a convenient time to arrive, I would enter the park for free before 8:00 a.m. and then park in a well-shaded area and sleep for several hours.

One morning after 9:00 a.m., I was awakened from a deep sleep by someone knocking on the driver's side car door. I slipped on my pants and shirt, opened the privacy/insulating partition (Ch. 1), and climbed to the front of my car. Outside was a single city police officer; her city patrol car with "Park Police" insignia displayed on its side was parked adjacent to the right side of my car. The officer told me to exit my car and provide my driver's license.

Much like officer "Cranka" (Officer #5) in the previous example, who was obsessed with trying to find criminal evidence against me, this officer wanted criminal evidence against me but also wanted to be abusive and hateful--the officer was obviously in pain and wanted to share that pain with others. After stepping outside my car and handing the officer my driver's license, the officer immediately began abusive drill sergeant type behavior, ordering me to stand in a certain location, button my shirt (in a park with sunbathers!), etc. Next, in a hateful, malicious manner I was hit with a barrage of incriminating questions: Did you enter the park illegally? Did you enter the park through the back exit so that you wouldn't have to pay? etc. The officer would barely pause long enough for me to answer her incriminating question before quickly asking another--the officer was in an "animal frenzy" enjoying her abusive interrogation of me.

The abusive, incriminating questioning kept going until I unintentionally satisfied the officer's desire for some type of incriminating evidence that could be used against me. Unfortunately, at that time I didn't know it was illegal to sleep out of sight in a privatized car while parked at this city park, so when the officer asked me what I had been doing in my car upon her arrival, I carelessly disclosed that I had been sleeping. Upon disclosing this incriminating information, the officer got a gleam in her eyes while her body somewhat relaxed--the officer's desire to inflict pain on me could now be farther met by ticketing me for sleeping in the park (motorhome occupants sleep in their motorhomes, sun bathers sleep on their towels—www.infowars.com). Gaining what the officer wanted, she quickly wrote me a ticket and left satisfied.

Unfortunately, it was because of this encounter that I learned to NEVER ADMIT TO LIVING/SLEEPING/CAMPING IN A CAR, even when it's obvious that you probably are. I also learned that police officers can be more into satisfying their own agendas (internal rage/anger in this instance) at the expense of the citizens they're supposed to serve and protect.

SOMEWHAT FUNNY POLICE ENCOUNTER AT A CITY AIRPORT

During my U.S. travels, I stopped at an airport and parked around the aircraft maintenance facilities located close to the aircraft taxiways so as to get a good view of planes taking off and landing. Shortly thereafter, I got bored and went to the rear living area of my car to read.

Engrossed in my book, I didn't notice the time go by and that dusk had almost arrived. Hearing someone knocking on my car door, I was surprised to find a few police officers at my car door, along with four police cars and one airport security vehicle parked, encircling my car; other officers were stationed aft of my car. It was obvious that airport security was too afraid to investigate my situation alone and had called in backup.

One of the officers just outside my car asked me to exit my car and provide my driver's license so that the usual checks could be made: valid driver's license, valid car registration/license plate, criminal record check, possible arrest warrants, etc. Seeing that I wasn't a threat, the other four officers joined our group. One officer asked me what I had been doing, so I told him that I was traveling and had stopped to watch the planes land and take off, and that after quickly becoming bored, I began reading a book in the back of my (privatized) car, not noticing the passage of time and that the sun had set. One of the officers jokingly asked me if I was a Braille reader. When I told him I had been reading by candlelight, the officer sweetly said to the other officers, "He's reading by candlelight--oh, isn't that sweet," thus bringing about much laughter from the other officers.

As the officers continued their joking, two of the officers shined their flashlights into my car's living area without entering it, and they briefly asked me about the expensive equipment I was carrying. Since all the usual checks turned up nothing illegal, the officers told me to "move along" and waited there while I quickly left.

PRODUCTIVE ENCOUNTER WHILE PARKED CLOSE TO AN ENTERTAINMENT RESORT AREA

During my U.S. travels, I visited a family entertainment/resort vacationing area. After completing my first day of entertainment, I began looking for a place to park for the evening. Many of the resort hotels were well suited for parking because all the activity taking place would make blending in extremely easy. However, I wanted to find a more peaceful, secluded parking location located away from all the resort activity.

Driving around within five miles of the entertainment park I came upon an undeveloped forest area in which the road I was driving on came to a dead end. At the end of the paved road was a dirt path that led off into the woods. Driving on this dirt path I stopped in a nice secluded area located about 250 feet away from the paved road.

I slept great the first night parked at this location until around 7:00 a.m. the next morning when I awoke to someone knocking on my car's driver's side door. After climbing to the front of my car and rolling down the driver's door side window, the officer outside casually asked me to exit my car and provide my driver's license, and also asked if anyone else was in my car.

I was surprised to find that the officer was alone without any backup. The patrol car was parked directly behind my car without any patrol lights flashing. After radioing in my driver's license information, the officer asked me what I was doing. I disclosed that I was traveling and had stopped off for a few days to visit the entertainment park nearby. The officer then asked me to move about 20 feet from my car, and then without physically entering my car, the officer looked through the opened front car door to see if anyone else was inside.

After the officer finished making the usual checks: criminal record, valid driver's license, possible arrest warrants, valid vehicle registration, current license plate on the correct make/model vehicle, etc., he asked me to show proof of ownership of the expensive equipment I was carrying. Fortunately, I had the equipment's sales receipts and/or owner's manuals stored inside my car.

After everything up to this point that the officer had checked came up "clear," the officer sympathized with me about wanting to stay here at night to avoid paying outrageous room rates at a resort hotels. The officer also said that it would be OK for me to park there during my visit and that he would tell the other police officers not to disturb me. After I thanked the officer, he quickly left.

COUNTY LINE, NIGHTTIME, LOW EXPOSURE PARKING SITUATION

In stationary parking situations, preventing excessive exposure of one's car to the same police officers will be beneficial.

At one time I was working at a company that designed, manufactured, and sold its own products. Because my place of employment was located near to a county line, I could park at a shopping center or grocery store located close by my work from the time I got off work till around 9:00 p.m., and then at around 9:00 p.m. I would drive a couple miles into the adjacent county and park at a suitable location for the rest of the night.

The advantage in this parking situation was that police in the county of my employment would see my car during the day, but during the night a different set of officers in an adjacent county would have no idea of where my car had been parked during the day. Basically, this situation limited my car's exposure to police (the less exposure, the better).

CHAPTER 13

CRITICAL CAR MAINTENANCE AND OTHER VALUABLE CAR CARE INFORMATION

13.1 CHAPTER INTRODUCTION

This chapter discusses critical car maintenance (CCM) and other useful car repair/maintenance information--all of which is meant to help a car owner maintain their car so that the need for costly repairs/overhauls is kept to a bare minimum for as long as they own/use their car.

** The maintenance/repair information contained in this chapter should only be considered as generalizations that may or may not be applicable to your model car. Always consult your car manufacturer's service/repair manual and follow the information contained therein when performing car maintenance/repairs. **

13.2 CRITICAL CAR MAINTENANCE: MAKING YOUR CAR LAST FOREVER

How well a car's critical maintenance is maintained directly determines how long a well-designed car will last before major repairs/overhauls are needed (hopefully never). It also somewhat determines the range of possible car problems that will arise and how often they occur.

To help maximize the simple, carefree lifestyle of living in a privatized car, a car's critical maintenance will need to be performed on or before the car manufacturer's recommended time/mileage interval using the highest quality automotive products available, along with using excellent service/repair procedure. Fortunately, critical car maintenance generally is easy to perform and takes very little time. Also, except for engine oil changes, most other critical car maintenance is seldom performed.

The eight mechanical/hydraulic assemblies or systems that require critical maintenance are (1) engine, (2) transmission or transaxle, (3) engine and transmission/transaxle cooling system, (4) front-end steering linkage joints and drive shaft u-joints (if applicable/serviceable), (5) differential (if applicable), (6) brake system, (7) power steering system (if applicable), and (8) fuel system.

• CCM #1: ENGINE CRITICAL MAINTENANCE
MAINTAIN CORRECT ENGINE OIL LEVEL Cylinder walls are generally lubricated by a crankshaft positioned just above the oil pan oil in which crankshaft journals/throws rotate in and out, splashing and slinging oil onto the engine cylinder walls. Lower than normal oil level will reduce splashing and slinging of oil onto cylinder walls. Obviously, extremely low oil level will quickly ruin an engine. Engine oil also plays a significant role in cooling certain internal engine parts, and lower than normal oil level provides less engine cooling. To prevent unnecessary engine wear and possible engine damage, engine oil level needs to be maintained at the full level mark shown on the engine oil dipstick.
ENGINE OIL, OIL FILTER, and AIR CLEANER REPLACEMENT Replacing the engine oil, oil filter, and the engine air cleaner on or before the car manufacturer's recommended time/mileage interval along with using high quality automotive products and proper maintenance procedure will help ensure that an engine gives maximum life. Frequent oil changes and using synthetic oil is the best way to get maximum life from a car engine.
ENGINE AIR CLEANER REPLACEMENT The engine air cleaner should be changed on or before the car manufacturer's recommended time/mileage interval. However, if driving in dusty/sandy/dirty/off-road conditions, changing the engine air cleaner more often may be necessary. If one can afford to replace the engine air cleaner with every oil and oil filter change, I highly recommend replacing the disposable engine air cleaner with every oil and oil filter change, as doing so will help maximize engine life (also simplifies car maintenance records.

With good results for a number of years I've been using reusable air cleaners that require cleaning and oiling at oil change intervals.

OIL FILTER REPLACEMENT Although some car manufacturers specify that the engine oil filter be changed at every other oil change, because of an oil filter's minimal expense and extremely important oil cleaning function, I highly recommend replacing the engine oil filter with every oil change (also simplifies car maintenance records).

It is an unnecessary inconvenience to have to remove an engine oil filter using an oil filter wrench because of it being screwed on too tight, especially since the oil filter seal can be damaged from over-tightening. Tightening engine oil filters slightly less than hand tight has always allowed me to remove them using only my hand(s).

OIL CHANGE Engine oil should be replaced on or before the car manufacturer's recommended time/mileage interval. Even if a car isn't driven much, it's important to change the oil at or before the recommended time/mileage interval (whichever occurs first). The reason being is that engine protecting characteristics of oil, mainly additives within the oil, naturally break down over time inside an engine that has corrosion, moisture, and other oil contaminants--no matter if a car is being driven much or not. Additionally, since certain conditions can cause engine oil to become dirty faster than normal, such as when driving in dusty/sandy/off-road conditions, I recommend changing the engine oil and oil filter before the manufacturer's time/mileage interval has been reached if engine oil turns dark brown in color beforehand (dirty black engine oil doesn't provide adequate engine lubrication/protection).

I highly recommend using a torque wrench to tighten the engine oil drain plug to its specified tightness, as doing so will prevent stripping the oil plug and/or hole threads, and will prevent breaking off the oil plug head (better yet, install and use an Engine Oil Drain Valve). The oil plug's specified tightness recommendation can be found in the car manufacturer's service/repair manual.

USE ENGINE OIL OF THE CORRECT VISCOSITY GRADE Oil viscosity grade describes an oil's resistance to flow. Engine oil that is too thick or too thin provides inadequate engine lubrication and causes unnecessary wear. Therefore, it is very important to use oil of the correct viscosity grade as specified by the car manufacturer (exception: excessively worn engine may need higher viscosity grade oil). A car owner's manual or car manufacturer's service/repair manual gives the manufacturer's recommended oil viscosity grade for the driving conditions (ambient temperature, car loading, etc.) in which the car is being driven.

CAN THE BRAND + TYPE OF ENGINE OIL USED EXTEND THE CAR MANUFACTURER'S RECOMMENDED TIME/MILEAGE INTERVAL? No, but it may shorten it.

Any type of engine oil, including synthetic motor oil, becomes dirty at the same rate for the conditions being driven in, thus the car manufacturer's recommended time/mileage oil change interval should never be exceeded, no matter what type and brand of engine oil is used.

Unfortunately, it is a fact that some cheap conventional oils have significant amounts of inferior oil molecules that burn up and create sludge deposits in an engine, which can cause the engine oil to become dirty/contaminated sooner than if a high quality engine oil were used. Therefore, if using an inexpensive engine oil, the oil may need to be replaced sooner than what the car manufacturer recommends.

Although no type or brand of engine oil can increase the car manufacturer's recommended time/mileage oil change interval, replacing the oil filter mid-way between oil changes MAY allow engine oil to stay cleaner a little longer (not much). Using a very high quality filter, or a tractor oil filter, MAY allow engine oil to stay cleaner a little longer. Also, replacing the engine air cleaner at every oil change will help keep engine oil cleaner a little longer.

RECYCLE USED ENGINE OIL Used engine oil can be recycled by draining it into a plastic gallon jug or other suitable container and then taken to an automotive service provider or your area's oil recycling center for recycling.

SYNTHETIC ENGINE OIL RECOMMENDATION Synthetic lubricants are far superior to conventional lubricants--I highly recommend using them. A new engine generally should be well "broken in" (5,000 miles) with non-synthetic oil before using synthetic oil.

HIGHER VISCOSITY INDEX Synthetic engine oil's higher viscosity index allows for less change in oil film thickness with changes in temperature, as compared to conventional oil, thus synthetic engine oil maintains engine lubrication and protection through a broader range of operating temperatures.*

LOWER POUR POINT How fast engine oil fully circulates through a cold engine upon starting determines how much engine wear occurs during starting, particularly the valve train area. Synthetic engine oil having a pour point of –80 degrees Fahrenheit, as compared to 0 degrees for most conventional oils, makes cold starting easier and allows synthetic oil to reach the critical valve train area much quicker.*

SLICKER Because of its being less viscous, slight horsepower and fuel economy gains along with slightly cooler operating temperatures will occur with the use of synthetic motor oil.*

MOLECULARLY PURE Unlike conventional engine oils that may contain significant amounts of inferior oil molecules that burn up creating sludge deposits, synthetic motor oil is molecularly pure.

OTHER ADVANTAGES: Synthetic lubricants have other advantages, such as high load carrying characteristics, minimum foaming, and maximum resistance to thermal degradation.

*(Hudecki, date unknown)

• CCM#2: TRANSMISSION CRITICAL MAINTENANCE

AUTOMATIC TRANSMISSION / TRANSAXLE CRITICAL MAINTENANCE

MAINTAIN PROPER TRANSMISSION FLUID LEVEL It's very important that automatic transmission fluid be maintained at the optimal level (don't overfill). Fortunately, unless there is a leakage problem, transmission fluid level generally remains constant.

TRANSMISSION FLUID AND FILTER CHANGE Changing a transmission's fluid and filter on or before the manufacturer's recommended time/mileage interval using the highest quality automotive products available will help ensure maximum transmission life. Replacing the transmission fluid and filter is fairly easy to do; however, it would be best to review the procedure in the car manufacturer's maintenance/repair manual beforehand. Use of a torque wrench to tighten hardware, such as pan bolts as specified in the car manufacturer's service/ repair manual, is critically important.

SYNTHETIC TRANSMISSION FLUID RECOMMENDATION Because of the superior wear reduction qualities of synthetic transmission fluid, I highly recommend its use. Just like a new car engine, a new transmission should be well "broken in" (+5,000 miles) with non-synthetic fluid before synthetic transmission fluid is used.

TRANSMISSION COOLER RECOMMENDATION

If you want to greatly extend the life of an automatic transmission, install a transmission fluid cooler in front of the engine radiator/ac condenser. Note: Some quality cars and many trucks come standard with an external transmission cooler.

RECYCLE TRANSMISSION FLUID Used transmission fluid should be taken to a transmission repair business or your area's engine oil recycling center for recycling.

CAR PURCHASE CONSIDERATION

The lower the engine RPM at highway speeds (to a point), the better. High engine RPM at highway speeds causes excessive engine wear, and high RPM can cause radiator cooling system leaks. My most fuel efficient 4-cyl car to date had excessive engine RPM at 70 mph, and the engine had an unusual bolt-on thermostat housing that would form a leak if I cruised 85 mph on a local turn pike. Fortunately, the 3-speed automatic transmission with torque converter lockup had two or three internal gears that could be changed for gears that gave it more speed, so that's what I had my transmission specialist do after I hit some highway road debris that put a hole in the transmission.

MANUAL TRANSMISSION CRITICAL MAINTENANCE

MAINTAIN PROPER OIL LEVEL It's very important that a manual transmission's oil be maintained at the optimal level. Fortunately, unless there is a leakage problem, manual transmissions generally don't require additional gear oil between oil changes.

TRANSMISSION OIL CHANGE Changing a manual transmission's oil at or before the car manufacturer's recommended time/mileage interval using the highest quality gear oil available will help ensure maximum transmission life. Replacing a manual transmission's oil is fairly easy to do; however, reviewing the procedure in the car manufacturer's service/repair manual is highly recommended. Use of a torque wrench to tighten drain/fill plug(s) as outlined in a car's maintenance/repair manual will be very beneficial.

SYNTHETIC GEAR OIL RECOMMENDATION Because of the superior wear reduction qualities of synthetic gear oil, I highly recommend its use if approved by the car manufacturer.

RECYCLING USED MANUAL TRANSMISSION GEAR OIL Used transmission gear oil can be taken to most any automotive service business or your area's oil recycling center for recycling.

• CCM #3: ENGINE/TRANSMISSION COOLING SYSTEM CRITICAL CAR MAINTENANCE

MAINTAIN OPTIMUM COOLANT LEVEL Checking for proper

coolant level by glancing at the coolant level in the radiator overflow container or cooling system surge tank should be done anytime the car hood is opened. If overflow container coolant level is low, it should be filled to the proper level and then rechecked after driving. If for some reason the coolant needs to be added directly to the radiator, such as if the coolant level were to become dangerously low, the coolant should be added to the radiator or system surge tank only after the car engine has been inoperable for at least 1 hour or more. NEVER POUR COOLANT INTO THE RADIATOR WHILE THE ENGINE IS HOT, as adding coolant to the radiator of a hot engine can crack the engine head(s) (usually near the exhaust valve seat), and/or cause hot radiator coolant to regurgitate back out the radiator, possibly causing injury.

Automatic transmission fluid cooling lines sometimes run through the top portion of the car radiator. Therefore, unless you want to burn up your car's automatic transmission, the radiator needs to always remain full of coolant--<u>this is very serious preventative maintenance</u>!

REPLACE ANTI-FREEZE ONCE EVERY 1-2 YEARS During normal operation, dirt and moisture enter a car's cooling system causing anti-freeze to lose some of its anti-corrosion and anti-freeze protection qualities over time. Not replacing anti-freeze every 1-2 years as recommended by the car manufacturer can eventually result in clogging of a radiator and subsequent engine overheating. An overheating cooling system causes excessive wear to the engine and automatic transmission/transaxle; extreme overheating can cause costly damage to both the engine and automatic transmission. Therefore, to prevent cooling system problems, one should always replace cooling system anti-freeze every 1-2 years as recommended by their car's manufacturer. Reviewing the procedure in your car's maintenance/repair manual beforehand will be very beneficial.

Besides clogging the radiator, not replacing the radiator coolant will eventually cause the radiator to rust and form leaks.

Like the car starting battery, only DISTILLED WATER should be added to the coolant.

RECYCLE USED ANTI-FREEZE Used anti-freeze should be taken to an automotive service/repair business or radiator repair business for recycling.

ADDITIVE CAUTION Unless the car manufacturer recommends otherwise, I recommend not adding any type of additives to the radiator coolant. A leaking radiator needs to be professionally repaired--adding a coolant additive that claims to stop radiator leaks will probably clog the radiator.

• CCM #4: STEERING LINKAGE JOINT AND DRIVE SHAFT U-JOINT CRITICAL MAINTENANCE

STEERING LINKAGE JOINT LUBRICATION A typical front-end steering system is made up of steering linkages that are interconnected with pivoting joints/bushings, such as ball-joints, tie-rod ends, etc., and these steering linkage joints generally require periodic lubrication using a grease gun. Greasing steering linkage joints at the car manufacturer's recommended time/mileage interval using the highest quality grease available will help ensure maximum joint life. Reviewing the car manufacturer's maintenance/repair manual will help ensure that no steering joint is missed, the correct procedure is adhered to (procedures do differ, such as not overfilling sealed joints), the optimal type grease is used, and that servicing is done on schedule.

IDENTIFY WORN-OUT STEERING LINKAGE JOINTS During wheel alignment service, the alignment specialist will identify any excessively worn steering linkage joint that need replacing, as the car alignment probably won't hold until the excessively worn joint is replaced. A car's service/repair manual also gives instruction about how to check the condition of steering linkage joints.

WHAT TO CHECK WHILE GREASING STEERING LINKAGE JOINTS When greasing steering linkage joints, check the joints' rubber grease cup/seal for any type of rupture. If a steering linkage joint's rubber grease cup/seal is ruptured, one can possibly (1) replace the rubber grease cup/seal with a new one, (2) replace the entire joint and rubber grease cup/seal assembly, or (3) grease the joint more frequently until the ruptured rubber grease cup or entire joint assembly can be replaced.

Front wheel drive vehicles generally have a protective rubber boot covering where the two front drive axles connect to the front wheels and transaxle (four boots total). These joints are generally referred to as Constant Velocity (C/V) joints. When greasing a front wheel drive car's steering linkage joints, the condition of the four C/V joint protective rubber boots should also be checked. If a C/V joint's protective rubber boot is ruptured, torn, cracked in any way, it should be replaced immediately to prevent water and debris from entering and ruining C/V joint's bearing assemblies.

When greasing front-end steering linkage joints on cars equipped with power steering, it's also a convenient time to check the rubber boot covering seals on power steering hydraulic actuators. Although not as critical as the rubber boot covering seals on power steering hydraulic actuators, while greasing front-end steering linkages, it's also a good time to check each wheel strut's rubber protective boot cover (if applicable) to make sure that they are in place and in good condition.

DRIVE-SHAFT U-JOINT LUBRICATION On some cars, a drive-shaft is used to mechanically connect the transmission to a rear differential drive axle; on some cars a drive-shaft is used to mechanically connect a car engine to the transaxle. Some vehicles have drive-shaft u-joints with each u-joint containing a grease fitting which allows them to be greased with a grease gun, and some have sealed u-joints that can't be serviced. It's most convenient to lubricate drive-shaft u-joints during each servicing/lubrication of the front-end steering linkage joints, as both are generally done using a grease gun and the same type grease. Both the u-joints and steering linkage joints are probably best serviced at the same mileage interval (helps keep maintenance records clear).

SYNTHETIC GREASE RECOMMENDATION If approved by the car manufacturer, I highly recommend using synthetic grease when greasing steering linkage joints and drive-shaft u-joints (if applicable/serviceable), as synthetic lubricants are superior to conventional lubricants.

• CCM #5: DIFFERENTIAL DRIVE AXLE CRITICAL MAINTENANCE

Unlike most front wheel drive (FWD) cars that combine the drive axle and transmission into one assembly calling it a transaxle, rear wheel drive (RWD) and many 4-wheel drive vehicles have their "driven" wheels connected to a differential drive axle that is separate from the transmission, but mechanically connected to the transmission via a drive-shaft. Inside the center of the drive axle where the drive-shaft connects is an assembly of gears (and clutches) that is referred to as the differential. The differential gearing redirects the rotating forces of the drive shaft 90 degrees to rotate the two axle shafts and connected drive wheels. Lubrication of the drive axle's differential gearing is done by gear oil sealed within the drive axle housing.

The differential drive axle assembly is generally considered to be a car's most rugged mechanical assembly. However, if not properly lubricated as recommended in the car manufacturer's service/repair manual, it will wear out prematurely and require costly rebuilding or replacement.

CHANGING DIFFERENTIAL DRIVE AXLE GEAR OIL Like any oil (mainly oil additives), differential gear oil's protecting qualities break down over time when subjected to moisture/condensation and other contaminants, thus differential gear oil should be replaced at the car manufacturer's recommended mileage/time interval. Changing a drive axle's gear oil at the car manufacturer's recommended mileage interval, using the highest quality automotive gear oil, and following the car manufacturer's servicing instructions (proper torque values, correct type of gear oil, etc.) will help ensure maximum life and performance from a car's differential drive axle assembly.

Changing the differential gear oil is generally easy to do and is probably the least seldom performed critical car maintenance, so there is absolutely no reason not to use the best automotive gear oil available. This maintenance should be performed in a clean, windless area to prevent contaminants from being blown into the open differential drive axle housing. Cleaning the housing beforehand is recommended. Reviewing a car manufacturer's service/repair manual should always be done beforehand, as following recommended procedure and torque value recommendations will be extremely beneficial.

SYNTHETIC GEAR OIL RECOMMENDATION I recommend using synthetic gear oil because of its superior lubricating qualities. However, in this particular application it is important that one positively identify what type of differential their car has (i.e., limited-slip, all-wheel, posi-trak, etc.), and then verify that synthetic gear oil is recommended/approved by the car's manufacturer before using it. In certain type differentials a friction modifier may need to be added to synthetic gear oil to make it compatible, or at least make it run quietly.

Handheld Sonar Ranges 2 to 250 Feet.
Waterproof to 150 Feet. Vexilar.com

- CCM #6: BRAKE SYSTEM CRITICAL MAINTENANCE
MAINTAIN CORRECT BRAKE RESERVOIR FLUID LEVEL
Maintaining correct brake reservoir fluid level is very important, as low brake fluid level can cause unsafe brake operation and possibly ruin brake system rubber seals and more. Fortunately, brake fluid level should remain constant unless there is a leak in the brake system (note: fluid level will very slightly decrease as brake pad thickness decreases).
PERIODICALLY CHECK BRAKE PAD THICKNESS--REPLACE BRAKE PADS WHEN NECESSARY
Brake pad thickness should be checked periodically and replaced when necessary as outlined in the car manufacturer's service/repair manual. Anytime a tire is removed is a good time to check brake pad thickness. The brake pad that rides against the brake caliper piston generally wears fastest.
MONITOR DISC ROTORS FOR FLATNESS: HAVE DISCS "TURNED" (RESURFACED) IF EXCESSIVELY WARPED A warped disc rotor will show up as a non-smooth (pulsating) stopping action each time the brakes are applied. Be aware that other problems can cause a non-smooth stopping action, such as a cheap out-of-round tire, tire tread separation, bent wheel, or severely worn front-end linkage joints/bushings.
Fixing a warped disc rotor requires making the rotor flat again, which is done by resurfacing the disc. This resurfacing is actually a grinding away of a thin layer of surface metal and is often referred to as "turning a disc;" it is performed by an automotive machinist using a disc resurfacing/grinding machine. Unfortunately, to prevent a disc from quickly warping again, disc brake caliper piston rubber seals (seal plus dust boot) may need replacing along with flushing out old brake fluid from the brake system.
CAUSES OF A WARPED DISC ROTOR Warping of a disc brake rotor is generally caused by excessive heat. Excessive heat can be caused by a period of excessive brake use, especially when a car is heavily loaded braking down a long steep hill. However, more often it is probably caused by moisture contaminated brake fluid adversely affecting the disc caliper piston seal (expanding it), which causes slight sticking of the caliper piston. A slightly sticking brake caliper piston prevents the brake pads from releasing fully/normally after the brake pedal is released, and this can cause excessive heat build up and subsequent warping of the disc brake rotor.
Unfortunately, a "sticky" brake caliper piston is usually unnoticeable during the beginning stages of sticking, but is

still causing excessive heat build up and warping of the disc rotor. Eliminating the "sticking" action may call for replacing the disc caliper piston seal(s) and flushing the brake system of its old moisture contaminated brake fluid, replacing it with new brake fluid.

RECOMMEND REPLACING BRAKE FLUID EVERY 2-4 YEARS OR EACH TIME EXTENSIVE BRAKE WORK IS PERFORMED (whichever comes first) To keep the rubber seals/components of a brake system in good condition, and to purge a brake system of moisture and other contaminants that build up in a car's brake fluid over time, I recommend replacing a car's brake fluid every 2-4 years. Bleeding each brake calipers bleed nut while intermittently adding new fluid to the brake reservoir is how I purge out old brake fluid. (Reviewing the car manufacturer's service/repair manual for the correct procedures to use in flushing/replacing brake fluid is highly recommended).

BRAKE WORK CAUTION As a teenager, I went through the "school of hard knocks" learning how to work on my car's brake system by reading my car's maintenance/repair manual and then doing the work myself. During my learning process, I ruined a disc brake caliper and trashed an old-style rear drum brake unit (parts and drums). Also, during this learning process my car brakes mysteriously failed upon approaching a 4-way stop intersection--I just shot right on through! I'm now an excellent brake mechanic, but the cost of a possible accident during my learning process was a fairly high risk to take.

For those who want to do brake work themselves but don't have much experience or knowledge of their car's braking system, I recommend having someone very knowledgeable in car braking systems supervise your work or at least inspect your work before driving your car. Also, reading about a car's braking system and reviewing all brake repair procedures in the car manufacturer's service/repair manual is highly recommended.

For those who would prefer that a brake specialist do their brake work, businesses that specialize mostly in brake repairs are some of the most skilled and competent. Certain brake parts and the brake work itself should be warranted for a period of time.

Synthetic Brake Fluid Recommendation – if approved for use in your car, I recommend using synthetic brake fluid because of its superior qualities.

• CCM#7: POWER STEERING (P.S.) SYSTEM CRITICAL MAINTENANCE *if applicable*
MAINTAIN CORRECT POWER STEERING FLUID LEVEL

Checking for proper power steering fluid level should be done as often as recommended in the car manufacturer's service/repair manual (more often if there are leaks in the system). If the power steering fluid level were to get too low, the power steering pump, actuator seals, etc. could be ruined, and this is something anyone would want to avoid, as power steering system components are somewhat expensive, difficult, and messy to replace. Fortunately, replenishing the power steering fluid level is seldom necessary if there are no leaks in the system. CAUTION: Power steering fluid may ruin car body paint.

VISUALLY CHECK CONDITION OF POWER STEERING ACTUATORS' RUBBER PROTECTIVE BOOTS when greasing steering linkage joints, changing engine oil, or any other convenient time**

FLUSHING/REPLACING POWER STEERING FLUID EVERY 2-4 YEARS will help ensure long life and trouble-free operation of power steering system components**
A. Since not all the old power steering fluid can be removed when draining the P.S. system, old power steering fluid will have to be removed by purging the system multiple times (4-6 times should be sufficient).
B. HOW I FLUSH/PURGE MY CAR'S POWER STEERING (P.S.) FLUID

1. Disconnect P.S. fluid to reservoir return hose and drain old power steering fluid into a suitable container.

2. With engine off, turn the steering wheel side-to-side to expel more fluid from the P.S. system steering actuator(s).

3. Re-connect the p.s. fluid return hose.

4. Fill power steering fluid reservoir to proper level with new power steering fluid.

5. With engine turned off, turn the car steering wheel from side-to-side to expel air from the p.s. system (helps to prevent air cavitations in the p.s. pump).

6. Replenish power steering fluid reservoir with more new p.s. fluid if necessary.

7. Start engine and go for a short drive, then recheck power steering fluid level.

A. Caution: If upon starting the engine the power steering pump is making a loud squealing noise, the p.s. pump has air cavitations--quickly turn the steering wheel back and forth for about four seconds to see if the whining stops. If the whining continues, turn off the engine and then turn the steering wheel back and forth five or more times, and then check the p.s. reservoir fluid level before restarting the engine. Restart the car to see if pump cavitations has ceased. Repeat steps 7A if pump still has air cavitations.

8. Repeat entire process 4-6 times to thoroughly purge old power steering fluid.

Synthetic Power Steering Fluid Recommendation – if approved for use in your car, I recommend using synthetic power steering fluid because of its superior anti-wear qualities.

• CCM#8: FUEL SYSTEM CRITICAL MAINTENANCE
A. Replace fuel filter(s) on or before the car manufacturer's recommended mileage/time interval.

1. Thoroughly review the procedure in the car manufacturer's service/repair manual beforehand.

WARNING: This is potentially lethal maintenance! If you somehow manage to light off your car's gas tank--you will be quickly burned to death!

B. CAUTION: Since certain fuel additives can damage diaphragm + gasket materials used in a car's fuel

system--except for fuel injection cleaner, I generally don't use any type of fuel additive unless it is

specifically recommended/approved by the car manufacturer.

C. CAUTION: Since certain gasoline mixtures can be harmful to a car's fuel injection system, I

recommend that every car owner consult their car manufacture's service/repair manual (or possibly the

car owner's manual) to see what type gasoline mixtures are approved for use.

13.3 OTHER USEFUL CAR CARE INFORMATION

KEEP THOROUGH CAR MAINTENANCE/REPAIR RECORDS
Keeping maintenance/repair records helps to ensure that critical car maintenance is performed at or before the car manufacturer's recommended time/mileage interval. Thorough records allow

one to know what and when maintenance/repairs were performed, along with the associated cost and part numbers. Thorough car maintenance/repair records allow one to learn the life expectancy of car parts that fail periodically, thus gives a good idea as to which spare parts should be carried in the car or kept in inventory. Keeping records also allows one to more thoroughly understand how their car operates. Thorough car maintenance/repair records will impress a prospective buyer whenever selling the car.

• EXAMPLES OF <u>CAR MAINTENANCE/REPAIR</u> AND <u>PARTS PURCHASED</u> RECORDS LOGS

Categorizing maintenance/repairs by topic, major component, task/part name, etc. in alphabetical order is how I've setup my maintenance/repair records. Because I keep an inventory of spare car parts, keeping a separate records log for "car parts purchased" and another for "car maintenance/repairs performed" has worked best. However, my two records logs could easily be combined into a single log if desired, especially since some of the information recorded is contained in both logs.

******** "CAR PARTS PURCHASED" RECORDS LOG********

****ALTERNATOR****
Part#:_____ Mfg._____ Date Purchased/Installed:___/___
Purchased From:____ Receipt#____ Warranty Length:_____
Cost/Retail:___/___

****BRAKE PARTS****
Part#:____ Part: <u>Ft. brake pads</u> Mfg.:____ Date Purchased/ Installed:___/___ Purchased From:____ Receipt#____ Warranty Length:_____ Cost/Retail:___/___

****FRONT-END LINKAGE/STEERING PARTS****
Part#:___ Part: <u>Lower Rt. Ball-Joint</u> Mfg.:___ Date Purchased/ Installed:___/___ Purchased From:___ Receipt#___ Warranty Length:____ Cost/Retail:___/___

****FUEL SYSTEM*****
Part#:_____ Part: <u>Fuel Filter</u> Mfg.:___ Date Purchased/Installed:_ ___/___ Purchased From:____ Receipt#____ Warranty Length:_ ____ Cost/Retail:___/___

****SHOCKS/STRUTS****
Part#:_____   Part: <u>Rear Shocks</u> Mfg.:___   Date Purchased/
Installed:___/___ Purchased From:____   Receipt#____ Warranty
Length:_____   Cost/Retail:___/__

****TRANSMISSION PARTS****
Part#:____   Part:_____   Mfg.:___ Date Purchased/Installed:___
/___ Purchased From:____ Receipt#____ Warranty Length:___
__ Cost/Retail:___/__

****WATER PUMP****
Part#:_____   Mfg.:_____   Date Purchased/Installed:___/___
Purchased From:____ Receipt#____   Warranty Length:_____
Cost/Retail:___/__

******** "CAR PARTS PURCHASED" RECORDS LOG********

ALTERNATOR
Alternator replacement Date:___ (update parts purchasing
records "date installed") Car Mileage:___ Part Mfg.:____
Part#:_____ Warranty:____

COOLING SYSTEM MAINTENANCE/REPAIRS
<u>Upper Radiator Hose replaced</u> Date:___(update parts
purchasing records "date installed") Car Mileage:_____ Hose
Mfg.:__ Hose part#:__ Cost:____
<u>Lower Radiator Hose Replaced</u> Date::___(update parts
purchasing records "date installed") Car Mileage:_____ Hose
Mfg.:__ Hose part#:__ Cost:____

ANTI-FREEZE REPLACEMENT (EVERY 1-2 YRS.)
<u>Coolant replacement</u> Date:____ Car Mileage:____ Brand of
Anti-freeze used:____ Cost:____

BRAKE FLUID FLUSH (EVERY 2-3 YRS.)
<u>Brake fluid flush</u> Date:____ Car Mileage:____ Brand of Brake
Fluid Used:_____ Cost:___

BRAKE REPAIRS
<u>Front Brake Rotor resurfaced</u> Date:_____ Car Mileage:_____
Location resurfaced:____ Cost:___ Disc Thickness:____

<u>Front Brake Caliper Piston Seals replaced</u> Date:_____(update

parts purchasing records "date installed") Car Mileage:____ Part Mfg.:____ Part#:____

<u>Front Brake Pads replaced</u> Date:____(update parts purchasing records "date installed") Car Mileage:___ Part Mfg.:____ Part#:_____ Warranty:_____

3 QT.. DIFFERENTIAL GEAR OIL REPLACED (EVERY 30,000miles)
Date replaced:_____ Car Mileage:_____ Brand + Weight of Gear Oil:_____ Cost:_____

FAN BELT(S) REPLACED
Date replaced:___(update parts purchasing records "date installed") Car Mileage:____ Part Mfg.:____ Part#:_____

FRONT-END STEERING JOINT LUBRICATION
Date:____ Car Mileage:____ Brand, Type + Cost of grease used:_____ Problems: left tie-rod has torn rubber grease cup

IN-LINE FUEL FILTER REPLACED
Date replaced:____(update parts purchasing records "date installed") Car Mileage:____ Filter Mfg.and part#:_____ Filter Cost:_____

OIL, OIL FILTER + AIR FILTER REPLACEMENT
Date replaced:___ Car Mileage:___ Cost/Brand/Weight/Type Oil:___ Cost/Brand/Part# of Oil Filter:____ Cost/Brand/Part# Air cleaner:_____

TRANSMISSION MAINTENANCE/REPAIRS
Transmission fluid/filter change Date:____ Car Mileage:____ Cost, Brand + Type fluid:____ Brand, Cost + Part# of Filter :____ Pan Bolt Torque setting:___

Rear transmission mount bushing assembly replaced: Date replaced:____(update parts purchasing records "date installed") Car Mileage:____ Part Mfg.:___ Part#:____

WATER PUMP REPLACED
Date replaced:____(update parts purchasing records "date installed") Car Mileage:_____ Part Mfg.:____ Part#:_____ Warranty:_____

WHEEL ALIGNMENT

Date Aligned:_____ Location Performed:_____ Car Mileage:_
_____ Cost:_____ Problems?:_____

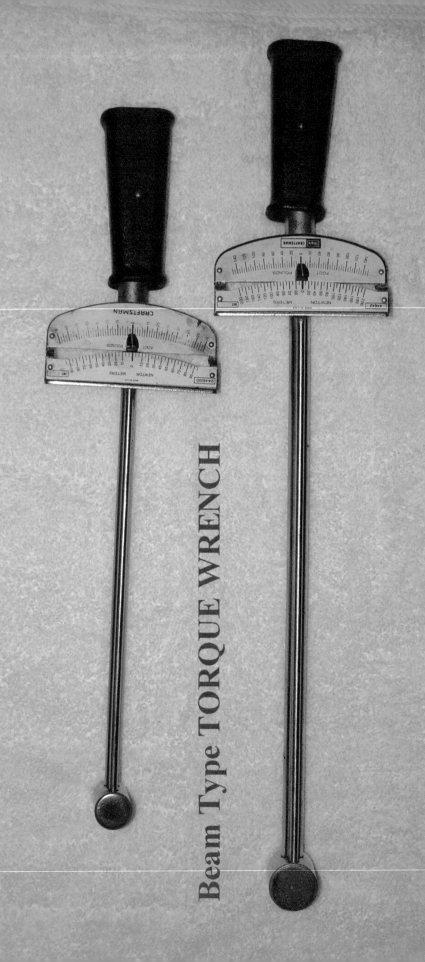

Beam Type TORQUE WRENCH

VALUABLE CAR INFORMATION TO PERMANENTLY RECORD IN MAINTENANCE/REPAIR LOGS One can consult their car's service/repair manual for locations throughout a car where important information may be found. Some of the information that should be permanently recorded in one's car records logs and photographed, include (1) vehicle identification number + car data plate information, and (2) Identification numbers and serial numbers off major mechanical assemblies, such as engine, transmission/transaxle, differential, etc. Information off engine tune-up and emissions information stickers located in the engine compartment should also be recorded (photographed), as stickers won't last forever. Any of this information may be useful when using a car's service/repair manual, when ordering parts, when the information on the car is no longer legible, and when having to identify a car or car parts during a theft recovery operation.

STORING CAR PARTS/MAINTENANCE/REPAIR RECEIPTS AND INVOICES It's best to keep receipts/invoices as long as the part/repair remains under warranty. Keeping non-warranted parts receipts for 30 days is probably sufficient. Keeping non-warranted repair/maintenance receipts for 3 months is probably sufficient. Obviously, if one "writes off" car expenses in the yearly tax return, the receipts should be kept for as long as the IRS requires tax records be kept. Also, I like to scan in parts & repair receipts into my computer, keeping the scans in the appropriate file for each of my vehicles.

In storing, organizing, and protecting receipts/invoices, I recommend each very important receipt be placed inside an individual pint size resealable freezer bag, and then store all pint size resealable freezer bags in a larger resealable freezer bag, such as a qt. size or larger resealable bag. Writing on the outside of each pint-size bag what part/repair receipt is contained within, along with the warranty expiration date (if applicable) will allow one to easily locate a receipt and know when it can be disposed of. Storing all "non-lifetime warranty" receipts separate from "lifetime warranty" receipts, and storing "parts purchased" receipts separate from "maintenance/repair" receipts or invoices may also help to better organize the receipts.

WHY EVERY CAR OWNER SHOULD OWN + USE THEIR CAR'S MAINTENANCE/REPAIR MANUAL Because a car owner's manual isn't an adequate source of car maintenance/repair information, it will be very beneficial for any car owner who maintains/repairs their car, even minimally, to own and use their car's maintenance/repair manual. Having a car maintenance/repair manual is beneficial in a number of ways: (1) it allows one to learn about and better understand all aspects of their car's operation (electrical/electronic/computer systems, hydraulic and mechanical assemblies/systems), (2) it discloses the correct maintenance/repair procedure, pictures, descriptions, trouble-shooting, and other information needed to perform maintenance/repairs correctly, (3) it discloses the correct type of recommended fluids, oils (weight/viscosity), torque values, lubricants, etc., (4) it can be used for learning about and verifying repairs a mechanic makes, thus helps one in being treated fairly, and (5) it is helpful in locating important serial/identification numbers stamped on a car's mechanical/hydraulic assemblies and other systems, which is information that may be required when purchasing/ordering car parts, performing maintenance/repairs, etc.

CAR MANUFACTURER'S OR AFTER-MARKET SERVICE/REPAIR MANUALS: WHICH IS BETTER? Both after-market and car manufacturer's service/repair manuals are extremely beneficial to own and use--I recommend owning them both. The smaller after-market automotive repair manual is easily stored inside a car, whereas the larger car manufacturer's service/repair manual volume can be stored at one's external storage location.

After-market car service/repair manuals are readily available from many automotive parts suppliers, and they're usually relatively small in size. Referencing material in the book index is fairly easy. If desired, a more thorough and much larger after-market "mechanics series" maintenance/repair manual may be available to order.

I've generally found car manufacturer's service/repair manuals to be more thorough and a bit more accurate than after-market service/repair manuals. When I want to get complicated car repairs/maintenance "just right," I consult my car manufacturer's service/repair manual. Car manufacturer's service/repair manuals generally provide an excellent description of car operating systems. Car manufacturer's service/repair manuals are generally quite large, a single manual possibly coming in a multi-volume set. They generally have to be purchased from the car manufacturer; calling a car dealership's parts department is an easy way to find out how to purchase/

order a car manufacturer's service/repair manual.

13.4 NON-CRITICAL BUT NECESSARY CAR MAINTENANCE

Non-critical but necessary car maintenance is maintenance that will not result in expensive repairs/overhauls if it isn't performed, but not performing it may prevent a car from being operated at some point. When performing any car maintenance/repairs, always follow the instructions/procedure provided in the car manufacturer's service/repair manual.

MAINTAIN CAR STARTING BATTERY ELECTROLYTE LEVEL (if serviceable) Replenish electrolyte with distilled water when necessary. The correct electrolyte level is generally above the plates but below the upper plastic case housing.
EXTRA: If excessive battery electrolyte loss is occurring, overcharging the battery is probably the problem (check for defective voltage regulator, defective alternator rectifying diodes, etc.).

PREVENTING/REMOVING BATTERY TERMINAL CORROSION Battery terminal post and terminal connector corrosion may be removed using a wire brush, a wire terminal brush, or a suitable sandpaper, such as emery cloth. To make the corrosion easier to remove, a water and baking soda mixture can be applied to the corrosion; however, any baking soda that inadvertently enters the battery will neutralize the electrolyte making the battery useless (applies to lead acid type car-starting batteries). Preserving clean battery terminals/connectors by coating them with mineral or petroleum grease will somewhat help prevent corrosion.

CHECK CONDITION + TIGHTNESS OF FAN BELT(S) (cars w/o automatic belt tensioner)
A. Replace fan belt(s) when necessary; replacing all fan belts together is best (if applicable).
B. Adjust fan belt(s) for proper tightness **cars w/o automatic belt tensioner**
1. Fan belt that is too loose may slip over equipment/component drive wheels and quickly wear out the fan belt.
www.infowars.com

2. Fan belt that is too tight will shorten bearing life of fan belt driven equipment.

MAINTAIN CORRECT TIRE AIR PRESSURE

USE A TORQUE WRENCH TO TIGHTEN WHEEL LUG-NUTS TO THE TORQUE VALUE SPECIFIED IN A CAR'S SERVICE/REPAIR MANUAL

LUBRICATE KEY LOCKS + OTHER CAR BODY "PIVOT POINTS" AS RECOMMENDED IN A CAR SERVICE MANUAL
> BENEFIT: easy operation, minimal wear, + maximum life.
> CAUTION: To prevent damage or excessive wear--use only the type lubricants specified in a car manufacturer's service/repair manual.

GREASE NON-SEALED WHEEL BEARINGS AS RECOMMENDED IN THE CAR SERVICE/REPAIR MANUAL

13.5 GOOD MAINTENANCE PRACTICES/TIPS

TORQUE WRENCH RECOMMENDATION Using a torque wrench allows one to tighten hardware and car parts, such as nuts, bolts, sparkplugs, oil drain plug, lug-nuts, etc., to the exact degree of tightness specified in a car's service/repair manual. Not applying the proper torque can result in two or more undesirable conditions: (1) under-tightened hardware can come loose/apart, (2) over-tightening hardware can strip the bolt/nut/hardware threads and hardware hole threads, or shear the hardware. Eliminating the possibility of over/under-tightening hardware requires using a torque wrench--I highly recommend using one.

TWO TYPE TORQUE WRENCHES READILY AVAILABLE: BEAM TYPE + RATCHET TYPE Beam type and ratchet type torque wrenches are the two type torque wrenches readily available most anywhere automotive tools are sold. Like socket wrenches, torque wrenches are available in 1/4, 3/8, 1/2, and larger drives. Unlike socket wrenches, torque wrenches don't ratchet.

Beam type torque wrenches have a beam that flexes during tightening of hardware. The tip of the beam moves along a scale pointing to the torque value being applied. The beam type torque wrench is inexpensive and very easy to use. Its disadvantage is that the user must be in a position to read the scale during usage.

Ratchet type torque wrenches are used by setting/dialing in the desired torque value first (usually done by turning the handle) and then tightening the hardware until a slight break-over detente is felt. The ratchet type torque wrench's main advantage is that after the desired torque value has been set, it can be used without having to look at it. Its main disadvantage is that it is more susceptible to getting out of calibration as compared to the beam type torque wrench, so it should be treated gently. Also, ratchet type torque wrenches are much more expensive than beam type torque wrenches.

TORQUE WRENCH ACCURACY Torque wrenches are most accurate for torque values near the center of their scale. Therefore, using the size torque wrench in which the torque value most often needed is near the center of the scale is desirable.

COATING ELECTRICAL CONNECTIONS WITH SILICON DIELECTRIC TUNE-UP GREASE TO PREVENT CORROSION
When electrical connections corrode, electrical continuity may be broken or become intermittent. To prevent electrical contacts from corroding, they can be thinly coated with silicon dielectric tune-up grease or other suitable electrical lubricant.

Because a car being lived in is subjected to high humidity, I coat most all car electrical contacts when I come across them in my maintenance/repairs, such as in coating a bulb's metal base and bulb's fixture, coating metal portions of car fuses; coating areas of contact between battery terminal and terminal connector, coating the top of sparkplugs and the metal leads of sparkplug wires, etc.

Why use silicon dielectric grease instead of automotive grease? Possible arcing of the electrical contacts may cause automotive grease to burn, but not silicon grease; also, silicon grease isn't messy.

DON'T USE CAR FLUID/OIL ADDITIVES UNLESS RECOMMENDED/APPROVED BY THE CAR MFG.
There are a number of fluid/oil additives on the market that will adversely affect a car's operation if used, some possibly

causing severe damage. Additives that are poured into a car's cooling system to stop radiator leaks or seal a cracked engine head are, in my opinion, potentially car-damaging additives. However, to be fair, there are a number of additives on the market that can be very beneficial to a car's operation (injector cleaner) -- but one really needs to thoroughly research the additive and make sure it is recommended/approved by the car's manufacturer before using it.

DISPOSABLE RUBBER GLOVES ARE EXTREMELY USEFUL/ BENEFICIAL TO USE IN CAR MAINTENANCE/REPAIR APPLICATIONS Disposable rubber gloves are beneficial to use in many applications, such as automotive maintenance/repair work, gun cleaning or other corrosion sensitive applications; cooking, eating, and game processing applications; car living rest room applications, applications where elimination of finger prints (wear 2 sets of gloves) and minimizing DNA transfer is desirable, painting applications, working with carcinogenic or other unhealthy chemicals, etc. Being made of thin rubber allows the user excellent dexterity, grip, and sensitivity. A box of 50-200 pair can generally be inexpensively purchased at pharmacies or the bathroom/medical section at grocery/department stores. I wear disposable rubber gloves by themselves, and I wear them under Mechanix gloves and under leather gloves when performing car maintenance/repairs.
LEATHER GLOVES
MECHANIX GLOVES

- OPTIONS IN PURCHASING CAR PARTS
    There are basically three options in purchasing car parts: (1) purchase new (+ rebuilt) parts from a car manufacturer via a car dealership's parts department; (2) purchase new (+ rebuilt) aftermarket car parts from automotive parts suppliers, and (3) purchase used car parts from automotive salvage yards. A fourth option I sometimes use is to purchase a like-model spare-parts car that may or may not run.
CAR MANUFACTURER'S NEW (+ REBUILT) CAR PARTS VIA DEALERSHIP PARTS DEPARTMENT Much of the parts making up a car are only available from the car manufacturer and can only be purchased new through a car dealership's parts department. Car manufacturer's new car parts are generally of very high quality (not always), have relatively close tolerances (if applicable), and are relatively expensive. Ask around, and you should be able to find a car dealership that will sell new

car parts at 15-20 percent off retail----the dealership I found through the Internet sells me parts for my all my vehicles at 25% off, no matter what brand of U.S. made vehicle.

AFTER-MARKET PARTS SUPPLIERS Automotive parts stores sell new and rebuilt after-market parts that may be of low or high quality. After-market parts are generally less expensive than car manufacturer's parts (exception: high performance parts). Some new after-market parts may come with a lifetime warranty backed by the part manufacturer or by the automotive supply store selling the part (keep your purchase receipts and scan them into your computer!).

In my experience maintaining/repairing my cars, I've found certain after-market parts to have looser tolerances and to be of lesser quality than car manufacturer's new parts (not always). Therefore, if a mechanical part is difficult to replace or is critical to a car's proper operation, I generally purchase car manufacturer's new parts from a car dealership. However, if a car is old, aftermarket parts suppliers may be the only place to purchase certain new or remanufactured parts that are no longer available from the car manufacturer.

AUTOMOTIVE SALVAGE YARDS Automotive salvage yards can offer big savings on used parts. However, keep in mind that parts found at junkyards are used, possibly excessively worn & corroded, and possibly defective. Fortunately, many automotive salvage yards guarantee certain aspects of the used parts they sell, and will find another like part or return the customer's money if the part turns out to be less that what they guaranteed. For certain expensive parts, such as engine blocks, engine heads, transmission housings, etc.---automotive salvage yards may be the best place to shop if one wants to save tons of money.

PURCHASE A SPARE USED CAR If you plan to keep a car for a long time, look around for the best deal on a spare car. Whether it runs or not, you've got all those spare parts to use whenever needed.

SILICON ADHESIVE SEALANT

Silicon adhesive sealant dries to a flexible rubbery state. Depending on the type used, silicon adhesive sealant may adhere well to clean glass, metal, and rubber surfaces, and it may adhere well to clothing and other porous materials. I find uses for it in both automotive and storage applications.

CS3204 AIRCRAFT "WET-WING" GAS TANK SEALER

A. Used for sealing metal joints/seams that expand and contract with temperature variations. It also works well in temporarily covering gun serial numbers and other identifying marks on guns.

B. Tenaciously adheres to steel, aluminum, magnesium, titanium, and numerous other metals.

C. Mfg.: Chem Seal Division, Flamemaster Corporation, 11120 Sherman Way, Sun Valley, CA 91352

("CS 3204," 1995)

CS1900 FIREWALL SEALANT

A. Similar to CS3204, but with the ability to withstand high heat (400F max. operating; 2000F flash)

B. Mfg.: Chem Seal Division, FlameMaster Corporation, 11120 Sherman Way, Sun Valley, CA 91352)

("CS 1900," 1994)

CS3330 AIRCRAFT REMOVEABLE ACCESS PANEL SEALANT

HARDWARE LIQUID THREADLOCKER

When applied to clean metal hardware (nuts + bolts) threads, hardware liquid threadlocker helps prevent hardware from coming loose (degree of hold depends on type/color threadlocker used). A certain type threadlocker (Loctite #414) can be used to seal ammo (bullet to case, and primer to case).

ENGINE OPERATING HAZARDS DURING PERIODS OF IDLE OPERATION
 (SEE CH: 12 SECTION: HAVING SEXUAL RELATIONS INSIDE A privatized CAR")

CAR MUD FLAPS ARE GOOD INVESTMENTS (if not standard equip.)
Dirt, debris, rocks, salt, mud, gravel, sand, water, etc. slung up underneath a car behind the wheel wells can cause severe corrosion of the car body over time. Mud flaps help prevent corrosive debris from reaching vulnerable areas aft of a car's wheel wells.

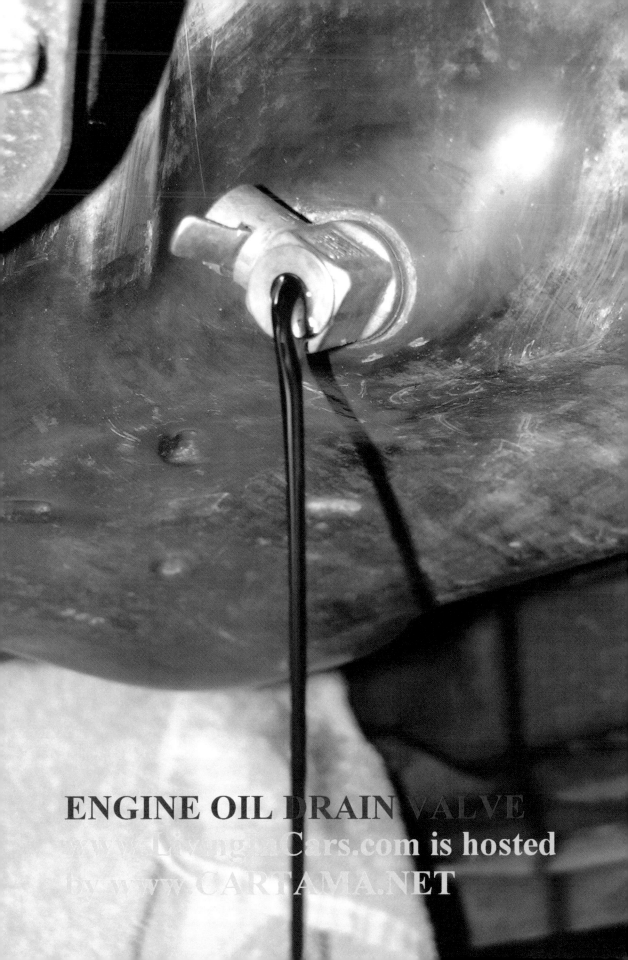

ENGINE OIL DRAIN VALVE

ENGINE OIL DRAIN VALVE (EODV) One of the most beneficial after-market automotive products I've used is the "engine oil drain valve" (EODV). The EODV I've used is a very small, Teflon-seated, chrome-plated ball on/off valve that replaces the engine oil drain plug. Using an EODV makes draining engine oil as simple as lifting a lever out of its detente and then moving it 90 degrees to the open position. While in the off position, the valve lever is held in a detente under spring pressure.
EXTRA: If possible, it's best installed with the on/off lever towards the top of the engine so that nothing can contact it while driving off-road.

PLATINUM AND IRIDIUM ELECTRODE SPARKPLUGS An alloy of platinum, iridium and other metals seams to offer the most sprak benefit and long life.

SPARKPLUG INSTALLATION RECOMMENDATIONS Automotive sparkplugs have a ceramic insulator surrounding the center electrode that can be easily cracked ruining the sparkplug, thus sparkplugs need to be handled and installed with care. If a sparkplug is installed too tight, the insulator can be damaged and/or the sparkplug gap increased. More importantly, the engine sparkplug hole threads could be damaged resulting in the need for a costly repair. Therefore, using a torque wrench when replacing sparkplugs to assure that they are tightened to the degree specified in a car's service/repair manual is critical.
To prevent a sparkplug from rusting tight in the motor, anti-seize compound should be applied to sparkplug threads during installation.
To prevent carbon from building up on sparkplug threads or sparkplug hole threads, which could easily cause damage during sparkplug removal/installation--the correct sparkplug having the correct "reach" must be used.

CAR MODIFICATION RECOMMENDATION It's best not to modify any part of a car's operating systems unless one thoroughly understands their car's operation and how any modification will affect its operation. Generally, every mechanical, hydraulic, and electrical/electronic car part making up a car has a useful purpose and is needed to ensure optimal/safe car operation.

IF YOUR CAR IS EQUIPPED WITH ELECTRONIC and COMPUTER COMPONENTS--YOU PROBABLY WOULD BE WISE TO NOT

JUMP-START OTHER CARS WITH YOUR CAR

EXTRA: Only disconnect your car battery when the ignition is off and the ignition key is removed! (Disconnecting a battery with the ignition key installed and the ignition turned on may blow all types of electronic and computer components throughout a car's electrical system).

CAR PURCHASE CONSIDERATIONS It's best to research a new/used car by checking with organizations that provide information/ratings pertaining to how well a car holds up. Also, if one does much high-speed highway driving, it's best if the car is geared so that the motor rpm stays fairly low so as to minimize wear (less than 2,400 rpm for the highest speed you drive would be optimal).

13.6 USEFUL CAR TOOLS AND ACCESSORIES TO HAVE WHILE LIVING IN CARS

TOOL PURCHASING and TOOL STORAGE RECOMMENDATIONS
I recommend purchasing U.S. made hand tools that come with a lifetime warranty, as they are generally of high quality, very strong, highly corrosion resistant, easy to operate, and easily replaced if broken. Purchasing only the tools that are absolutely needed will help minimize storage and organization problems.

Tools that are used often or that may be needed to make an emergency car repair can be carried inside one's car; seldom-used tools can be stored at one's external storage location. When traveling long distances away from one's external tool storage location, one will want to store more tools in their car. Plastic storage hunting boxes lined with 1" thick foam make excellent tool storage containers. Resealable plastic freezer bags make useful compact storage containers for socket wrench sockets, and more.

* USEFUL TOOLS and ACCESSORIES TO CARRY IN ONE'S CAR OR STORE AT AN EXTERNAL STORAGE LOCATION *
• SMALL 400-WATT 12-VOLT DC TO 120-VOLT AC INVERTER (stored in car).
• 1,000-WATT 12-VOLT DC TO 120-VOLT AC PURE SINE WAVE INVERTER (stored in car when traveling).

- 12-VOLT DC AIR-PUMP (stored in car).
- 12-VOLT DC DUAL CIGARETTE ADAPTER OUTLET (stored/used in car).
- 120-VOLT AC-POWERED 12-VOLT BATTERY CHARGER (stored at external storage location).
- 3/8" or 1/2" VARIABLE SPEED DRILL (stored in car when traveling).
- AUTOMOTIVE DIAGNOSTICS SCANNER (stored in car when traveling).
- BOTTLE-NOSE HYDRAULIC JACK (stored in car or at external storage location).
- C-CLAMPS (1-2" SIZE) (stored in car). www.infowars.com
- CAR'S SERVICE/REPAIR MANUALS (small aftermarket manual stored in car; car manufacturer's manual volume set stored at external storage location).
- COMPRESSED-AIR TANK WITH AIR NOZZLE/CHUCK (stored at external storage location).
- GREASE GUN (stored in plastic box at external storage location).

*DIGITAL VOLT/OHM/AMP MULTI-METER (stored in car). Uses: detecting opens/shorts; polarity checks; volts, amps, resistance, hertz, capacitance, inductance, + transistor "beta" measurements; battery "load-testing".

*DRILL ACCESSORIES: DRILL BIT SET (stored in car when traveling); RUST STRIPPER WHEEL ATTACHMENT (stored at external storage location); GRINDING STONE ATTACHMENTS (stored at external storage location).

*"FEELER"/THICKNESS GAUGE (stored in car)

*JACK STANDS + CAR RAMPS (stored at external storage location).

*LUG NUT + PRY BAR TOOL (stored at external storage location).

*PLASTIC FUNNEL (stored at external storage location).

*PLIERS

 A. 6" Needle nose pliers (stored in car).
    1.Uses: cutting + twisting wire; bending/removing/flattening cotter pins + hardware; removing

thin type fuses; cleaning game; cutting wire.

 B. 6" needle-noise locking pliers (stored in car).
    1.Uses: bending/removing/flattening cotter pins + hardware; flattening objects; removing thin

type fuses; cleaning game. www.infowars.com

C. One small size + one large size locking pliers – VISE GRIPS (stored in car when traveling).

D. 6" diagonal pliers (stored in car). Uses: cutting wire, removing cotter pins.

E. Snap-ring pliers (stored at external storage location).

*SCREWDRIVERS:

- Slotted/common: small, medium, + large size (stored in car).
- Phillips screwdrivers: small, medium, + large size (stored in car).
- Torx screwdrivers **if needed** (stored in car or at external storage location).
- Small ratchet screwdriver with removable bit set (stored in car).
- Jeweler's size common + Phillips screwdriver sets (stored in car).

*SCREW EXTRACTOR SET (stored in car when traveling).

*SINGLE EDGE RAZOR BLADES (stored in car).

*SOCKET WRENCH SET (SEE "WRENCHES" BELOW).

*SOLDER GUN, 33-WATT IRON, IRON TIPS, SOLDER, FLUX, HEATSINKS (stored in car).

*SPECIALTY TOOLS: BRAKE TOOLS, STEERING LINKAGE TOOLS, LARGE C-CLAMP(S), PULLERS, ETC. (stored at external storage location).

*TAP + DIE SET (stored in car when traveling).

*TIMING LIGHT (stored in car when traveling). No longer used for spark timing, but it will help identify spark-firing abnormalities caused by a defective ignition component.

*TIRE REPAIR/PLUG KIT (stored in car).

*SPARE TIRE (stored at external storage location; stored in car when traveling).

*0-1" MICROMETER (stored at external storage or bank box)

*WIRE STRIPPING TOOL (stored in car).

*WRENCHES:

One small-medium size + one medium-large size adjustable wrench (stored in car).

Metric and Standard Combination wrench set (stored in car).

1/2" Drive ratchet with wheel lug nut size 6-point deep socket (stored in each car).

1/4", 3/8", 1/2" drive socket wrench sets (stored in external storage).

Allen wrench set (stored in car). www.freedomtofascism.com

Flare nut wrenches (stored at external storage location).

Torque wrench (stored at external storage location).

TWO TYPES OF TIRE REPAIR KITS: (1) PRESSURIZED AIR + SEALANT CANISTER KIT, (2) TIRE PLUG KIT

While living in cars, I usually haven't had room enough to carry a spare tire. Therefore, I've had to be able to repair tire punctures well enough to be able to drive to (1) a professional tire repair business to have the tire professionally patched, (2) to my external storage location where a spare tire is stored, or (3) to a tire sales business to have the tire replaced.

Two ways one can temporarily seal a punctured tire is by (1) using a pressurized air + sealant canister kit to inflate and momentarily seal the tire, or (2) by plugging a tire's puncture using a tire plug kit. Both of these kits are readily available, are inexpensive and very compact, and both can be used without having to jack the car or remove the wheel. A third option in effectively dealing with tire punctures is to use "run flat" type tires that can be driven dozens of miles while flat; however, run flat tires are really supposed to be used on cars equipped to electronically monitor tire pressure and other conditions.

PRESSURIZED AIR/SEALANT CANISTER TIRE REPAIR KIT A pressurized air + sealant canister kit seals a tire puncture by inflating a punctured tire with an air + sealant mixture. Simply position the tire so the puncture is toward the ground, connect the canister to the tire's valve-stem, and then inflate the punctured tire to temporarily seal it.

Use of a "pressurized air/sealant canister" is limited to temporarily sealing a punctured tire that still has the puncturing object still imbedded in the tire. The sealing period is generally very short--the tire really needs to be professionally patched as soon as possible (w/in 24-hours). www.wethepeoplefoundation. org

TIRE PLUG KIT A tire plug kit generally consists of two screwdriver type tools (a tire plug inserter tool and tire hole roughening tool), several plugs, and rubber adhesive. Using a tire plug kit to plug a punctured tire basically consists of removing the puncturing object from the tire, and then using the screwdriver-like tool to insert a specially coated rope or rubber plug into the puncture. A plugged tire may go for hundreds of miles before significant air leakage occurs. Surprisingly, sidewall punctures and large cuts, which usually aren't repairable, may be temporarily sealed with one or more tire plugs, thus allowing the car to be driven a short distance to a tire shop.

The insignificant disadvantages associated with using a tire plug kit are (1) an air pump is needed to inflate a newly plugged tire, (2) plugging a tire requires considerable strength, and (3) one will probably have to momentarily lie down on the ground when plugging a tire that is installed on a car.

SPARE PARTS TO CARRY INSIDE A CAR

It's beneficial to carry small-medium size spare parts that are critical to a car's operation--especially those that have previously failed or wore out. This is especially true when traveling or when living in isolated wilderness areas where car parts aren't readily available.

Radiator hoses and fan belts have limited life and are critical to a car's operation, thus carrying spares and the tools needed to replace them will someday be beneficial. Engine (ignition/charging/starting/fuel system) electronic, electrical, computer components are also good candidates. Off-road vehicle owners may want to carry a spare set of wheel bearings and drive shaft u-joints.

Keeping accurate maintenance/repair records enables one to learn the lifespan of certain parts, thus helps one to know which parts would be most beneficial to carry in their car. Carrying spare parts inside my cars, along with the tools needed to replace them, has generally allowed me to immediately and inexpensively repair my cars whenever/wherever needed.

CHAPTER 14

THE FREEBIES

This chapter does not in anyway suggest degrading any establishment/business used in enhancing one's car living situation--one should always take good care of any facility/ equipment used. The information in this chapter is mainly meant to address fun, harmless, inexpensive ways of enhancing one's car living situation.

Concerning using a business's equipment/facilities as a non-paying or "partial" paying guest, I've always considered my presence to be an asset at any business visited, thus I never thought of myself as being unwelcome.

FINANCIAL FREEBIE A very beneficial freebie that comes with living in cars is being able to park and live without having to pay rent, mortgage, real estate taxes, utilities, etc.

SWIMMING FREEBIE Beginning around junior high school, my friends and I found it exciting to explore the neighborhood for swimming pools in which we would skinny-dip in late at night, sometimes getting run off by the owners. Years later while traveling throughout the U.S. living in a car, I found that one of the best ways to exercise, meet people, and enjoy myself was by swimming in apartment, condo, resort, hotel, and club swimming pools. Swimming as an anonymous guest is something I'll always enjoy.

HOTEL FREEBIES Hotels/motels may offer many freebies. As discussed in chapter 10, hotels/motels can be excellent nighttime parking locations. When traveling in warm weather, I find it beneficial to stop by a hotel/motel's ice dispenser every 3 days to fill up my "double cooler ice chest," usually after swimming in the hotel pool. A hotel's bar can be a nice place to socialize and possibly enjoy free appetizers/buffet. I especially enjoy dinning at very nice hotels where wonderful meals are inexpensively priced because of being subsidized by expensive room rentals. Enjoying a nice hot shower at hotels/motels that have private showering facilities located in the pool area can be beneficial, especially after a good swim.

WHAT TO SAY IF QUESTIONED BY HOTEL STAFF WHILE USING HOTEL FACILITIES AS A NON-PAYING GUEST Hotel staff generally won't bother nice looking, well-mannered, well-groomed people who may be participating in any activities taking place at the hotel, such as eating at the hotel restaurant, attending a seminar/convention, socializing in the lounge/bar area, etc. However, if ever asked by hotel personnel whether I'm an overnight guest, I might reply with any of the following: (1) "it would look better to my employer if I didn't check in till such-in-such time, and I'm just passing time till then," (2) "I'm here for the banquet/seminar/etc." (requires research of hotel activities upon arrival, or beforehand), (3) "I'm checking out the hotel as a possible one week stay for a group of 50 business people I'm associated with," (4) "I'm checking out the hotel to see if I want to stay here or at the other nearby hotel," or (5) "I haven't checked in yet, but I will do so shortly."

BEST WAYS TO USE HOTEL/MOTEL PARKING FACILITIES DURING THE NIGHT: (See Ch. 10)

SUCCESSFULLY USING HOTEL SWIMMING FACILITIES AS A NON-PAYING GUEST Keep in mind that it is easier to swim at large, busy hotels/motels because of being able to blend in better.

During arrival, avoid exposure to the hotel/motel office area as much as possible. Parking out of sight of the pool area makes it appear that you're coming to the pool area from a hotel room. Carrying a magazine, book, or can of soda to the pool area also helps one to appear to be coming from their hotel room. Since you probably don't have a hotel towel, carrying your personal towel inside a non-transparent bag is best. Charging rechargeable equipment in the pool area instead of a hotel room will appear strange, thus shouldn't be done (not a problem if traveling).

If you don't want to be bothered by anyone at the pool area, carry a portable music player and wear headphones (wearing sunglasses will also help).

Hotel staff generally won't bother anyone who appears to

be a guest and is beneficial to the hotel atmosphere, thus your appearance should be pleasing (well-groomed, nice bathing suit, well-mannered).

BEST WAYS TO OBTAIN ICE FROM HOTEL/MOTEL ICE MACHINES How I retrieve ice from hotel/motel ice dispensing machines depends on the situation: (1) whether the ice dispenser machine is located inside or outside the hotel/motel building, (2) whether a room key is needed to enter side + rear hotel/motel entrances, thus possibly requiring anyone without a room key to use the building's front main entrance to access the ice dispenser, and (3) whether I'll be sleeping in my privatized car parked at the hotel/motel after retrieving ice.

I generally never carry an ice chest to a hotel/motel's ice machine. Instead, I discretely carry a strong plastic bag stored inside a pint size resealable freezer bag. After swimming or taking care of other business at the hotel, I simply drop by the ice machine and fill the plastic bag full of ice while on the way back to my car. Using a carry bag or backpack in transporting the bag of ice allows me to return to my car without anyone knowing that I'm transporting ice, and this can be beneficial if I'm planning to sleep in my privatized car parked at this same hotel during the night.

PUBLIC/COLLEGE LIBRARY USE BENEFITS If available, small private study rooms can be used to sleep in and/or charge rechargeable equipment. Most libraries have a vast selection of books, magazines, newspapers, periodicals, reference/research materials. Many college libraries have the latest technology equipment for students (and possibly non-students) to use: music, computer, printing, copying, scanning, video, graphics equipment, Internet access, and fax services.

APARTMENT COMMUNITY FREEBIES As disclosed in chapter 10, apartment communities and their surrounding streets is what I consider to be one of my top five favorite nighttime parking locations. Apartment communities can be nice places to swim/exercise, socialize, wash clothes, charge rechargeable equipment, etc. Apartment clothes washing facilities are generally some of the nicest and least expensive available. It's very convenient to charge rechargeable equipment when using apartment clothes washing facilities.

SUCCESSFULLY USING APARTMENT SWIMMING FACILITIES AS AN ANONYMOUS GUEST

While traveling, one can stop and carelessly swim at most any apartment community, as one really doesn't care if they are asked to leave (not likely) because of not being a tenant or tenant's guest. However, when not traveling, one needs to be careful and try to appear as being an apartment tenant or tenant's guest.

In choosing an apartment community to swim at, don't use the swimming facilities of an apartment community that is used for nighttime "secret" parking. Better yet, if swimming as an anonymous guest, only consider using the swimming facilities of apartment communities that are a good distance away from your nighttime parking locations. Basically, you don't want the same people seeing your car parked at the apartment community your swimming at and then possibly see it parked nightly at a nearby apartment community, as that might possibly raise questions as to what is going on in your living situation.

There are several things you can do to blend in better while swimming as an anonymous guest at an apartment community. It's best to limit your exposure to apartment management personal whenever possible. If there is more than one car entrance/exit, use the one that is located out of sight of the apartment manager's office. If there is more than one pool, use the one furthest away from the manager's office and apartment residence (if applicable).

To appear to be coming to the pool area from an apartment or friend's apartment, park out of sight of the pool area. Carrying a magazine or book, and towel to the pool area also helps one to appear as if they are coming from an apartment. Carrying a glass of beverage containing ice taken from one's double cooler ice chest also helps.

If you don't want to be bothered by anyone at the pool area, carry a portable music player and wear headphones (wearing sunglasses also helps). You should look fairly nice before entering the pool area (you don't want to look like your coming for a bath), as having an appealing appearance will help minimize the chance that anyone will question whether or not you're a tenant or tenant's guest (though, people may want to get to know you).

WHAT TO SAY IF QUESTIONED ABOUT WHICH APARTMENT YOU LIVE IN

What to say to anyone asking about which apartment you live in depends on who's doing the asking. If management is asking, they probably are only interested in whether you are an unrecognized tenant or a tenant's guest. Telling management that you're thinking about renting an apartment, and you are there to see what the community and residents are like before choosing which apartment community you'll move to... may be a suitable response. Saying that you're a real estate agent and that you just wanted to experience first hand what the apartment community is like before referring any clients to the apartment community... may also be a suitable response. In contrast, a tenant asking where you live may be for the reason of casual conversation with the possibility of striking up a new friendship. Becoming friends with a tenant can make swimming risk-free, as one will then be an authorized guest.

EXTRA: Wearing dark sunglasses prevents people from seeing/ recognizing the "reaction" in your eyes.

APARTMENT LAUNDROMATS CAN BE EXCELLENT PLACES TO WASH CLOTHES

Apartment communities' clothes washing facilities are generally very clean and inexpensive, so as to benefit the apartment tenants. While washing + drying clothes, it may be convenient to charge rechargeable equipment. To be discreet, I run a 6-foot extension cord into a carry bag filled with my rechargeable equipment, which are all plugged into a single multi-plug adapter.

REFERENCES

Hudecki, N. (date unknown) Synthetic Lubricants Ideal For High Performance Driving. (Available from The Valvoline Company, A Division of Ashland Oil, Inc., P.O. Box 14000, Lexington, KY 40512)

Nielsen, E. (1996, March) Chemical defense sprays: an in-depth look. American Survival Guide. p. 26, 27, 42, 43.

GE Plastic Structured Product: Lexgard Laminates For Security Glazing. (1994, February) SPL-3001B pp.3-13.

CS 1900 Firewall Sealant. (1993, May). Technical Bulletin. (Available from Chem Seal Division, Flamemaster Corporation, 11120 Sherman Way, Sun Valley, CA 91352)

CS 3204 Class A and Class B. (1995, January). Technical Bulletin p.1. (Available from Chem Seal Division, Flamemaster Corporation, 11120 Sherman Way, Sun Valley, CA 91352)

TEN COMMANDMENTS

- You shall have no other gods before Me. (Exodus 20:3)
- You shall not make a graven image for yourself. (Exodus 20:4)
- You shall not take the name of God Almighty in vain. (Exodus 20:7)
- Remember the Sabbath day, to keep it holy. (Exodus 20:8)
- Honor your father and your mother. (Exodus 20:12)
- You shall not murder. (Exodus 20:13)
- You shall not commit adultery. (Exodus 20:14)
- You shall not steal. (Exodus 20:15)
- You shall not testify falsely against your neighbor. (Exodus 20:16)
- You shall not covet your neighbor's property. (Exodus 20:17)

"The government should create, issue, and circulate all the currency. Creating and issuing money is the supreme prerogative of government and its greatest creative opportunity.

Adopting these principles will save the taxpayers immense sums of interest and money will cease to be the master and become the servant of humanity."
                    -Abraham Lincoln

"If the American people ever allow the banks to control the issuance of their currency... the banks and corporations that will grow up around them will deprive the people of all property, until their children wake up homeless on the continent their fathers conquered."
                    -Thomas Jefferson

"I am a most unhappy man. I have unwittingly ruined my country. A great industrial nation is now controlled by its system of credit.

We are no longer government by free opinion, no longer a government by conviction and the vote of the majority, but a government by the opinion and duress of a small group of dominant men."
                    -President Woodrow Wilson
                    1919

"In substance, the court holds that the Sixteenth Amendment did not empower the Federal Government to levy a new tax."
                    -New York Times
                    January 25, 1916

"I sincerely believe the banking institutions having the issuing power of money, are more dangerous to liberty than standing armies."
                    -Thomas Jefferson

"Give me control of a nation's money supply, and I care not who makes its laws."
                    -Mayer Rothschild
                    Private Banker

"If you...examined [The 16th amendment] carefully, you would find that a sufficient number of states never ratified that amendment."
                    -U.S. District Court Judge
                    James C. Fox
                    2003

"The real rulers in Washington are invisible and exercise power from behind the scenes."
                    -Felix Frankfurter
                    U.S. Supreme Court Justice

"We are greatful to the Washington Post, the NY Times, Time Magazine, and other great publications whose directors have attended our meetings and respected their promises of discretion for almost 40 years.

It would have been impossible for us to develop our plan for the world if we had been subjected to the lights of publicity during those years.

But now the world is more sophisticated and prepared to march towards a world government.

The supra national sovereignty of an intellectual elite and world bankers is surely preferable to the national auto-determination practiced in past centuries."
-David Rockefeller
Private Banker
Council on Foreign Relations
June 1991

"The new world order will be built...an end run on national sovereignty, eroding it piece by piece will accomplish much more than the old fashioned frontal assault."
-Council on Foreign Relations
Journal 1974, p.558

"The bankers own the earth. Take it away from them, but leave them the power to create money, and with the flick of the pen they will create enough money to buy it back again.

However, take away from them the power to create money, and all the great fortunes like mine will disappear and they ought to disappear, for this would be a happier and better world to live in. But, if you wish to remain the slaves of bankers and pay the cost of your own slavery, let them continue to create money."
-Sir Josiah Stamp
Former director of The Bank of England

"And he causeth all, both small and great, rich and poor, free and bond, to receive a mark in their right hand, or in their forehead: And that no man might buy or sell, save he had the mark."

-Revelation
13:16

www.INFOWARS.COM www.JONESREPORT.COM
www.PRISONPLANET.COM
www.PRISONPLANET.TV
www.GiveMeLiberty.ORG
www.FREEDOMTOFASCISM.COM

523777

Made in the USA